HEARTH & HOME
Preserving a People's Culture

AMERICAN CIVILIZATION
A Series Edited by Allen F. Davis

Gospel Hymns and Social Religion:
The Rhetoric of Nineteenth-Century Revivalism
by Sandra S. Sizer (1978)

Social Darwinism: Science and Myth
in Anglo-American Social Thought
by Robert C. Bannister (1979)

Twentieth Century Limited:
Industrial Design in America, 1925–1939
by Jeffrey L. Meikle (1979)

Charlotte Perkins Gilman:
The Making of a Radical Feminist, 1860–1896
by Mary A. Hill (1980)

Inventing the American Way of Death, 1830–1920
by James J. Farrell (1980)

Anarchist Women, 1870–1920
by Margaret S. Marsh (1981)

Woman and Temperance:
The Quest for Power and Liberty, 1873–1900
by Ruth Bordin (1981)

Hearth and Home:
Preserving a People's Culture
by George W. McDaniel (1981)

The Education of Mrs. Henry Adams
by Eugenia Kaledin (1981)

Class, Culture, and the Classroom:
The Student Peace Movement of the 1930s
by Eileen Eagan (1981)

HEARTH & HOME
Preserving a People's Culture

George W. McDaniel

Temple University Press ● Philadelphia

Temple University Press, Philadelphia 19122

© 1982 by Temple University. All rights reserved

Published 1982

Printed in the United States of America

Library of Congress Cataloging in Publication Data

McDaniel, George W.
Hearth and home, preserving a people's culture.

Bibliography: p.
Includes index.
1. Historic buildings—Maryland. 2. Farmhouses—
Maryland. 3. Afro-Americans—Housing—Maryland.
4. Maryland—Rural conditions. I. Title.
F182.M32 975.2 81-13627
ISBN 0-87722-233-9 AACR2

Publication of this book has been assisted by a
grant from the Publication Program of the National
Endowment for the Humanities.

To

James G. and Marguerite McDaniel

and to

Mary Sue

CONTENTS

Chapter V
Houses of Landowners:
"The Colored People Want Land"
187

Epilogue
Celebrating the People's History:
"From Somebody Who Wore the Shoe"
240

Appendix I
Sites Surveyed in Southern Maryland and
Montgomery County, Maryland
251

Appendix II
Oral Informants and Interviews
261

Notes
267

Bibliography
285

Index
293

ILLUSTRATIONS

PREFACE

There is history in all men's lives.
William Shakespeare[1]

In the winter of 1974, while in graduate school in history at Duke University, I went out in the country to conduct my second oral interview, in this case with an elderly black tenant farmer, and to photograph his house for a study of farm tenant houses that I was writing. I had been given his name in confidence by a Farm Extension Service agent, who told me not to tell the farmer how I had learned of him. This presented a problem: how in the world to explain how I had arrived at his doorstep on a backwoods road to interview him about tenancy without knowing he was a tenant farmer. Some friends advised me to say I was a journalist looking for a story. Off I went. I arrived at his place but could not drive in. I did not want to establish the relationship on a lie. So I drove around the country roads asking myself, "What am I doing here?" And the answer eventually became clear: "I am a historian interested in learning about the way it was years ago. I am especially interested in telling the story of the houses and ways of life of ordinary people so younger generations can see how their ancestors lived. I'm concerned that this history is rarely told in school textbooks, museums, and history books; and an important step in getting that story is to talk to the people who knew and lived it." Of course, I could not say all this in one breath, but that was the underlying thought behind my work. So I drove back, introduced myself to the farmer, and was warmly received. I've been at it ever since.

Over the years, I have interviewed scores of people in North Carolina, Maryland, Virginia, and Washington, D.C. Though I have met with a few hostile receptions, the overwhelming majority of people have been cooperative because they have been concerned about recording the history they knew. Some may have had reservations because I was white, from Georgia, too conservative, too radical, a stranger; but more important, it appears, was the fact that I was there and sincere. Better me than nobody. They opened up their store of knowledge and led me to old-time houses and people they knew in their communities. This book is just one example of what can be produced. There remains so much more to be done by utilizing these local resources, especially the elderly, not only in southern Maryland, but throughout the nation.

It has been my experience as a high school teacher and a student that history is usually taught apart from the local setting, so that students get a very clear idea that history is something that happened somewhere else to somebody else. But this study is intended to help us realize that history is something that has happened to each of us. In short, it is an effort to help democratize our concept of history.

As a teacher, I learned that historical artifacts, old photographs, and museum exhibits are valuable teaching aids because they can be interpreted on different levels according to students' abilities and make it easier for students to relate to their past. However, what was available was severely limited. Few of the findings of the recent historians about American social history were reflected in the exhibits that existed, and the heritage they conveyed still tended to focus on the white affluent. In the American South, most of the historical homes on exhibit were the main houses of plantations and the homes of the merchant class, to the exclusion of the homes of agricultural workers, whether slave or free, black or white, even though their houses often constituted the majority of homes on the site and were integral to the world in which the affluent whites lived. At these sites the presence of black people was rarely exhibited accurately, if at all. For example, historian Peter Wood tells of visiting Thomas Jefferson's remarkable home, Monticello, and overhearing a visitor say to her friend: "It's a beautiful place; do you suppose he had any help?"[2]

The exclusion of black people and their contributions to the built environment fosters a false picture of the historical reality of blacks and whites. As historian C. Vann Woodward wrote in *American Counterpoint*:

> The ironic thing about these two great hyphenate minorities, Southern-Americans and Afro-Americans, confronting each other on their native soil for three and a half centuries, is the degree to which they have shaped each other's destiny, determined each other's isolation, shared and molded a common culture. It is, in fact, impossible to imagine the one without the other and quite futile to try.[3]

A major purpose of this work, therefore, is to join others in returning ordinary black people to the stage of history, so that all of us, black and white, may more fully understand the world our ancestors knew.

Essential to this endeavor is the study of the historical houses of black families in all their variety—as slaves, as tenants, and as landowners. Such a study can help us see the physical world in which black people lived, especially their domestic world of hearth and home. Viewing history in this way produces two distinct layers of evidence—the material evidence contained in the houses, and the even richer story of the people who lived in them. Both have concrete historical utility. It is important to examine the houses as structures, so that we can understand how they were constructed, what was typical, and how they changed over time. But we also need to understand the houses as homes of families that, together with furnishings and work places, constituted the stage on which black families acted out their lives.

Two elements are interwoven throughout this study. The first is an examination of material culture. The second is an analysis of how the houses were lived in and the objects used—that is, a social history. It is hoped that these two elements together can help us to visualize more completely the world of our ancestors and to convey more accurately the ways of life of black people in historical literature, museums, and schools.[4]

The area investigated is southern Maryland, which consists of five traditionally rural counties south of Washington, D.C., and Baltimore (see figure 1). These counties are St. Mary's, Charles, Anne Arundel, Prince George's, and Calvert. They form a long peninsula bordered by the Chesapeake Bay on the east and the Potomac River on the southwest and bisected by the Patuxent River. With its rich soil and waters abundant with fish, the region has supported generations of Euro-American and Afro-American farmers and fishermen since the seventeenth century.

Historical black culture is rich in southern Maryland. Blacks were among the first immigrant settlers from across the Atlantic. At least one black arrived in Maryland before the *Ark* and the *Dove*, ships which are to Maryland what the *Mayflower* is to Massachusetts. But unlike other immigrants, the Africans came as slaves. From the mid-seventeenth century onwards, the slave population steadily increased due to the demand for slave labor for tobacco plantations until, by the end of the eighteenth century, Maryland and Virginia had the largest black population in the United States. In much of southern Maryland, a black majority existed from the late eighteenth century through

the nineteenth. From throughout Maryland there arose a number of
black people of national fame, prompting historian Benjamin Quarles
to observe, "Few other states can boast so many black men of mark,
including a quartet as diverse in generation and calling as surveyor-
mathematician Benjamin Banneker, orator Frederick Douglass, North
Pole explorer Matthew Henson and Supreme Court Justice Thurgood
Marshall."[5]

What was the physical environment of the ancestors, not only of
these famous men, but of ordinary black people? Unfortunately,
none of the seventeenth- and eighteenth-century houses of black
families are known to have survived, and the few written descriptions that I found provided the measurements and types of construction of comparatively few examples. Consequently, an analysis of
seventeenth- and eighteenth-century houses of black families that is
comparable in scope and detail to that of extant nineteenth-century
houses is not possible at this point. Also, only one surviving dwelling
of an ante-bellum free black family was located in southern Maryland, but it was built as a post office and converted to a dwelling
in the 1850's.[6] This study, accordingly, concerns the houses of the
ante-bellum nineteenth-century slaves and post–Civil-War farm tenants and landowners.*

A word about the development of this study. It began as an ex-
ploratory survey to locate and record whatever slave houses might
still be standing in southern Maryland as part of a graduate internship in historical archaeology with the Smithsonian Institution and
the St. Mary's City Commission, St. Mary's City, Maryland, during
the summer of 1974. In 1975–76, I continued the survey while a
predoctoral fellow with the Smithsonian, and in 1976–77 I worked
as a historic sites surveyor in southern Maryland for the Maryland
Commission on Afro-American History and Culture and the Maryland Historical Trust. At the outset there were few sources to guide
me. In fact, the houses in this study were unknown to most historians
and to myself when I began. None of the oral informants had been
featured in a newspaper, cited in a secondary source, or mentioned
in a manuscript collection. Fortunately, people of both races in southern Maryland, including county historians and community leaders,
were concerned about the preservation of their history and led me
to local sites and informants.

Thanks to these leads, I extended the survey to include the houses

---

*A list of all the sites that I have recorded in the Southern Maryland Afro-Ameri-
can Survey is given in Appendix I.

of post–Civil-War black families and their ways of life. In the search for "old-time houses," local people took me to sites that when researched turned out to be post-bellum farm tenant houses rather than slave quarters. But it seemed important to record them because most would soon be destroyed. Some already have been. The lifestyles of families that continued to live in traditional ways were also recorded, for their uses of space and everyday activities suggest how the old houses were lived in. Local people also took me to rural communities founded by freed slaves, not mentioned in Maryland history texts. Their houses and material culture furnished significant contrasts with those of slaves and tenants. It may be said, therefore, that this study evolved from field work and the people of southern Maryland, rather than a preexisting conceptualized model.[7]

This book deals with problems in the research, analysis, interpretation, and exhibition of black material culture and houses. The Introduction, which focuses on the Prince George's County, Maryland, farm tenant house on exhibit at the Smithsonian Institution, acquaints the reader with the problems and methods of researching and exhibiting the houses of black families. Chapter I sketches the African and European origins of Afro-American slave houses and their development in Maryland. Chapter II explores slave house design and construction in southern Maryland in the nineteenth century, the period for which we have the most complete sources of evidence. Chapter III portrays the slave houses as more than bare structural shells by describing their furnishings and the ways of life associated with them. Chapter IV portrays the houses and lifestyles of black farm tenants after "freedom," and focuses on two specific case studies. Chapter V provides a counterpoint by depicting black landowners' material culture and houses in the same period, focusing on two case studies. It is also a saga of the struggle of blacks for the measure of autonomy that private property provides. The Epilogue celebrates the return of this people's history to the people via the Festival of American Folklife at the Smithsonian Institution in 1978, which featured the farm tenant house, its former residents and neighbors, and other oral informants you will get to know in this book. The chapter concludes with a discussion of the challenges faced by all of us concerned with preserving the people's history.

A word about method. The results of this study are derived from a combination of sources: houses, artifacts, documents, oral informants, and photographs. The first three are invaluable, but the vast majority of the houses and furnishings of slaves and tenants have not survived and were not documented sufficiently to enable comprehensive descriptions. As a rule, tax assessors, slaveholders, landowners, neighbors, and travelers did not consider them to be of sufficient worth to warrant recording. Moreover, the slave and tenant residents were often illiterate, and did not leave wills, write and keep letters or diaries, or gain the attention of archivists in the event they might have written collections to preserve. If they died intestate, their houses and their contents were not inventoried and appraised, as was customary with the more affluent. For example, among the free antebellum population of St. Mary's County in the early 1800's, as many as 40 percent of the free householders listed in the censuses were too poor to warrant notice by the tax assessor; this group included virtually all the free black population and 45 percent of female householders. Since approximately half of the total population was slaves, the houses and possessions of roughly 70 percent of the entire society were documented in official records in a cursory manner or not at all. Such gaps in recording probably occurred in other areas in the South.[8]

How, then, are we to know of the life of this historical majority? Additional sources were needed, so I turned to the testimony of oral informants, such as former slaves interviewed by the WPA in the 1930's, and elderly blacks born in the late 1800's and early 1900's whom I interviewed. The informants gained their expertise over the course of long lifetimes during which they became thoroughly familiar with the houses and material culture of black families. The stories and customs that other former slaves and "old-time people" passed on to them gave historical depth to their knowledge. As a result, the informants can describe scores of small wooden houses that have left little or no trace on the landscape or in documents.

Old photographs supplemented the informants' recollections and showed how such houses appeared in the nineteenth century while they were occupied. Unfortunately, only two old photographs of houses of Maryland blacks were found, and they were too dark to be reproduced; but I did find a score of pictures of houses from Virginia and elsewhere in the South, houses that matched the informants' descriptions. Together, all these sources help provide a more comprehensive portrait of the historical houses of black Marylanders.

There may be uncertainties about the reliability of the recollections of the oral informants in this study. To minimize errors, I tested informants' recollections against written records to the extent possible, and against a careful examination of the houses themselves for evidence of dates of construction and changes in the houses. I tried to select knowledgeable, conscientious informants who would not hesitate to say "I don't know" rather than invent an answer. Also, I asked for descriptions of houses, building techniques, and ways of life, rather than evaluations of whether conditions were "good" or "bad" or whether people were "happy." Answers to questions about further details—such as the frequency and causes of chimney fires in log chimneys, the longevity of thatched roofs, and so forth—indirectly reveal how "good" or "bad" life actually was.

This story's implications go beyond the limits of Maryland, the American South, or even of black America. The lives of the residents of these houses were similar in many ways to those of peasants of all eras. They built their homes themselves of wood and earth; they depended on a fire from locally available fuel for heating and cooking; they raised and preserved most of their own food. For the most part they traveled by foot or horse, that is, at a rate of speed no faster than that available to, say, the ancient Egyptians. Their principal destinations were the market, the church, the fields, and home again.

The remnants of that way of life are fast disappearing as the houses are torn down and the elderly pass on. Those still living can testify to radical changes in their way of life: farmland has been "developed" into shopping centers and subdivisions; hand labor has been replaced by machine, firewood by oil and electricity, horses by automobiles, homemade log houses by prefabricated mobile homes of synthetic materials. "It's not just one thing that's changing," said James Scriber, looking back over his hundred years of life. "It's everything."[9]

ACKNOWLEDGMENTS

This book is a product of the cooperation of many people and organizations that have cared about preserving and conveying a more democratic history. Among these are:

Lay people

Anne Arundel County

Captain John Bowie
Arthur Smith

William Smith
Mary Warren

Calvert County

Edward Bourne
McKinley Gantt
Albert Johnson

"Hopsie" Johnson
Jennie Tongue Reichart
Blanche Wilson

Charles County

Lloyd Bowling
Rachel Diggs
Benjamin and Nellie Ross
Mary Stokeley

Luther Stuckey
Joe Tolson
Royal Tolson
Preston Williams

Prince George's County

William Butler
Octavia Proctor Carter
Oscar and Sadie Crump
Edward and Vivian Harley
Richard and Helen Turner James
Elizabeth "Mamie" Johnson
George and Elizabeth Johnson
Elizabeth Parker Merrill

Mary Parker
Octavia Parker Proctor
Mary Agnes Savoy
Samuel Spragins
James R. Taylor
Eugene Wood
Joe Wood

St. Mary's County

J. Gwynn Buckler
Colonel Colin Burch
George Carroll
James G. Curtis
Elwood Cusic
Nora Cusic
Clem Dyson
Zachary Fowler

Holger Jansson
Joseph Julius Johnson
Edward Knott
Abraham Medley
Charles A. Medley
Amanda Nelson
James Scriber
Howard Young

Montgomery County

Ethel Foreman
Lemuel Graham
Florence Hallman
Ida Hallman

Hester Hamilton
Evelyn Herbert
Tilghman and Bessie Lee
Howard Lyles

Historians, editors, and administrators

Kenneth Arnold
Silvio Bedini
Edwin Beitzell
Cary Carson
Aylene Cooke
Allen Davis
William Day
William Diggs
Mark Edwards
Scott Ellsworth

Lawrence Goodwyn
Mary Sue Nunn McDaniel
Sydney Nathans
Wayne Nield
John Pearce
Rodris Roth
Gail Rothrock
Orwin Talbott
Wilcomb Washburn
Peter Wood

Organizations

The Smithsonian Institution, Washington, D.C.
Maryland Commission on Afro-American History and Culture,
Annapolis, Maryland
Maryland Historical Trust, Annapolis, Maryland
St. Mary's City Commission, St. Mary's City, Maryland
Sugarloaf Regional Trails, Dickerson, Maryland
Center for Southern Folklore, Memphis, Tennessee

HEARTH & HOME
Preserving a People's Culture

INTRODUCTION
The Farm Tenant House at the Smithsonian Institution: "You've Got It Backwards"

In the Hall of Everyday Life in the American Past at the Smithsonian Institution, scores of visitors each day tour a series of exhibits, including a seventeenth-century New England home, an eighteenth-century Virginia parlor, a Delaware log house, a Victorian library, a California rancher's kitchen, and a farm tenant house—the Smithsonian's acknowledgment of rural working-class Southerners. The Smithsonian rescued the then-abandoned tenant house from oblivion in 1969. It had stood on a farm in Mitchellville, Maryland, about thirty miles east of Washington, D.C., in Prince George's County (figure 1). It was a small, plain dwelling, of a type commonly thought of and referred to as a "shack" (figure 2). Indeed, as with most "shacks," the history of this house was for the most part a blank. There were no readily available documents on which the Smithsonian could base the exhibit. From the materials used in construction, the Smithsonian staff could see that the dwelling was built after the Civil War, in a style common to the mid-Atlantic region. Its location on the farm, not far from the main house, indicated that it had been a tenant house, instead of the landowner's, and local people said that it had been occupied by black tenant families. No one knew any more.

Even as workers dismantled the house, the land around it was being cleared for development; today, the site's pre-1960's history is almost invisible. The farm's main house, now the offices and sales room of a commercial nursery, stands in the wide median of a four-lane highway, U.S. 301, and busy traffic rushes along the lanes in front of and behind the house. Not far away, where tobacco and corn fields once surrounded the tenant house, now sprawls the Pointer Ridge Shopping Center and a subdivision of hundreds of small ranch-style houses developed by Levitt, Inc. (figure 3). The site of the

Figure 1
Map of Maryland.

Figure 2
The farm tenant house in situ near Mitchellville, Maryland, after
it was abandoned, 1968. Photo: George Watson. Copy photograph,
reproduced through the courtesy of The Smithsonian Institution.

tenant house itself is now part of a parking lot. The obliteration of this farm is a striking illustration of the transformation of the modern American landscape.

Spared from the bulldozer, the tenant house stands inside the National Museum of American History on the Capitol Mall. Piece by piece, workers reassembled it in a wide corridor in the Hall of Everyday Life with its front length facing into the corridor; its rear length, flush against the wall, cannot be seen (figure 4). The two gable ends can be viewed, but several feet were removed from the top of the structure to conform to the museum's ceiling. A small side yard enclosed by a fence was created. Unlike many period exhibits, which are closed off behind a glass wall or rope cordon, visitors to the tenant house can enter through the front door. Approximately four feet inside they are contained by a glass barrier, about four feet

Figure 3
Site of the tenant house in 1978. Photo: author.

Figure 4
Reassembled tenant house on exhibit in the National Museum of
American History. Photo: author.

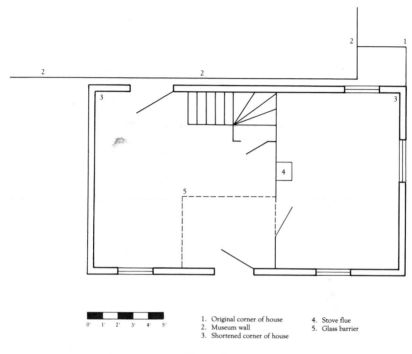

1. Original corner of house   4. Stove flue
2. Museum wall   5. Glass barrier
3. Shortened corner of house

Figure 5
Floor plan of the reassembled tenant house.

high, over which they can look into both refurnished downstairs rooms.

The house is a small, one-and-a-half-story frame dwelling with two rooms down and two up (figure 5).* Its frame is sheathed with board-and-batten siding of naturally weathered wood—the original sheathing, which preceded the horizontal weatherboards present when the house was last lived in. The front door is located in the middle of the length and is flanked by a sash window on either side. Overall, the house is plain in appearance and has no structural or decorative

---

*Definitions of one-story and one-and-a-half-story vary. I use a structural definition, as employed by other architectural historians in Maryland. In a one-story house, the ceiling joists and rafters rest on the same horizontal timber, or plate, while in a one-and-a-half story dwelling, the rafters rest on a timber above the one supporting the joists with less than a full story between the two timbers. A one-and-a-half story house need not have dormer windows.

features outside, such as a front porch, window shutters, or door or window trim. New plank steps with a narrow rail—intended to sim- ulate the plain steps on tenant dwellings—lead into the house.

Inside, the original frame and woodwork have been rebuilt, but the rooms are shallower than in the original, as the house had to be squeezed into the museum's space. The "front room"—the one into which the door opens—is larger than the narrow side room. Between them is a thin partition of tongue-and-grove siding, with a door lead- ing between them. Visitors look through this opened door in order to view the side room. A brick stove flue with openings for stove- pipes in each room is located in the side room in the middle of the partition. In the side room is a small wood-burning stove with two lids, and in the front room a small, potbellied, coal-burning stove with one lid. A small quarter-turn stairway boxed with tongue-and- groove siding is located against the back wall in the front room. In the space underneath the stairway is a small closet (figure 6). The interior siding of the walls is of tongue-and-groove boards of irregular widths, which have not been painted or whitewashed since the house was dismantled. Although traces of paint of different colors remain along some sections of the walls, they are exhibited as faded and quite drab.[1]

From the beginning, some members of the Smithsonian staff felt that something was missing. The exhibit, it was thought, had been put up in too much haste, partly in response to pressures on the Smithsonian. Little scholarly research had been conducted on the history of the house, or on the furnishings of houses like this one— elements of research basic to most Smithsonian exhibits. The rooms were too bleak to show much sign of family life. Probably there were more household furnishings and activities than the few objects on display reflected. Perhaps the objects were too "high style." Also, the side yard seemed to be more an empty space used to exhibit a few farm implements than a farmhouse yard where outdoor activities took place. These were important concerns of the Smithsonian staff, but other museum priorities intervened, so the tenant house remained as it was.[2]

In 1978, ten years after the abandoned house reached its strange new location, the Smithsonian hired me as a consultant to help reinterpret the house. I was charged with three responsibilities: to re- search the history of the house, to submit a furnishings plan and a list of artifacts for a more authentic interpretation of the two rooms downstairs, and to submit plans to interpret the side yard. For several years I had been studying in their native habitat tenant houses sim-

Figure 6
Front room of the farm tenant house as exhibited in 1978. Photo: author.

ilar to the one that the Smithsonian now had in captivity. Such houses had been home for thousands of landless farm laborers, both black and white, and exhibits of their homes, I felt, could reflect their history back to their descendants, as well as convey it to thousands more.

But in order to exhibit this house properly, its history first had to be researched. How to do so? The Smithsonian files contained no historical documents related to it, and current staff members knew only that the house was moved from Mitchellville, Maryland, but not the exact location of its original site. Without knowing the location of the property, there was no way to trace deeds, learn the names of earlier owners, or research probate inventories and other documents in courthouses and archives.

My several years of field work, and the suggestions of Silvio Bedini, then deputy director of the National Museum of American History, prompted me to think that there might be some people living in Mitchellville, perhaps former neighbors or even former residents, who knew of the house. Beginning with the names in the Smithsonian files of persons from the community who had been involved in rescuing the house, I contacted Ellis Yochelson, a Smithsonian geologist. He said that the in-laws of his housekeeper, Edith James, were somehow associated with the house, and a short while later introduced me to her. She in turn introduced me to her husband, Bill James, who was well acquainted with the house. They led me to the original site, and then to meet Bill's parents, Richard and Helen (Turner) James, born in 1892 and 1896 respectively. They knew even more about "that old house," for they had visited it in the 1930's, when Mrs. James's brother, Tom Turner, had lived there, and again in the late 1940's, when one of their sons, Frank James, lived there. My hopes for interviewing these residents and learning precisely how it was furnished during their occupancy were dashed, however, as both had died recently. Mrs. James had pictures of them both, which I copied. I interviewed Mr. and Mrs. James about the history of the house and its community and invited them, along with Bill and Edith James, to the museum, where they were interviewed as they toured the house (figure 7). Richard and Helen James recalled how Tom Turner and his wife had furnished the rooms, as well as the layout of the farm and the locations of other houses and buildings of the historical community. Since the Jameses were children of tenant farmers and had grown up nearby, they were asked also to describe the furnishings of similar tenant houses they had known in

Figure 7
The James family and Smithsonian staff by the tenant house on
exhibit in February 1978. Left to right: Richard James, Edith James, Helen
(Turner) James, Bill James, Rodris Roth, and Anne Golovin.
Photo: author.

the early 1900's. Their recollections were highly informative in regard to reinterpreting the house.[3]

Interviewing older people always presents the problem of distance between interviewer and interviewee, so it is important that both have common visual reference points to minimize the possibility of confusion in describing artifacts. We therefore went through a series of photographs of tenant houses and interiors from the 1890's and early 1900's, and reprints of the mail-order catalogs of Sears, Roebuck from the same period. This way the Jameses, and other informants later, could specify the particular type of a given artifact they recalled seeing in tenant houses. They also used the illustrations as a basis for describing artifacts that did not appear in the catalogs or photographs. For example, an informant could refer to several types of plain kitchen chairs in pictures to create a composite.

While this visual aid dramatically improved the precision with which informants identified objects, it should be noted that it may also have skewed their memories. To satisfy the interviewer or to paint a brighter picture of life, informants may have selected finer objects than were actually present. Realizing this possibility, I did not press them for answers if they were not sure, and I presented them with a variety of illustrations of tenant houses, interiors, and objects from the turn of the century and later, in order to increase the chances of their seeing objects that had actually been in their houses. Also, I tried to make clear that we were most concerned with recording what they were sure about, because the goal was to exhibit the house as closely as possible to how it actually appeared. Most informants understood this and cooperated, because they were concerned about "getting down the history of that house," and getting it straight. Many saw the house as an object lesson for their descendants as to how they "came along." While this method of research may appear too subjective, no other sources—written records or photographs—specifically identified the furnishings of this house. Without the informants' help, most of the history of the dwelling and its furnishings would have remained unknown.

After Bill James had identified the site of the tenant house, I was able to research deeds in the courthouse and weave together the history of landownership for 150 years, with special attention to the post-bellum era, since the house was built in that period. Part of a 400-acre plantation during slavery times, the farm had descended to Beale D. Mulliken in 1876 and to his nephew, Samuel Spragins, Sr., in 1909. Beginning in the 1950's, the Spragins family began to sell portions of the farm, and in 1959 the 7.3-acre tract on which the tenant house stood was sold to land developers, and eventually to Levitt, Inc. As is often the case with tenant houses, landowners' wills and probate inventories did not contain information about this or any other tenant house on the farm, or identify residents. A reprint of an 1878 atlas of Prince George's County did show the location of the Mulliken farm and the main house, along with churches, schools, and stores, but the location of tenant houses on this farm and on others did not merit inclusion.[4]

The James family put me in contact with the Parker sisters, whose father had been manager of the farm and who had lived in the house

Figure 8
The Parker family outside the tenant house. Left to right: Mary
Parker, Octavia Parker Proctor, Jillet Earnest (a family friend), Octavia
Proctor Carter, Elizabeth Parker Merrill, Marie Parker Hall.
Photo: author.

next to this one from about 1912 to 1920. I invited them to the
museum, reviewed the mail-order catalogs and old photographs with
them, and taped an interview about the furnishings and ways of life
on the farm (figure 8). They could not clearly remember the furnishings in this house since they were young when they moved away,
but Mrs. Octavia (Parker) Proctor sketched an informative map of
the Spragins farm as she remembered it from around 1920.[5]

Still missing was an interview with a person who had actually
lived in the house, who could remember specific artifacts, household
activities, and feelings about the house. The Parker family told me
about Edward Harley, a resident from about 1941 to 1946, who still
lived just a few miles up the highway from the original site of the
house. I asked him and his wife, Vivian, to the museum for interviews (figure 9). Because he was young when he lived there, he did
not remember many details about furnishings, but he did recall how
the rooms were used. He was somewhat reticent to talk about life
there, perhaps because the house had negative connotations, or per-

Figure 9
The Harley family inside the tenant house. Left to right: Vivian Harley,
Edward Harley, and their daughter, Judy. Photo: author.

haps he was simply a quiet, almost reserved man. His reticence, however, was in part compensated for by his wife, who coincidentally had been the social worker for the family that had resided in the house in the 1960's, the Savoys. She volunteered important recollections about the house's appearance and about family life there, based on what she had seen in the 1960's and what she had heard from the Harleys.[6]

To cast a wider net, I requested that an article on my research appear in the local Prince George's County newspaper, the *Bowie News*. The story elicited a telephone call from Mrs. George Johnson, who said that her husband was born in the house in 1929—a report that was music to my ears. The Johnsons came to the museum, bringing George's mother, Elizabeth "Mamie" Johnson, who had lived in the house twice—in the 1920's and again in the 1940's. The Johnsons brought their children, and their son Terrence remembered that he had seen the house on a previous school trip to the Smithsonian, but had had no idea that his father was born in it. In fact, none of the informants had an inkling that the house was preserved at the Smithsonian.

The Johnsons also brought "Mamie" Johnson's sister, Mary Agnes Savoy, the last resident of the house. Mrs. Savoy gave me snapshots taken of her family in the two rooms downstairs in the 1960's, showing the presence of modern, inexpensive, mass-produced furniture. She also explained the numbers written in pencil on the kitchen wall as the telephone numbers of neighbors and relatives, evidence of modern culture that I recommended be preserved rather than painted over in the reinterpretation.

Mrs. Savoy and Mrs. Johnson added that another sister, Gertrude Butler, had lived in the house in the 1950's, and that they were first cousins to a previous resident, Edward Harley. These connections were but one example of the kinship network that was eventually revealed among black families on this farm. All of the historical information the Johnsons supplied is a telling commentary on the potential value of oral informants.[7]

The Harleys and Parkers told me of the Wood family, the first residents they remembered, and directed me to Joe Wood, who happens to work at the Mobil station in the Pointer Ridge Shopping Center, a few yards from where the house once stood. He was born in 1917, just one year after his family moved out of the house. He gave me the address of his brother, Eugene Wood, born in 1896, who lived on Long Island, New York. After I telephoned him, his son drove him and his family from New York to the Smithsonian (figure 10). Wood, confined to a wheelchair, suffered from chronic emphysema and could not converse for a sustained period of time. Nonetheless, he was the earliest resident still living and the only one who could describe its furnishings before the 1920's. An important interview was taped with him at the house. He remembered, for example, that the walls inside were newspapered and whitewashed. Today they are drab, with only traces of faded paint. To learn about the objects of young residents, I asked him, for instance, "When you were living here, what would you have wanted most to save from the house in case of fire?" He replied, "My .22 rifle!" No evidence of any such prized possession, or of the presence of a boy, is on display.[8]

Thanks to the assistance of a neighbor of the old farm, Mrs. James Hamilton, I located the descendants of the landowners in hopes that they might have family papers or even old photographs of the house or its residents. They had not known that the tenant house was preserved at the Smithsonian, but Sam Spragins, Jr., said that dur-

Figure 10
Former resident Eugene Wood (in wheelchair) with his family in front
of the tenant house. Photo: author.

ing a visit to the museum he had seen the house and remarked to his wife, "That looks like one of our houses." He and other family members volunteered to search their collections of family memorabilia, but they found no records. Spragins, who had known the farm from the 1920's to its sale in the 1950's, did sketch a map based on his recollections of the farm in around 1925, before the Crain Highway cut across the front yard, a time when "we could stand on our front porch and see only the smoke from two chimneys."[9]

I also tried to locate old stores and storekeepers with whom the tenant families traded, since their records might document the things in this tenant house or in others like it. Richard James gave me the names of the two Slingluff brothers, furnishing merchants, and I contacted their sister, who said that all their papers had been thrown out upon their deaths a few years before. James also directed me to an old community store that still stood, but no account books remained, and the owners of more than twenty years before had passed away. However, I did locate and interview Zack Fowler and Preston Williams, two elderly storekeepers from elsewhere in southern Maryland, who came to the Smithsonian and identified typical artifacts sold to tenants during their youth in the early 1900's.[10]

Once I had the names of former residents, I returned to the courthouse and searched the lists of wills for their names. None were listed. Nor were their estates inventoried by the state when they died intestate. Also, no living resident had a collection of artifacts or family papers, such as letters, diaries, or journals, or any photographs of the house before the 1960's. If one were to categorize the existence of the residents of this alleged "shack" upon the availability of conventional historical sources, it would appear that they were the flotsam of history.

But were they? They owned no real estate, paid no real estate taxes, and had little money to buy things and few educational opportunities. Their houses were ordinary, slow to change, and difficult to date. In terms of historical records, their condition resembled that of landless peasants throughout the world. But an imaginative use of evidence from a combination of sources, I hoped, could enable us to exhibit their homes and their lifestyles.

Since the Smithsonian staff intended to refurnish the house to the earliest period of occupancy, the date of construction was important. But it was difficult to fix precisely, due to the absence of written records and the lack of datable architectural or decorative "styles." In 1968, the Smithsonian staff had identified the house as being built between 1865 and 1885. However, my own survey of southern Maryland sites found that farm tenant houses that had a hall and parlor floor plan, a one-and-a-half story height, a stove flue instead of a chimney with fireplace, and other features similar to those of this house, were usually built after 1875 and became the common type by the 1890's in many parts of the mid-Atlantic region. Other evidence, such as the original tongue-and-groove interior siding and partitions, supports at least a late-nineteenth-century date. Though the framing members were hewn timbers joined by traditional mortise and tenon joints, pegged through, open mortises along their lengths showed they were reused from an earlier structure and so could not be used to date the house. The rafters were attached by machine-cut nails of the post-1830 type, which continued in use throughout the nineteenth and twentieth centuries, so they provide no datable "stops." The house was therefore built most likely after 1875, but could have been built in any year since so far as structural evidence is concerned.[11]

Dating the house by oral sources also proved perplexing and at times contradictory, but most sources reliably point to a late-nineteenth-century date of construction. Richard James, who was born on a farm not far from the house, had first recalled that the house was built when he was about twenty years old, or around 1912. Mary Parker (figure 8), who lived next door as a young girl from roughly 1912 to 1920, disagreed, saying that it was an "old house when I was young." However, it is possible that this unpainted wooden house became old by the late teens, when Mary Parker remembered it best. As sociologist Arthur Raper found in the rural South in the 1930's, "tenant houses ten years old appear fifty." Sam Spragins and his cousin, Mrs. Walter Heidelbach, helped clarify the discrepancy by recalling that the house on exhibit was the oldest of the three tenant houses along the farm lane, and that the other two were built in the early 1900's. These were probably the ones whose construction Richard James remembered. Mrs. Heidelbach specifically remembers this house when she lived on the farm in the early 1900's, and, like Mary Parker, said it was considered to be old, and a "slave cabin" at that. However, its hall and parlor floor plan, one-and-a-half story height, glazed windows, tongue-and-groove siding inside, and original stove flue make this dwelling too "high style" to be a likely candidate for a slave house. Combining the structural and oral evidence, the maximum range in date of construction is between 1875 and 1900, and the most likely date is the 1880's.[12]

From the time it was built, the house was an integral part of a larger farm community. It did not stand alone as it is exhibited today. Sam Spragin's sketch, together with the recollections of other informants, shows a setting quite different from the cramped space in the museum. This house was part of a complex of three almost identical tenant dwellings, and stood at the intersection of two farm lanes facing east (figure 11). To the north of the house was a small kitchen garden and a chicken house. Behind it was a small yard, unfenced and without grass, with paths worn to the woodpile, the privy, and beyond to fields planted in corn and tobacco. In front of the house was a small, unfenced dirt yard with a path leading up to the front

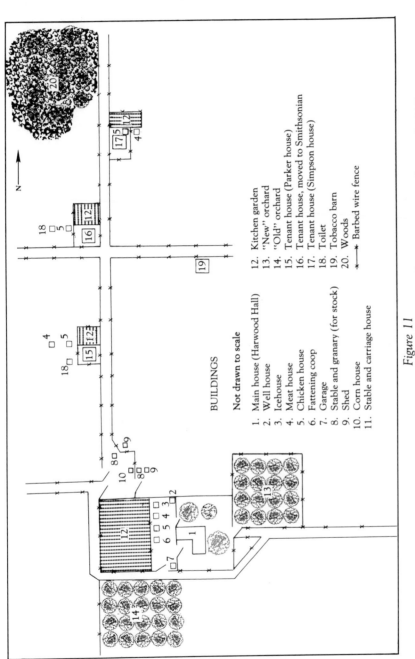

BUILDINGS

Not drawn to scale

1. Main house (Harwood Hall)
2. Well house
3. Icehouse
4. Meat house
5. Chicken house
6. Fattening coop
7. Garage
8. Stable and granary (for stock)
9. Shed
10. Corn house
11. Stable and carriage house
12. Kitchen garden
13. "New" orchard
14. "Old" orchard
15. Tenant house (Parker house)
16. Tenant house, moved to Smithsonian
17. Tenant house (Simpson house)
18. Toilet
19. Tobacco barn
20. Woods
✳ Barbed wire fence

Figure 11

Sketch of the Mulliken-Spragins Farm, from which the tenant house was removed, around 1925;
based on sketches by Samuel H. Spragins and Octavia Parker Proctor.

steps. Every day the residents, especially the children, trekked down the lane to the spring; there was no well.

In the opposite direction from the spring, the farm lane led up the hill to the main house, where the Mulliken and later the Spragins families lived. Behind the main house was a large vegetable garden and a complex of outbuildings: well house, icehouse, meat house, chicken house, fattening coop, garage, stable and granary, sheds, corn house, and stable and carriage house. On the west side of the farm lane was the hog pen, where hogs were raised for both land-owning and tenant families.

The rest of the land was planted in tobacco and corn, interspersed with vegetable gardens that the tenants cultivated for themselves. There was also a separate large garden. Common types of vegetables were grown and would have been found on the table: turnips, carrots, onions, beans, peas, peppers, collard greens, tomatoes. Two orchards south and east of the main house supplied the sharecropper families and the landowners. The residents of the tenant houses preserved their own food by canning vegetables and fruit and by digging vegetable kilns in which root vegetables, such as parsnips and turnips, were stored for use throughout the winter. They also made "cabbage pens" near their gardens to protect cabbage from the frost.[13]

In terms of everyday labor, most of the crop management and cultivation was the responsibility of the tenants, because during the twentieth century the owners were absent much of the year. From 1912 to 1920, the Spraginses left the day-to-day operation of the farm in the care of a black tenant, Lewis Parker, whose family (including young Octavia, Elizabeth, and Mary) lived in the first tenant house. About 1920, the Spragins family sold Parker an eighty-acre portion of their land to which he moved, and he became a successful landowning farmer himself.[14]

Throughout the second quarter of the twentieth century, the responsibility for cultivating the crops and managing the land remained with the tenants. In the absence of an overseer or owner looking over their shoulder, they had an added measure of autonomy, unlike sharecroppers or field hands who still worked in large, supervised gangs.

If white control was not felt daily, it was certainly felt at least once yearly. Former residents and neighbors agree that the occupants of the house were sharecroppers—that is, they shared with the owner the profit of the crop and received a specific portion, or share, as their pay. According to Richard James, whose brother-in-law, Tom Turner, lived in this house, and to George Johnson and Edward

Harley, both former residents, the sharecroppers on the Spragins farm were on halves. This was the usual percentage in the Queen Anne District of Prince George's County. Since the tenant families on this farm supplied their own stock, one would have thought that, according to custom, they would have had to give only a third or a fourth of their crop to the owner for use of the land and for rent, but James said, "that was just the way it was." Since the farm's profits were usually small, the tenant's half was small indeed, and the family had little surplus cash to buy furnishings or other things.[15]

The principal institutions that linked residents of this house to their community were church and school. Not far from the farm, a country road led to the Mt. Nebo A.M.E. Church, and further away, in Mitchellville, was the Carroll Chapel, a United Methodist Church, which other residents attended. Like many blacks in southern Maryland, some of the residents were Roman Catholic and attended the community Catholic church, along with whites. In front of the Mt. Nebo Church stood the one-room black school, which the children in this house attended. Behind the church was a cemetery with many small, simple tombstones. Several miles distant was the small town of Mitchellville, with its railroad station and cluster of stores where resident families purchased goods.

From the interviews with former residents and neighbors, it became obvious that the house, like most, knew the wide range of activities inherent in family life. As exhibited, the house lacks the clutter that a family living in such cramped quarters would have produced. Former residents recall that they cooked food, ate meals, washed dishes, bathed, sewed, took medicine, played music, churned butter, swept floors, rested and relaxed, washed clothes, and slept. Babies were conceived, and families heard the first cries of the newborn. In 1929, twenty-one-year-old Elizabeth "Mamie" Johnson gave birth to her second son, George, in the upstairs of this house, and in the months afterward rocked him to sleep in a cradle in the side room downstairs.

Death visited this house. Around 1917, young Octavia Parker, whose family lived next door, was brought here by her mother to view the first dead person she ever saw—a small baby, the daughter of the Wilson family, laid out on a cooling board between two chairs in the "front room." She has never forgotten the sight of that tiny, still baby. It resembled a "little doll."[16]

In addition to recording these everyday events for the exhibit, it was necessary to identify family composition, as this would determine the types of artifacts present. How many children were there? What were their ages? Were both parents present, or only one? Did relatives live there too? As the list of residents shows (table 1), two-parent households were the rule (only one exception), and there was not one example of grandparents, aunts, uncles, or cousins living in the house. Children were present throughout much of its history, ranging in age from infants to teenagers. In slightly more than half the years after 1912, there were five or more children in residence. This made living conditions in this four-room house rather crowded, a feature not seen in this exhibit or in most museums, even though large families living in one- to four-room houses and tenements have been commonplace throughout American history.[17]

No family remained in this house for more than ten years; most stayed less than five. A family in a neighboring house, the Furrs, lived there for fifteen or twenty years, so there was at least one long-term resident family in the neighborhood that provided stability to the farm community.

But the tenants brought with them an important source of continuity—they were kin to one another, and this farm was part of their extended family circle. For example, from 1932 to 1937 all three tenant houses along the lane were occupied by brothers and sisters, and all the black children then on the farm were first cousins. In fact, all of the known residents of this house were kin to one-time residents of one of the three houses, as shown in the kinship list below. Looking back over his fifteen or twenty years there, Frank Furr observed, "Everybody was kin."[18]

1. Families: Parker family (house #1) and Wood family (house #2).
   Period of residency: the Wood family was resident from about 1912 to 1916, and the Parker family from 1914 to 1920.
   Kinship: Lewis Parker's father and Charles Wood's father were half-brothers. Same mother. Thus, Lewis Parker and Charles Wood were half first cousins.

2. Families: Thomas family (house #1), Owens family (house #2), and Furr family (house #3).
   Period of residency: the 1930's.
   Kinship: Sally Owens Thomas, Promise Owens, and Elizabeth Owens Furr were brother and sisters, and their children were first cousins.

3. Families: Johnson family, Butler family, and Savoy family (all house #2).

Table 1

Residents of the Tenant House, c. 1912–67

Family	Dates	Number of Children	Source*
Wood M: Charles Aubrey F: Mary Lizzie	c. 1912–16	9	Joe Wood (son)
Wilson M: Arthur F: Carrie	1916–18	0 (all died)	Octavia and Mary Parker (neighbors)
Gross M: George F: Mary	1919–?	c. 5 or 6	Octavia and Mary Parker (neighbors)
Queen M: William F: Violet	c. 1927	?	Octavia and Mary Parker (neighbors)
Johnson M: James Edward F: Elizabeth "Mamie" Butler	1927–32	2	Elizabeth ("Mamie") Johnson (resident)
Owens M: Promise F: Louise	c. 1932–37	1	Mary Harley Octavia Parker (neighbors)
Turner M: Thomas F: Martha	c. 1937–40	0 (all grown)	Helen Turner James (sister)
Harley M: George F: Mary	c. 1941–46	13	Edward and Vivian Harley (son and daughter-in-law)
Johnson M: James Edward F: Elizabeth "Mamie"	c. 1947– c. 1949	2	Elizabeth "Mamie" Johnson (resident)
James M: Frank F: Hattie	c. 1949–51	3	Helen and Richard James (parents)
Butler M: absent F: Elizabeth "Gertrude"	1956–57	1	Elizabeth "Gertrude" Butler
Savoy M: Richard F: Mary Agnes	1957–67	8	Mary Agnes Savoy (resident)

*Name of informant, and informant's relationship to heads of household.
Note: M = male head of household; F = female head of household.

Period of residency: the three families were intermittent residents from 1927 to 1967.

Kinship: Elizabeth "Mamie" Butler Johnson, Elizabeth "Gertrude" Butler, and Mary Agnes Butler Savoy were sisters; hence many of the children living in this house were first cousins to previous or future residents.

4. Families: Butler family and Harley family (both house #2).

   Period of residency: the Butler sisters were intermittent residents from 1927 to 1967, and the Harleys from about 1941 to 1946.

   Kinship: the Butler sisters were the nieces of George Harley and first cousins to his children.

5. Families: Harley family (house #2) and John William Wallace (house #3).

   Period of residency: the Harleys were residents from about 1941 to 1946, and John Wallace through the 1940's.

   Kinship: Mary Harley was the daughter of John William Wallace, and her children were his grandchildren.

6. Families: Turner family and James family (both house #2).

   Period of residency: the Turner family was resident from 1937 to 1940, and the James family from 1949 to 1951.

   Kinship: Tom Turner was the maternal uncle of Frank James.

Thus tenants who came to this farm were not uprooted, aimless transients without ties to family or community, as farm tenants are usually perceived. And when they moved, families tended to remain within the northeastern portion of Prince George's County, so ties were not broken. If families took jobs in nearby Washington or Baltimore, their connections to the community were sustained by their returning to church, family reunions, parties, funerals, and by participating in the grapevine of gossip and news about relatives and friends. It was this continuity in the old community—still extant in 1978—that enabled this research to proceed so rapidly once its purpose and I were accepted. The first informants had only to put me in contact with a few others, who led to still more, until by the end of the research project three months later, so many potential informants had been located that there was time for only one interview per person, and some were not interviewed at all.

By the 1960's, much had changed on the farm. The land around it was being sold to developers, and the two flanking tenant houses

Figure 12
The front of the tenant house during occupancy (mid-1960's).
Copy photograph, reproduced through the courtesy of ESEA Title I Operation
Moving Ahead, Prince George's County Public School System.

were abandoned. Electricity, telephone service, and oil heat had been added. The house was photographed extensively in the mid-1960's for a filmstrip on the rural poor entitled "Operation Moving Ahead," a federally funded Title I compensatory education project. Most of the pictures were thrown away because the filmstrip was considered too negative. Vivian Harley, wife of former resident Edward Harley, participated in the project as a social worker for the resident family, and she managed to locate the few images that had been kept by the Prince George's County Public School System. The print from a slightly out-of-focus slide (figure 12) reveals the house as it last looked when families lived there. No one could have foreseen its future.[19]

The Smithsonian's Hall of Everyday Life in the American Past, where the house was brought, was one of the first exhibit halls of its kind. In the past, museums had traditionally set up old houses or rooms and furnished them "to the period," with the principal criteria being beauty and fine craftsmanship, rather than representation of an authentic way of life. But the Hall of Everyday Life strove to create a setting that former residents could enter and say, "Yes, that's the way it was. This is home." When I brought my informants to view their former home on exhibit, their reaction fell somewhat short of the ideal.

Their response can be illustrated by comparing it to circumstances described in Claire Cooper's study of Easter Hill Village, a California housing project designed to provide a humane environment for working-class families. She found serious discrepancies between how designers and scholars think houses ought to be lived in, and how they are actually inhabited. Perceptions, values, and uses of space vary with class, culture, and individual tastes. Such discrepancies can too readily appear in museum exhibits, when exhibit designers make assumptions, rather than base the exhibit upon historical research. The exhibit of the tenant house is a case in point.[20]

If one were to choose a side of the tenant house to be the front, the length with the door centrally located, flanked by two windows, is the more symmetrical, stylish, and formal. It "should" be the front (figure 4). The other length has a door near one corner, a window near the other, and no opening in the center. It is off balance, unwieldy in appearance, and "should" be the back (figure 12). Indeed, there are examples of houses in Prince George's County and elsewhere in the mid-Atlantic region of this very design, with the symmetrical length as the front. This was the way that the house was reassembled in 1968. But when Elizabeth "Mamie" Johnson saw the house ten years later, she politely declared in a rather puzzled tone: "You've got it backwards" (figure 13). The back of the house was exhibited as the front, and the original front of the house was placed against the wall and was not on view at all.

This recollection is supported by all other former residents and neighbors and by Sam Spragins, Jr., son of the landowners. Their memories are confirmed by the measured drawings of the house *in situ* by George Watson, the restorationist the National Museum of American History hired to dismantle and reassemble the house. The result is a house exhibited with symmetrical and formal facade representative of this house type, but not true to the actual, historical orientation of this particular house.[21]

When Helen James toured the house, she pointed out that the rooms downstairs are exhibited backwards. The larger room, or "front room," is furnished as the sitting room and dining room, and the side room as the kitchen. But Mrs. James, Edward Harley, and other

Figure 13
The Johnson family inside the tenant house. George Johnson,
who was born in the upstairs of this house in 1929, is shown with
his hand on the shoulder of his mother, Elizabeth Johnson. In the
center of the the group and in front of the door is Mary Agnes Savoy,
the last resident of the house and her sister Elizabeth Johnson. Shown
with them are: George Johnson's wife, Elizabeth (standing next to him), his
younger sister, Elizabeth Geraldine (by the door), his son, Terence, and
his two daughters, Delores Marie Rita and Faustine Denise
(foreground). Photo: author.

residents and neighbors remembered the front room as the kitchen as well as the dining room, family room, wash room, and work room. The small side room was the parlor. If families were small, children slept upstairs in one room, and parents in the other. But if the family was large, as was more often the case, the side room doubled as the parents' bedroom.[22]

There are many examples of one- or two-room rural houses with a small shed kitchen, so the assumption that a small room could be used as the kitchen was not without historical precedent. But in this case there was no attached shed kitchen, just a two-room floor plan. In houses of this type, the more spacious room customarily served as the kitchen, multipurpose room, and center of ordinary family life in the way the former residents remembered, while the smaller room served more private and formal purposes and was used less often. Exhibiting the cramped side room as the kitchen repeated the misperceptions of the architects of Easter Hill Village, who designed kitchens too small for the many ways in which working-class residents preferred to use them, and who designed too-large living rooms that were rarely used. The result in both cases was a serious reversal of traditional uses of rooms in working-class homes.[23]

What then could be done to correct the exhibit? Although I made a number of recommendations that would have enlivened the exhibit and would have conveyed more accurately the life of the people who had inhabited the house, shifts in museum priorities and a lack of funds prevented the implementation of those suggestions. The house remains as it was first exhibited in 1968. It is still an important example, however, of an attempt to exhibit the lives of ordinary people, especially the poor, the landless, the servants, or agricultural or industrial workers.*

An exhibit of this sort can represent an important change in the way we think about the past. It can symbolize the democratization of history that has been going on for several years. Behind a museum exhibit—behind the decision that something is *worth* exhibiting—are cultural assumptions and historical research that can lead us to a new appreciation of ourselves and of those we have forgotten. The black families studied here did not live in "shacks." They are not stereotypes, mere ciphers. They are people whom we can know in remarkable detail by examining what they left behind.

To go back to the beginning, it is necessary to go back to Africa and Europe, for there is the origin of much about the black families that concern us here.

---

*In 1981, the Smithsonian announced plans to disassemble the house to make way for a new exhibit, and to reassemble it elsewhere in the Hall of Everyday Life.

CHAPTER I
Exploring the Origins of Maryland Slave Houses: "Every Man a Sufficient Architect for the Purpose"

Slave houses were once an integral part of the landscape of Maryland and the South; in such houses lived the majority of the population on many plantations, and frequently the majority of whole counties and regions. These enslaved workers raised the tobacco, rice, and cotton that produced the wealth. Without them, the history of Maryland, the South, and America would have been dramatically different. Yet it is difficult for us to imagine their homes with historical accuracy. We know little about the origins of slave houses or about traditional African house types and building methods, traditions that may have continued in some fashion in America. How did slave houses evolve over the century and a half from the early colonial years to the pre–Civil-War decades? How were slave houses designed and built? What were the different types? How were they furnished? What were the ways of life associated with them? Last, how did they evolve after "freedom"?

Definitive answers to such questions elude us at the moment due to lack of evidence, but we must begin somewhere, and the place to do so is Africa. Like Kunte Kinte of *Roots*, many enslaved Africans retained strong memories of their homeland. How were those memories expressed? And what exactly were they memories of? Charles Ball, a fugitive slave from Maryland, wrote that his grandfather, an "African of rank in his native land, . . . retained his native traditions respecting the Deity and hereafter." Folklorist John Vlach has recently pointed to African continuities in boat-building and boat-handling by slaves in the Chesapeake region, and to specific objects that were probably products of African traditions. Among them was a drum made by slaves in seventeenth- or early eighteenth-century Virginia that was a near copy of an Akan drum (from present-day

Ghana). Another was perhaps the most famous American contribution to the world of musical instruments, the banjo, which may have originated in Africa as the chordophone. According to Thomas Jefferson, "The Instrument proper to them [blacks] is the Banjar, which they brought hither from Africa." In regard to farming techniques, historian Peter Wood has shown that enslaved Africans in South Carolina shared knowledge of rice production brought from their homelands and were primarily responsible for the success of "white gold" in the colonial low country. Other scholars have demonstrated important African continuities in religion, music, language, family life, decorative arts, and architecture.[1]

In order to consider the possibility of African survivals in slave architecture, we must first examine traditional African architecture and learn the ideas and building skills that Africans might have brought with them. West Africans built a variety of buildings of formal and informal designs that were products of traditional ideas and community endeavor. Far more than the stereotypical "mud huts," they included temples, houses, granaries, palaces, forts, and mosques. Examples include a mosque in Timbuktu described in the early sixteenth century as a "most stately temple with walls of stone and lime." The fortified brick walls of Kano in northern Nigeria were begun in the twelfth century and enlarged through the fifteenth and seventeenth centuries. In the early nineteenth century, two-story buildings with arcades, galleries, and hand-sculptured walls lined the streets of Kumasi, the capital of the Ashanti kingdom in present-day Ghana (figure 14). Among the most impressive buildings of historical West Africa were the palace buildings of the Benin kingdom (figure 15), which a seventeenth-century Dutch writer described as a "collection of buildings which occupy as much space as the town of Haarlem," with many apartments and fine galleries "as big as those on the Exchange at Amsterdam."[2]

Today the vast majority of historical African structures exists only as archaeological sites, since most were made with wood or earthen walls and have been destroyed by the rigorous climate, by termites and other wood-boring insects, and by other natural forces of decay in tropical Africa, which are far more injurious to buildings than those in the temperate zone. Social and political turmoil among tribal groups resulting from the slave trade also wiped out buildings, as did attacks by European colonists. For example, jewels of African architecture were lost when the British destroyed the palaces of Kumasi in 1875, and sacked the city of Benin in 1897, burning its palaces. In that ancient cultural center of Africa, there had developed by

Figure 14
Ashante Street, Kumasi, Ghana, c. 1818. Reprinted with
permission from Susan Denyer, African Traditional Architecture *(New
York: Africana, 1978).*

the fifteenth century "well-organized guilds of brassworkers, blacksmiths, carpenters, weavers, leatherworkers, wood carvers, and pot-
ters." Other buildings in Africa, because they were not intended to
be permanent, died a more natural death. Permanent buildings were
unnecessary to migrant pastorialists or to groups that practiced land-
rotation agriculture and moved every four or five years. Also, the
houses of many groups were intended only to satisfy immediate family
needs; as families changed due to marriage, births, and deaths, old
houses were torn down and new ones built.[3]

The study of historical African architecture is only just now coming
into its own. Previous studies have tended to emphasize its primitive
qualities or the more photogenic features, with little historical or
architectural analysis. Others have focused on a few specific places,
making little reference to the whole. One result has been generaliza-
tion based on a narrow body of evidence. For example, one scholar
wrote that, "as a rule, traditional African houses are round in shape,"
in keeping with "nature's rhythm." Others have concluded the opposite, that rectangular houses were the norm and, more specifically, that
West African rooms were square, averaging 10′ x 10′ in size. How-

Figure 15
Benin palace, southern Nigeria, 1668. Reprinted with
permission from Susan Denyer, African Traditional Architecture
(New York: Africana, 1978).

ever, architectural historians have recently shown that there was a rich diversity of traditional house forms in West Africa—round, oval, square, rectangular—with rooms varying in size, usually from ten to twenty feet or more in length or diameter. Some dwellings were freestanding; others were joined and enclosed in a rectangular courtyard. More importantly, they have found that many traditional African societies did not think of a house as a single building; instead, homes consisted of clusters of buildings, the "rooms" for sleeping, eating, entertaining, and storage being located in the several buildings and in the spaces between them. The entire cluster was usually enclosed by an earthen wall or a wattle fence to create one overall entity, known as a compound. These architectural historians did find that Africans within the same ethnic group used the same design concepts and construction techniques, with the result that their dwellings were uniform in kind. Size and decorative expression increased in accordance with higher status. Also, buildings within a given cultural or geographical region usually had more similarities than differences. But there was apparently no standard type or size of dwelling across all West Africa.[4]

This architectural heritage had important implications for the development of black material culture and house types in Maryland and the rest of the nation. If large numbers of the same ethnic group or the same cultural or geographical region arrived in the same colony, they likely shared similar traditions, so the prospect of their continuing their customs in some form was enhanced. On the other hand, if small lots of Africans from different backgrounds or areas arrived, the chances of their continuing traditions were lessened. Thus, the patterns of slave importation and colonial settlement, the type of colonial economy, and the resultant composition of the colonial population strongly affected the character of African cultural survivals.

This can be demonstrated by comparing the situation of Africans arriving in Maryland with that of Africans further south. Throughout the eighteenth century in South Carolina, over 100,000 Africans arrived in Charleston and were then sold to low-country plantations. Due to the semitropical climate, the topography, and the demands of rice cultivation, these plantations were vast, isolated estates, rather than small, neighboring farms, and the slaves in the communities that developed often numbered in the hundreds. Their daily labor was supervised by black drivers year-round, while their white owners left the plantations at least during the summer, if not for longer periods. As a result of their isolation from white culture, their strong numerical majority, and the continued influx of imported slaves from Africa, rural slaves in low-country South Carolina "incorporated more of West African culture—as reflected in their language, religion, work patterns, and much else—into their new lives than did other black Americans . . . [and developed] their own distinctive culture."[5]

The extent to which South Carolina slaves built houses reflecting African traditions awaits a study of slave houses there, but a remarkable house in South Carolina, built by a former Bakongo slave and photographed in 1907, clearly illustrates African retentions (figures 16, 17). Translating Bakongo, we learn that the prefix "ba" means "people of" and "kongo" refers to the kingdom of the Kongo. Significantly, his house in South Carolina and the traditional Kongo house type are nearly identical in design, building materials, and methods of construction (figure 18). The former slave spoke the truth when he said that his house was modeled after the ones he knew in his homeland. No such houses are known to have been built in southern Maryland, but of course the possibility exists.[6]

The existence of this African-style house in fairly recent times can be explained in part by the sustained importation of slaves into South Carolina up to the prohibition of the African slave trade in 1807, and by the fact that boatloads of slaves were smuggled into South Carolina and Georgia up to the Civil War. The result was that African customs in these low-country areas were replenished from one generation to another, unlike in Maryland, where slave importation was halted by law in the 1780's. The story of Okra, a slave on a Georgia sea island plantation, illustrates the continued presence of African customs in black culture along the South Carolina and Georgia coast. Probably in the 1840's or 1850's, Okra constructed an African-style house with wattle-and-daub walls and a thatched roof of palmetto leaves, but his owner made him tear it down, saying he wanted no "African hut" on his place. The quarters that the owner did allow, excavated recently by archaeologists, were two-room houses with central chimneys with back-to-back fireplaces, an enlarged modification of a traditional Anglo-American tidewater cottage. But living in a house of a different cultural style did not end the African ways of Okra and the other African slaves on the plantation. As individuals and in groups, they continued to practice African customs in their religious practices, funeral services, music, dress, and language, as described by a former slave who knew the Africans as a youth.

"Now ole man Okra an ole man Gibson an ole Israel dey's African. . . . Dey tell us how dey lib in Africa. Dey laks tuh talk. It

Figure 16
House near Edgefield, South Carolina, built by a freed Bakongo slave.

Figure 17
House of Bakongo slave, near Edgefield, South Carolina.

funny talk an it ain so easy tuh unnuhstand but yuh gits use tuh it. Dey say dey buil deah own camp deah an lib in it. . . . Ole Israel he pray a lot wid a book he hab wut he hide, and he take a lill mat an he say he prayuhs on it. He pray wen duh sun go up and wen duh

Figure 18
Kongo house type, Angola, 1910. Reprinted with
permission from Susan Denyer, African Traditional Architecture
(New York: Africana, 1978).

sun go down. . . . He alluz tie he head up in a wite clawt an seem he keep a lot uh clawt on han. . . . Deah wuz a ole man . . . at the plantation wut wehn roun wid ole man Okra an I membuh well he call all duh fish an ting uh duh ribbuh by duh name uh "nyana" an den I heah pancake call 'flim.' . . . Ole man Okra he a great un fuh buil drum. He take a calf skin an tan it an make duh side uh maple. . . . It wuz bout eighteen inches wide an fifteen inches deep wen he finish it. He beat it wid a stick. Ole man Okra he sho kin chase a drum. Ole man Jesse he frum Africa too, an he make he own drum."[7]

Slaves in late seventeenth- and early eighteenth-century southern Maryland also made their own drums and used them to communicate. In fact, there were complaints of slaves getting "Drunk on the Lords Day beating their Negro Drums by which they call considerable Numbers of Negroes together in some Certaine places."[8]

On the island of Haiti, and later in New Orleans, Africans and their descendants may also have been able to sustain their traditional house forms and to establish them in America. According to folklorist John Vlach, large numbers of Yoruba slaves were sold to Haiti, where they lived in populous communities in relative isolation from whites. They blended their traditional house type with that of native islanders. In the late 1700's, they immigrated as free blacks to New Orleans, where their cultural cohesiveness enabled them to replicate their Yoruba-Haitian house type, which was one story in height, with the front door in the gable end, and with two or three small, square, approximately 10' x 10' or 12' x 12' rooms connected to one another front to back. According to Vlach, it was this African-derived house type that was the original "shotgun house," a common style of vernacular dwelling that eventually spread throughout the South.[9]

Slaves faced different circumstances in the Chesapeake region. The types of farms that developed, the topography, the patterns of slave settlement, and the colder climate worked against efforts to replicate African-style houses. In contrast to South Carolina or New Orleans in the late 1700's, blacks were sold in small lots directly to riverfront farms or in small port towns from ocean-going ships that sailed up the Bay and the many inland rivers, as illustrated by this advertisement: "Just imported from Africa a parcel of choice slave Negroes which will be to sale this day, on board the ship Kaulikan . . . on Patuxent River, for Bills of Exchange, money, or crop tobacco. . . ." The experience of Kunte Kinte, who was purchased in Annapolis by a Virginia planter and separated from his African shipmates, illustrates the dispersal of Africans by such sales in the Chesapeake region. The result was a diversity of tribal origins on Chesapeake plantations. One enslaved African, who was later manumitted, wrote that the mixture produced a "Babel of Languages," while blacks in South Carolina developed their own language, Gullah.[10]

Furthermore, the African population was not concentrated on large, isolated estates in southern Maryland, as in low-country South Carolina or Haiti. Between 1658 and 1710, almost three out of four slaves lived on farms with twenty or fewer slaves, two out of four lived on farms with ten or fewer, and nearly a third lived on farms with five or fewer. This thin distribution severely restricted social and cultural contact among Africans. The resultant difficulty in sustaining African cultural cohesiveness was compounded by the fact that the slaves' labor and everyday life was supervised not by black drivers but by whites—indentured servants, hired overseers, or the slaveowners themselves, who were more personally active in the acculturation process than their South Carolina counterparts.[11]

Though the slave population on farms did become more concentrated as the eighteenth century progressed, by 1730 over half the

slaves still lived on farms with twenty or fewer, and over a third on farms with ten or fewer slaves. Also, the number of imported Africans declined in proportion to the Maryland-born so that, by about 1730, Maryland-born slaves constituted the majority. Because of these factors—the demographic patterns of slave distribution, the daily supervision by whites rather than by blacks on relatively small estates, and the cold Maryland winters—it is unlikely that Africans were able to replicate their traditional house types in southern Maryland. But archaeological excavations of homes of black families should give us more definite answers.[12]

Rather than traditional house types, it is more likely that Africans in Maryland continued their traditional construction methods, since they were similar in several respects to the basic techniques of the British and colonial Anglo-Americans and could be utilized in the construction of early Maryland buildings. Because traditional African building methods are little understood, it is perhaps advisable to explain them, as well as how they were passed on.

Because of community cooperation in historical African societies, most African males who came to America would have participated in or at least have witnessed as youths building construction in their homeland, and therefore would have brought with them some knowledge of African architecture and building techniques. The description of an eighteenth-century Ibo (from present-day Nigeria) depicts traditional building methods both in his homeland and throughout West Africa: "Every man is a sufficient architect for the purpose. The whole neighborhood afford their unanimous assistance in building . . . and in return receive and expect no other recompense than a feast." In many African groups women participated in construction, particularly in its final phases, such as applying coats of plaster inside and out. Among some groups it was also the women's responsibility to decorate the exterior of the house by incising attractive designs into the plaster while it was still wet.[13]

Brick and stone masonry was one of the skills Africans brought with them. Contrary to the pejorative stereotype of "mud houses," many African structures were built of brick or stone. In the upper regions of the savannah and in the Sahel (the habitable fringes of the Sahara), sun-dried bricks and occasionally (in Bornu, for example) kiln-fired bricks were laid in courses and cemented by mud mortar to construct walls for houses, forts, granaries, and mosques. In the few places where stone was available, such as in the upper Niger regions and in Angola, stone walls were constructed for houses, compounds, and forts. The most famous examples of stone masonry are

the massive walled forts and buildings of Zimbabwe in East Africa.[14]

In the coastal and lower savannah regions of West Africa, the techniques used to build mud houses closely resembled those used to build wattle-and-daub dwellings in Britain and colonial America. These ancient techniques developed indigenously in prehistoric Europe and Africa and were continued in America. In all three places, a frame was first constructed of upright poles set into the ground. Then the interstices were filled in with a wickerwork of woven branches, and the walls heavily plastered with trampled wet clay to which lime, animal hair, cow dung, or chopped straw could be added for cohesiveness. Preferably, the walls were finished with a thin mud plaster that was washed and scraped regularly to maintain a smooth, water-repellent surface. In Africa the results could be quite impressive. A seventeenth-century Dutch writer reported of the palace buildings of Benin that "the walls were made of clay, very well erected, and they can make and keep them as shiny and smooth by washing and rubbing as any wall in Holland can be made with chalk, and they are like mirrors."[15]

In early Maryland, both houses and important public structures, such as the seventeenth-century courthouse of Charles County, were constructed of wattle and daub. It is possible—though as yet undocumented—that early Africans and their descendants assisted in the construction of at least some of these. Today examples of wattle-and-daub houses may be seen at the reconstructed settlement at Jamestown. (Yet in the interpretation of Jamestown by the National Park Service, there is little mention of the presence of blacks at Jamestown after their arrival in 1619.)[16]

Other traditional African construction methods were blended into those of the British and colonial Anglo-Americans. One was to build "cob" walls of trampled wet clay packed in courses up the height of the wall. Another was to erect houses of rammed-earth, or pisé, walls, where slightly moist clay was tightly compressed in wooden forms by a flat-surfaced beater, then set into place on the wall, like large bricks. There are a few examples of main houses in Maryland built of rammed earth, as well as nineteenth-century slave houses at the Four-Mile Tree Plantation and the Bremo Plantation in tidewater Virginia. Indeed, the owner of Bremo, John W. Cocke, considered pisé construction the "cheapest and best of all the permanent modes of building," and recommended it to other slaveowners. Robert Carter gave evidence that slaves were adept in these traditional methods of construction, and that their skills were valued, when he

asked a slave dealer for a black who "understood building mud walls," a man who was "an Artist, not a Common Labourer."[17]

Africans were also adept at building wooden houses, and had skills that they could have employed and modified in America, since their methods, though not identical to European or American techniques of log or frame construction, did have some basic features in common, a fact usually overlooked by historians. For example, Africans in the river basins and savannah regions built rectangular, gable-roofed houses with timbers horizontally aligned that somewhat resembled log houses (figure 18). Like single-unit houses in Maryland, they usually measured sixteen to twenty feet in length and fourteen to sixteen feet in width, and were one story in height. The corners of some examples were buttressed by posts, a technique also employed in some log houses in Maryland. Instead of being hewn, however, the timbers were left in the round and were lashed together with vines or strips of bark, since cutting into the diameter of bamboo or palm saplings weakens them.[18]

Africans in other areas of the coast and savannah also constructed frame dwellings, with different groups using different framing techniques. In some areas the frames consisted of large upright posts at each corner and in the center, with smaller posts serving as studs, similar to one type of traditional frame of Europe and America. "Houses of very regular dimensions and of extreme neatness and of sometimes imposing height or length" were constructed in this fashion. Another framing technique was to erect a series of upright studs of equal size, either adjoining one another or spaced a foot or so apart, and joined by smaller, horizontal poles. The frames were covered by a wicker or woven mat, sometimes of a highly decorative design, or by smaller poles laid horizontally. In the Sahel, more imposing structures were built of timber frames. For example, the Hausa of northern Nigeria used termite-resistant palm timbers to construct domes and clay roofs "of almost monumental dimensions . . . [and] of extraordinary symmetry" in the late fifteenth century. The Africans' skill in shaping wood was also illustrated in their sculpture, which included not only statues and masks, but architectural elements such as carved doors, pillars, and posts.[19]

Since African, British, and early American thatching techniques had similar features, Africans in Maryland could also continue their traditions in this endeavor, probably modifying them to suit the new environment. According to one Maryland architectural historian, "in the first few years after settlement there must have been literally thousands of thatched roofs." Though thatched roofs eventually lost favor, their use continued into the nineteenth century for some outbuildings, tobacco barns, and dwellings of slaves and post–Civil-War freedmen in Maryland, Virginia, and South Carolina. As we shall see later, some black families in Charles County, Maryland, continued to thatch the roofs of their log homes into the twentieth century.[20]

While thatched or earthen roofs were the most common types in West Africa, wood shingled roofs were not absent. For example, the palaces of Benin were most likely covered with wood shingles fastened by nails, as shown in sixteenth-century bronze plaques from Benin. Also, archaeological excavations of a fourteenth-century site at Ife in southern Nigeria have uncovered many iron nails, probably used to attach shingles. Thus, slaves from this region, and perhaps others, would possibly have known how to forge and shape nails and to split shingles or clapboards for construction. These techniques could possibly have been modified to help build the frame houses and buildings with split clapboard walls and shingles common to seventeenth-century southern Maryland. Further archaeological research of early African towns and cities should provide the evidence for a more complete and precise account.[21]

At this moment, it can be argued that early Africans in Maryland did not arrive in an alien world in which their traditions of construction had no use. Instead, the African and Anglo cultures shared elements that probably allowed Africans to utilize their building and design experience, despite the diversity of their tribal origins. As the historian Russell Menard has pointed out, the primary task of slaves in the seventeenth century and the first third of the eighteenth century was field labor, and the craftsmen identified in documents were almost exclusively whites.[22] But the majority of farms had only a small labor force, so it is likely that the slaves, many of them newly arrived from Africa, helped build the houses, outbuildings, and barns, adding new, Anglo building skills and design concepts to their own. The new synthesis could be passed on to the next generation. Nineteenth-century houses of Maryland slaves and freed families do not exhibit overtly African or Afro-American characteristics in construction or design; but an examination of African house-building traditions shows that these later-built houses, springing from less visible, shared traditions, were not as foreign to their inhabitants as they might appear.

At the moment, studies suggest the following course for the development of Maryland slave houses. Only a few slaves lived in "slave quarters" in the seventeenth and early eighteenth centuries, because the majority lived on farms with only a few slaves. Historian Cheryl Hayes's study of white property owners' houses in Queen Anne's County on Maryland's Eastern Shore has found that slaves typically lived in extra rooms dispersed about the farm, such as the lofts of barns and outbuildings and the main house's attic, basement, and storage rooms. Historian Eugene Genovese concurs that it was "all too common" in the eighteenth century for slaves to be quartered in "barn lofts and barrackslike makeshifts." However, Hayes found that by the mid-eighteenth century, slave quarters were becoming increasingly separated from the main house and specifically identified in the tax lists as "Negro quarters" or "Negro dwellings."[23]

Probably a major reason for this change in housing was the contemporary emergence of a more stable slave family. As historians Allan Kulikoff and Russell Menard have shown, most slaves lived on small plantations in the late seventeenth and early eighteenth centuries. Men substantially outnumbered women and usually lived with other unrelated men, presumably in rooms in the main house or in outbuildings. Due to the high proportion of men to women in this period, it was difficult for men to find spouses; when they did, the woman most often lived on another small plantation. Couples were rarely able to live together, and children lived with the mother on her plantation. Due to the natural decline of the first-generation male Africans, the sex ratios among slaves became evenly balanced by the 1750's, and the number of slaves who lived on plantations with more than twenty slaves increased. As a result, men had more opportunity both to marry and to marry a woman who lived on the same plantation. It is probable that slave couples sought separate houses, instead of rooms in the main house or outbuildings, since they could have more control over rearing their children and have at least a semblance of a place of their own, as their ancestors had had in Africa. It was at this time (the mid-eighteenth century) that tax records show specifically slave dwellings being constructed, as Cheryl Hayes found. It seems likely that the two developments in slave housing and family life are linked.[24]

The type of house that was built deliberately as "slave quarters" in the mid-eighteenth century is not yet clearly established, but at least by the early nineteenth century the single-unit log house became the standard. Log house construction was foreign to Anglo-American settlers in colonial Maryland, since it had not been used in Britain. The construction techniques were borrowed from German and Scandinavian settlers in America in the seventeenth and early eighteenth centuries, and, after the Scotch-Irish and other settlers adapted them, the methods spread rapidly across the frontier. As we have seen, Africans from certain regions used horizontal log construction, though the timbers were not hewn and notched at the corners. The log house would have been almost as new to Africans with different traditions as it was to Anglo-Americans. But its advantages for all were multiple: it could be made from locally available material at practically no cost, it was quick and relatively easy to construct, and it was durable. Its thick walls, if properly chinked with cohesive mud daubing (a technique known in Africa), provided insulation from cold weather.

By the last half of the eighteenth century, slaves had blended their traditional building crafts with those learned in Maryland, and they could readily erect the rectangular log walls, chink them with properly mixed clay, and cover the houses with gable roofs of thatch, boards, or shingles, as we shall see in the next chapter. The amount of living space that the dwelling provided approximated that of whites' log dwellings, as well as that of many African houses. As a result of all these factors, by the late eighteenth century and certainly by the early nineteenth, the single-unit log house had become the traditional house type of black Marylanders. Thus the "log cabin," commonly perceived as the home exclusively of white Americans on the frontier, has a long heritage for Afro-Americans as well.[25]

CHAPTER II
Slave Houses:
"My Lord, My Lord,
This Is It! This Is It!"

My Lord, my Lord, this is it! This is it! The old man says this is it!" exclaimed William Diggs, a sixty-two-year-old man from Charles County, Maryland. He was looking at a restored one-room log slave house at Sotterley, an eighteenth-century tobacco plantation in St. Mary's County, Maryland, now preserved as a private museum. Diggs himself was born in a log house similar to the one we had come to investigate. It was built by his grandfather, William Jordan, a former slave, a few years after emancipation, and modeled after the slave houses he had lived in and built as a youth. Diggs's mother was born in that house, too, in 1890. Almost all of those log slave houses are gone now in southern Maryland and elsewhere in the South, which explains Diggs's excitement in seeing on exhibit a house like that of his ancestors, and like those of the ancestors of thousands of other black men and women throughout Maryland and the nation.[1]

Such houses are rarely exhibited in historical museums or parks; when they are, the exceptional, better-built examples are usually preserved, as at Mount Vernon and Monticello, rather than the typical log houses in which the majority of slaves lived. Our main task, therefore, is to learn the design and construction of slave houses, especially of the typical ones, so that the historical houses of black people can be conveyed to the public. By describing the appearance of these houses, it is also hoped that we may see more completely the rural world of both blacks and whites.

Because of the more complete sources of evidence—extant structures, fugitive slave autobiographies, and WPA interviews of ex-slaves—our clearest view of slave quarters emerges in the nineteenth century. Also, elderly informants like William Diggs have provided specific details about nineteenth-century slave houses, since they saw

Figure 19
Unidentified log house, photographed near the turn of the
century, presumably near Richmond, Virginia. The common type of house
built as slave dwellings in nineteenth-century southern Maryland, Virginia, and
elsewhere in the South. Blacks inhabited houses of this type into the
early 1900's in southern Maryland. Photo: Huestis Cook.
Valentine Museum, Richmond, Virginia.

scores of them that remained standing into the early 1900's. Some informants actually lived as tenants in former slave houses. Unfortunately, only two old photographs of log houses of Maryland black families have been found that match the description of "old-time houses" given by ex-slaves and oral informants. All other pictures that did correspond to their descriptions were of houses in Virginia, North Carolina, and other Southern states, photographed after emancipation. But because they so clearly illustrate the houses described by the sources—houses no longer standing and difficult for us to imagine today—I use these photographs in this and subsequent chapters.

Slave quarters in nineteenth-century southern Maryland were rarely barracks or dormitories; instead, they were typically small, plain, freestanding dwellings, one story in height, with a gable roof and a chimney exterior to one gable end (figure 19). They were customarily of log construction, though there were some frame examples, and a very few of stone or brick. Whatever the construction, the floor plan typically consisted of one room down and a loft above. There was usually one door, centered in the long wall. There might be one or two windows on either side of the door, one in a gable end, or no windows at all. There were some examples in log, frame, and brick construction of two-unit (or double-pen) houses that consisted of two identical rooms on either side of a central chimney with back-to-back fireplaces, each room having its own front door. No two-story houses or dormitories were cited by freed slaves or by black oral informants today, though at Mulberry Fields in St. Mary's County there are brick piers of a structure that plantation tradition alleges to have been a "slave dormitory." Archaeological excavation of this and other slave structures would shed light on the neglected history of slave housing.[2]

Though only a small number of slaves were identified in written records as carpenters, slaves did make important contributions to the built environment of the plantation world. Most male and some female slaves were skilled in log construction, and some were especially trained by their owners or by other slaves as artisans to work on the plantation or to hire out. The fugitive slave Charles Ball was a stonemason, and the ex-slave James Wiggins from Anne Arundel County recalled: "My father was a carpenter by trade. He was hired out to different farmers by Mr. Revell to repair and build barns, fences, and houses." As an artisan, he learned to read and write and forged passes for slaves. Another former slave in Charles County told of a "very valuable slave, an expert carpenter and bricklayer, whose services were much sought after in southern Maryland." These skilled slaves built important work buildings as well as houses. For example, a slave named Charles from St. Thomas Manor built a windmill at St. Inigoes in St. Mary's County with "no instructions from anyone—the windmill [was] well built and answers well."[3]

Slaveowners actively sought to hire out skilled slaves, because they were profitable investments. Slave carpenters usually earned around one hundred dollars a year for their owners, while field hands hired out at around forty-five dollars a year. In 1821 the twenty-one slave carpenters in St. Mary's County constituted 23 percent of the total number of carpenters in the county, and their presence probably caused the decline in the number of free carpenters in the last decades before the Civil War.[4]

Some, if not many, slaves and free blacks from southern Maryland contributed to the construction of Annapolis, Baltimore, and Washington, D.C. In Annapolis, Caroline Hammond recalled that her father, George Berry, a free black, "was a carpenter by trade [and] had plenty of work . . . doing repairs and building both for the white people and free colored people." One observer in the nation's capital wrote, "A great portion of the labor of the different works now in progress in this city is performed by slaves," and among the public structures they helped to construct was the Capitol. Some of these slaves were probably from nearby southern Maryland. In Baltimore, city directories from 1819 to 1860 show blacks in a variety of trades related to either construction or woodworking: bricklayers, carpenters, caulkers, coopers, painters, plasterers, ship carpenters, ship joiners, stonemasons, stonecutters, sawyers, wheelwrights, and cabinetmakers. As ship caulkers, blacks "furnished nearly all the labor, until the middle of the nineteenth century," and held a "considerable share" of the blacksmithing trade. In fact, as much as 45 percent of all the blacksmiths in St. Mary's County in the ante-bellum nineteenth century were slaves.[5]

Slaves customarily constructed their own houses. "We had 60 slaves on the plantation, each family housed in a cabin built by the slaves to accommodate the families according to the number," said one former slave. The houses freedmen built after the Civil War are probably the most telling evidence that slaves built houses (Chapter V). Examples of their houses of log and frame construction still stand in the communities they founded: Ben's Creek and Ball's Graveyard in Calvert County; Beachville and Abell in St. Mary's; Muirkirk in Prince George's; and Sugarland, Jerusalem, Jonesville, Big Woods, and Martinsburg in Montgomery, to name a few.[6]

Figure 20
Facade, frame slave house at Grasslands, Anne Arundel County.
This single-unit house, built by slaves at Grasslands in the 1850's, had
glass windows, a brick chimney, and lathed and plastered walls in-filled with
brick. Located directly behind the main house, it served after emancipation
as quarters for the cook, Renie, who was born during slavery and
perhaps reared in this house. Photo: author.

Like Thomas Jefferson's slaves at Monticello, slaves in southern
Maryland built the main houses of their plantations, along with the
barns and other important farm buildings. Their skills are most
clearly illustrated and documented at Grasslands, a farm established
in the 1850's near present-day Fort Meade in Anne Arundel County,
where slaves constructed the brick main house and four frame slave
houses, whose walls they insulated with leftover bricks they had fired
for the main house (figure 20). According to the farm journal of the
owner, William A. Anderson, his slaves dug the ice pond, built the
dam and icehouse, "hewed and bored posts," split rails for fences,
and constructed farm buildings. One example was the corn house,
erected in 1854 and "finished" by a relative's "servant," who was
borrowed or hired for the purpose. In 1853, Anderson hired a Negro

Figure 21
Abandoned bank barn at Grasslands, Anne Arundel County. Photo: author.

named Elias Gardner—most likely a free black—and the slaves built an imposing two-story bank barn, probably under his supervision (figure 21). They quarried and hauled "100 wagonloads" of stone from nearby outcroppings and built massive ground-floor walls as the foundation for the tall upper story. The slaves hewed and squared impressive timbers—some as long as thirty or forty feet—and secured them by pegged mortise and tenon joints to other beams and braces. Anderson, Gardner, and the slaves "raised" the barn frame on August 29–30, 1853. They were probably proud of their accomplishment, for the barn was of fine quality; it remained in use and in sound condition for more than a century. Like so many other old Maryland farms where blacks constructed many of the buildings, Grasslands is no longer in operation, and the barn is abandoned and collapsing.[7]

The buildings at Grasslands are but a few of the thousands of structures throughout the South, including fine homes and interiors, that were built by slaves and free black artisans. In a world of severely limited opportunities, constructing these buildings gave free blacks and slaves an important measure of self-esteem. People in their community could see the products of their abilities. Their children and friends could point to their accomplishments with pride, and by association feel enhanced themselves; this is illustrated by the testimony of the former slaves in the WPA narratives. Today, the ante-bellum structures that survive continue to demonstrate not only the lives of the whites who owned them, but the workmanship of the black people who helped build the plantation world.[8]

The log house was the typical slave dwelling in nineteenth-century southern Maryland. The testimony of James Deane, a freed slave, introduces us to the common type: "I was born in a log cabin [in 1844], a typical Charles County log cabin at Goose Bay on the Potomac River. The cabin had two rooms, one up and one down, very large with two windows, one in each room. There were no porches. Over the door was a wide board to keep the rain and snow from beating over the top of the door, with a large log chimney on the outside, plastered between the logs, in which was a fireplace with an open grate to cook and to put logs on the fire to heat."[9]

Slaves inhabited similar log houses throughout Maryland and the South, revealing the common housing conditions of most slaves (figures 22 and 23). "I was born in a log cabin, with two rooms, one up and one down," recalled one former Maryland slave, and another, Richard Macks from Charles County, said he was reared in a "log cabin, built of log and mud, having two rooms." One former slave remembered living in "dingy little hovels which were constructed in cabin fashion and of stone and of logs with their typical windows and rooms of one room up and one room down." Slaves in Virginia also lived in log houses. "The log cabin, where we lived . . . contained two rooms, one up and one down, with a window in each room." Slave houses in Georgia were similar "two-roomed buildings made out of logs and daubed with mud to keep the weather out. At one end there was a chimney that was made of dried mud, sticks, and stones." Recollections of similar houses were given by ex-slaves in almost every Southern state.[10]

Among prominent black leaders born in Maryland during slavery who lived in log houses was Frederick Douglass. Born on the Eastern Shore of Maryland, he described his grandparents' dwelling, where he lived for a while, as a "log cabin that resembled the cabins in the western states built by the first settlers, except that it was smaller, less commodious, and less substantial. It was built of wood, clay, and straw." Abolitionist writer Josiah Henson, who was born in Charles County, grew up in a log house in Montgomery County, Maryland, and later lived in a log cabin in Kentucky. Because Harriet Beecher Stowe based her famous novel on his autobiography, *Father Henson's*

Figure 22
Single-unit log house photographed near the turn of
the century in Virginia. Except for its glass window, it is
representative of the type described by former slaves in the WPA
narratives. Unlike the log dwelling in figure 19, it has a board roof, no
porch, and a short chimney stack. It is not as well constructed as
those that have survived; it represents a type now vanished
from the landscape. Photo: Huestis Cook. Valentine
Museum, Richmond, Virginia.

Story of His Own Life, that log house was in fact "Uncle Tom's cabin."[11]

Descendants of freed slaves also recalled that log houses were the typical homes of their ancestors. William Diggs's friends Benjamin and Nellie Ross, born in 1883 and 1888 respectively in Charles County and the children of freed slaves, said the homes of their parents and of other "slavery-time people" were log houses with one room and a loft, a plan commonly called "one up, one down." James Scriber, born in 1878 and the son of former slaves who fled to St.

Figure 23
"Negro Shack (so called), Va.," c. 1897. This house is illustrative
of the "rough housing" James Scriber said existed in southern Maryland in
the 1800's. Courtesy Virginia Historical Society.

Mary's County from Georgia after the Civil War, grew up in a log slave house of this type on a farm where his parents were tenants. He said that most "slavery-time cabins" resembled his childhood home, which was similar to the house in figure 23, one of a series of photographs shown to him.[12]

In general, the overall design, floor plan, and size of slave houses were rather similar to those of the houses of the rural poor, even of small landowners. These dwellings were also one story in height, with a gable roof, a chimney exterior to one gable end, a central doorway, and a floor plan of one or two rooms (two rooms for a single family being larger than that provided for most slaves). As historian Bayly Ellen Marks found in her pioneering study of antebellum St. Mary's County, the homes of wealthy landowners were the most distinctive. They were typically of brick or frame construction (no log examples), and had the largest and most diverse floor plans, ranging from 18' x 26' to 26' x 36' to 48' x 30'. Homes of the

Table 2

Comparisons of Houses in St. Mary's County, Maryland

Types of Houses	1780–89	1790–99	1798
Houses of the wealthy			
Number of cases	1	3	56
Median dimensions	36 x 18	36 x 34	
Type of construction			
% brick		66	38
% frame		33	62
Houses of landowners			
Number of cases	33	12	179
Most common dimensions	16 x 20	16 x 24	
Type of construction			
% brick	18		16
% frame	63		81
% log	18		3
Houses of tenants			
Number of cases	18	7	251
Most common dimensions	16 x 16	16 x 16	
Type of construction			
% brick			20
% frame	66	50	79
% log	33	50	1
Slave quarters			
Number of cases	20	10	30
Most common dimensions	16 x 12	24 x 16	
Type of construction			
% brick			4
% frame		33	56
% log	100	66	40

Sources: These tables were compiled by Bayly Ellen Marks from the Valuations and Indentures 1780–1808, 1789 Federal Assessment, and Valuations 1807–26 and 1826–41, St. Mary's County. See Marks, "Economics and Society in a Staple Plantation System: St. Mary's County, Maryland, 1790–1840" (Ph.D. diss., University of Maryland, 1979), pp. 49–51, 53.

1800–9	1810–19	1820–29	1830–41
7	3	3	5
48 x 30	18 x 26	28 x 24	36 x 16
14		33	60
			20
44	18	31	54
16 x 24	24 x 26	16 x 20	16 x 24
16	25	10	21
58	37	68	70
25	37	21	9
46	13	45	24
16 x 24	16 x 20	16 x 16	16 x 16
8	16	15	
45	16	35	75
45	66	50	25
35	7	19	42
16 x 12	16 x 16	16 x 14	16 x 14
30		16	
70		84	100

landowning middle class were predominantly of frame construction, were markedly smaller than those of the wealthy, and were of a more uniform size, the most common dimensions being 16′ x 20′ and 16′ x 24′ (probably two rooms downstairs). Houses of free white and black tenants were commonly of frame or log construction (with only a few examples of brick), and were smaller than landowners' houses, typical dimensions being 16′ x 16′. Slave houses were predominantly of log construction with some frame and very few brick examples. Like the tenant houses, they were roughly square, usually 16′ x 16′ or 16′ x 14′ (table 2). My field survey of slave houses in southern Maryland found surviving examples of this type, such as the approximately square log slave houses at Sotterley (17′5″ x 15′8″), and the slave or possibly post–Civil-War tenant house at Collison Farm (16′7″ x 14′5″). In addition, there were examples of a more elongated, rectangular type, almost exclusively of frame construction, one side being four to six feet longer than the other. Examples included the slave house at Essex (19′2″ x 15′1″), at Grasslands (19′6″ x 13′4″), and the two houses at Wayson Farm (20′ x 13′4″). It is important to note that one-room houses of slaves were similar in size to those of tenants and small landowners. Thus, the vast majority of families in antebellum nineteenth-century St. Mary's County lived in small homes of only one or two rooms downstairs (figures 24–28).[13]

These small house types were not exclusive to southern Maryland. Instead, a variety of classes in the mid-Atlantic region, the Carolinas and Georgia, the Appalachian region, and the Ohio and Mississippi valleys, including slaves, tenants, and small landowners, built and lived in square or rectangular log and frame houses. The Abraham Lincoln birthplace, a single-unit log house with a log chimney, is perhaps the most famous example (figure 29).[14]

Significantly, no slave houses or houses of any black family in southern Maryland that were documented or surveyed had rooms of ten or twelve feet square, dimensions considered a survival of the African norm for room size. Such dimensions have been found in Afro-American houses in regions as diverse as Haiti, Louisiana, Massachusetts, and New York, and it may be that there were once examples in southern Maryland. However, the resident southern Maryland planters, who involved themselves personally in plantation life, likely imposed their ideas regarding house form upon the quarters of their slaves, as they probably did for their tenants. Also, since the sixteen-foot-square and the more elongated rectangular house forms were quite common in southern Maryland among most social groups,

Figure 24
The restored log slave house at Sotterley Plantation, St.
Mary's County, Maryland. Despite significant changes, the best-
preserved log slave house in southern Maryland.
Photo: author.

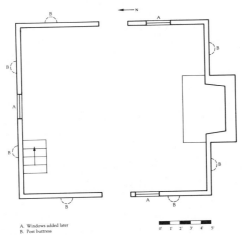

A. Windows added later
B. Post buttress

Figure 25
Floor plan of restored log slave house at Sotterley.

Figure 26
Facade of abandoned log slave house at River View, St. Mary's
County. This single-unit dwelling, probably built in the second third
of the nineteenth century, was representative of the log houses many slave
families occupied. The brick chimney that was on the gable end has been
removed, and the bottom logs have rotted away. The studs pegged
into the log wall on either side of the door braced the structure.
Photo: author.

it should not be surprising that these designs were used for slave houses. After all, slave carpenters helped build many houses for the larger society and most likely adopted the norm, as probably did many nonprofessional plantation slaves who built log dwellings also. In addition, one should remember that West Africa contained many traditional house types, including examples in different regions of one-story, one-room dwellings with a gable roof and with square and elongated rectangular proportions of roughly similar dimensions. Thus, it may be that these square and rectangular house forms were not simply imposed upon slaves, but rather that Anglo-American and Afro-American traditions coincided in some cases.[15]

For other slaves who had different housing traditions, these types would have been alien. Perhaps many of them—as suggested by

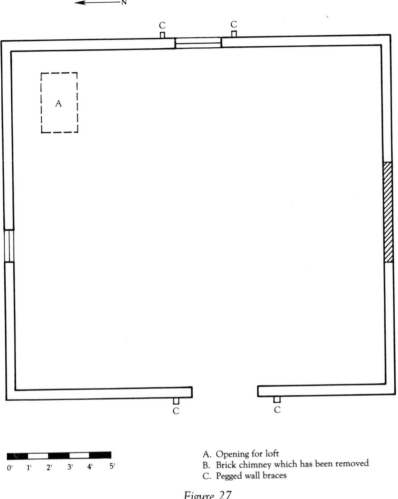

A. Opening for loft
B. Brick chimney which has been removed
C. Pegged wall braces

Figure 27
Floor plan of slave house at River View.

Okra, the Georgia slave whose African-style house was torn down—were able to continue with their own cultural traditions, even if they were forced to live in a house of a different cultural style. The likelihood of this is supported by the experiences of many European and Asian immigrants, who also were not able to replicate their traditional house types in America, but who did sustain their cultural

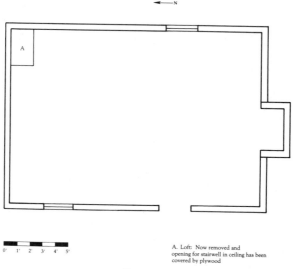

A. Loft: Now removed and
opening for stairwell in ceiling has been
covered by plywood

0'   1'   2'   3'   4'   5'

Figure 28
Floor plan of slave house at Grasslands.

identity. However, it should be remembered that for Afro-Americans the loss of control over the type of house they lived in was but one of many enforced losses they suffered during generations of slavery.

Let us now turn to the construction of log slave houses. We have learned that slaves customarily built their own houses, but what were their methods? What types of wood did they prefer? What kinds of floors, chimneys, and roofs did slave houses have, and how were they installed? Only after we answer questions such as these can we accurately recreate slave houses and assess the contributions of blacks to the built environment of the plantation world. Black building methods can probably best be described by reconstructing log slave houses feature by feature. Such descriptions have the added advantage of helping us see slaves engaged in important endeavors other than field labor, endeavors that enabled them to develop a collection of skills essential to their survival after emancipation.

Unfortunately, detailed descriptions of the actual construction of slave houses are limited by the absence of written evidence and by the fact that most slave houses have been destroyed, and all of the few that remain have been altered. Nonetheless, examination of their original elements, along with the recollections of former slaves, can shed light on the subject. These sources can be supplemented by

Figure 29
Abraham Lincoln birthplace and childhood home, near
Hodgenville, Kentucky. Like the tenant house at the Smithsonian,
this cabin was reduced in size, by one foot in length and four feet in
width. Photo: Ronald Guy. Courtesy Abraham Lincoln Birthplace
Historic Site.

the recollections of the children and grandchildren of freed slaves, some of whom, like James Scriber, lived in former slave houses, and all of whom watched freed slaves construct log houses and outbuildings using methods learned and practiced during slavery.

In explaining how "slavery-time people" evaluated wood for log construction, oral informants Benjamin Ross and James Scriber agreed that it was most important that the tree "be straight" and of a type that was durable, that would split properly, and that was fairly easy to hew. Trees with these qualities were plentiful in the southern Maryland woods, particularly pine, chestnut, oak, and poplar. The extant houses of slaves and freed black families are built of these woods and no others. Both Ross and Scriber added that the old-timers used to keep mental records of trees in the forest. "They may not cut it right then, but they'd have that in mind," explained Ross. He and William Diggs pointed out that their ancestors preferred oak because it was the most durable, while pine was less favored because it was softer, had more sap, and was more prone to rot unless the log was thick and hewed to its heartwood. "Hopsie" Johnson, the son of former slaves in Calvert County, disagreed, explaining that oak was "really hard to hew" and would not "score chip [hew cleanly] like chestnut or pine." Johnson learned about wood from his father, who used to supplement his income by splitting logs for crossties, fence rails, houses, and corncribs. Blanche Wilson from Calvert County said that her maternal grandparents, who were freed slaves, preferred chestnut because it "grew so tall and straight." In fact, the house of hewn chestnut logs her grandfather constructed after emancipation still stands. In contrast, the log house of a neighbor, also a freed slave, was built of pine. Thus people eveluted wood as individuals and followed their own judgments.[16]

Oxen, which were once common on southern Maryland farms, were the preferred work animals to "snake" the logs out of the woods. They were less excitable than horses and had common sense. Benjamin Ross and William Diggs explained that "horses didn't have enough sense to walk around the stumps, but oxen would walk around slow, and if the log ran up against a stump, you could pull it aside. But a horse, if he got tangled up, he would stomp and pull and jerk, and could break his leg."[17]

Slaves used the same basic methods to hew logs as black and white builders throughout America. First, said Ross, they stretched a string with powder or chalk on it along the length of the log. Then they plucked the string, leaving a colored line along the log that indicated the area to be hewed away (figure 30). "Then with an ax that had some weight to it [a poll ax], my father'd go down one side and notch it [cut perpendicularly into the log, at intervals of around six to eight inches]. Then with a broad ax [figure 31] he would come and chop them out. We called the chips 'scores' and we'd burn them in the wintertime to keep warm."[18]

After being hewed with the broad ax, the log was still rough.

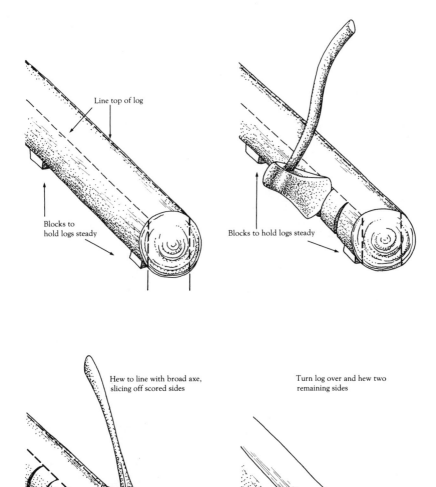

Figure 30
Methods used to hew logs.

Some builders used them in that condition (figures 19 and 22), while others preferred smoother logs and removed the rough gashes with a foot adz, which resembled a mattock or short-handled hoe with a curved chisel-like blade (figure 31). The length of the handle was usually custom-made according to the arm reach and height of its owner, Ross said. At all times, Diggs pointed out, "He had to be careful because if that adz got away from you, it'd cut your leg."[19]

Instead of a carpenter's level, the builders fashioned homemade devices to serve the purpose. "Hopsie" Johnson said "the people" used to fill a wide glass or bottle halfway with water, place something that would float in it, and set the glass on the log. If the float went to one side, that side was lowered. William Diggs's grandfather, the freed slave William Jordan, used a more accurate device, a "bubble bottle," which was more similar to a carpenter's level. It was a rectangular stoppered bottle (perhaps an old medicine bottle) filled with water except for a small air bubble. Jordan's bubble bottle, which Diggs has in his possession, is approximately six inches long, four inches wide, and one inch thick. The bottle was placed on its side on the log, and the log was adjusted until the bubble remained in the middle. As with many poor homesteaders in our history, these people did not have much in the way of materials, but they made do by their own ingenuity.[20]

To join the corners of the log houses, slaves used the types of corner notches typical of the mid-Atlantic region. The V-notch (figure 32) was the type most often found in slave houses in southern Maryland, as well as on houses built by freed slaves after emancipation. It is also commonly found on log houses built by whites. The half-dovetailed notch was used on a few houses of black families. One slave house with full-dovetailed cornering was found, while another had half notches. The first three types—V-notch and half and full dovetail—provide the strongest corners because the logs are locked together to create more stable walls.[21]

The most unusual feature found in the construction of log slave houses in southern Maryland was the use of upright posts placed against the walls and pegged into them as buttresses. Variations of this method were found in log slave houses at Sotterley, Blair's Purchase, and Gresham. James Scriber, a tenant farmer at Sotterley for thirty years, recalled that all seven of the single-unit log slave houses there were constructed with posts in a fashion similar to those on the sole surviving log house, which is now on exhibit. Oral informants in St. Mary's and Charles counties recalled in separate interviews that this practice of post-and-peg construction was common among

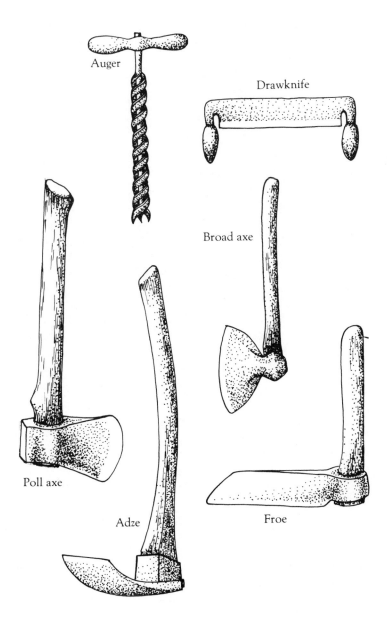

Figure 31
Principal tools used to build log houses.

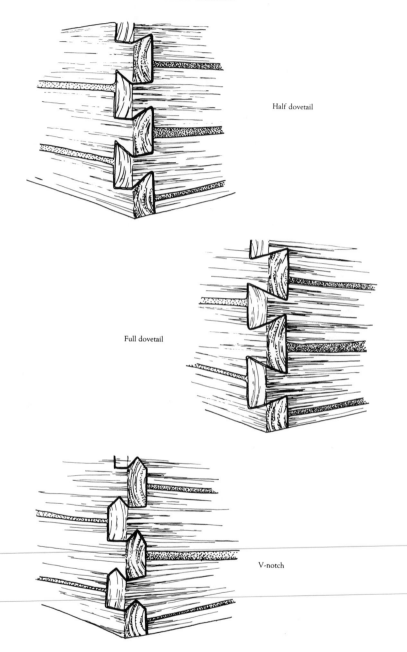

Half dovetail

Full dovetail

V-notch

Figure 32
Types of corner notches used in log construction.

log slave houses they remember. Cary Carson, architectural historian and former director of research for the St. Mary's City Commission, has reported this use of posts in log farm buildings as well as in log dwellings of white families in southern Maryland, and there are examples of log houses of white families braced similarly in Cecil County on the Eastern Shore of Maryland. Although this system was not unique to slave houses, it was widespread among them.[22]

The restored log slave house at Sotterley Plantation clearly illustrates one variety of post-and-peg construction (figure 24). Along each wall of the house are vertical debarked cedar posts set into the ground on either side of the principal opening—the door or chimney. They are split, and their flat surface is placed against the wall. Long, carved pegs pass through the post into each log in the wall. Rather than being aligned vertically, the pegs are staggered on the left and right sides of the post to prevent the post from splitting.[23]

The log slave house at Blair's Purchase in St. Mary's County (figure 33) is reinforced by a different method of post-and-peg bracing.* In each corner stands a debarked post. The bottom is sawn flat and simply rests on the sill (the bottommost log). Long pegs are inserted completely through the posts from each log in the wall. The top logs of the front length and back length (the plates) were lapped over the plates of the gable ends and pegged together. This is another example of a well-secured log house.[24]

Most southern Maryland slave houses apparently did not have front porches, since no slave houses remaining today originally had them, and elderly informants do not recall them. Where houses did have porches, they were not porches in the usual sense of a comfortable place where residents and visitors could sit and talk. Instead, they were intended to shelter the doorway. For example, one former slave said his log house had only a "wide board over the door to keep the rain and snow from beating over the top of the door." James Scriber recalled, "some of the old-time houses had a little overreach porch, but not all" (figure 19). Its absence on typical slave houses was probably due to the limitations placed upon housing for slaves, but could have also resulted from the traditional house style. Architectural historian Henry Glassie found front porches to be "not very common" on small houses of this square type in the upland South.

---

*Though one of the original two-unit houses has been removed, the construction of the remaining half is identical to that of the one removed, according to Clem Dyson, who was born in this house in 1890 and whose parents worked for the owners of Blair's Purchase (figure 34).

Figure 33
Facade of the northern half of the log double quarters at
Blair's Purchase, St. Mary's County. The vertical boards, the
window, and the tin roof have been added. Photo: author.

Abraham Lincoln's childhood log home in Kentucky is but one example. After emancipation, black landowners added front porches
on their homes as an improvement.[25]

William Diggs and Benjamin Ross recalled that log slave houses
typically had dirt floors, and their recollections are confirmed by
former slaves. "I lived in a log cabin . . . with a dirt floor," recounted
the ex-slave Richard Macks from Charles County. Josiah Henson, a
former slave from Montgomery County, said, "We lodged in huts on
the bare ground. Wooden floors were an unknown luxury." No log
slave houses with original dirt floors have survived unchanged. Since
the timbers of such houses were not adequately protected from termite infestation and water damage, most have been abandoned and
destroyed. However, if improvements were made, one of the first was
the addition of a plank floor, and archaeologists may yet locate the
original earth surfaces under the floorboards of existing dwellings.[26]

Figure 34
Clem Dyson, St. Mary's County, in front of the double
quarters at Blair's Purchase, where he was born in 1890. Photo: author.

A dirt floor tends to suggest something soft and insanitary, but this was far from the case. If properly prepared, the floor could be quite smooth, hard, and durable. All elderly informants who either lived in or visited former slave houses with dirt floors in the nineteenth or early twentieth centuries characterized them in similar terms: "hard as cement," "like asphalt," or "so hard you could hardly drive a nail into it." When William Diggs, who had lived in his grandfather's log house with a dirt floor, saw the loosely filled and dusty earthen floor in the slave house at Sotterley, he immediately recognized it as an inaccurate addition. His observation was confirmed by the caretaker of the plantation, who said he had been advised to add the dirt in place of a plank floor to make the cabin look more authentic.[27]

James Scriber said that the "old-time people" in St. Mary's County used to gather clay from river banks, mix it with water, "cook" it in pots over a fire in the yard, then pour it into place inside the house. They used the same method to make the mud plaster for the stick and mud chimneys. He said that they may have added something to make the mixture more cohesive, but did not know what it was because "when the old-time people were working, you better not stay around, you'd better get back. They didn't talk to young folks like they do today."[28]

Fortunately, "old-time people" did talk to William Diggs. In fact, his paternal grandmother, who spent her first fifteen years as a slave, lived with Diggs's family "until we were over half grown," and "she was the daily television show." In addition to hearing and remembering her stories, Diggs saw his maternal grandfather, William Jordan, also a former slave, at work. Diggs explained Jordan's methods of installing a dirt floor, methods he learned as a youth during slavery.

"The clay that you would get was from the river bottom or run bottom and would already be mixed, already wet."

"First, how did you get it up out of the bottom and then how did you get it from the edge of the river or the run to the house?"

"Well, they had oxen that they would drive out into the creek or river and then on low tide . . . ."

"Pulling something?"

"Yes, pulling an oxcart. They'd catch it on the low tide, and then they would either have shovels or buckets or anything that would get the clay up. Preferably the shovel. With the shovel they'd put the wet clay onto the oxcart. Then when they got as much as they thought the ox could pull, they'd carry it right on up to the site. . . ."

"How many oxcart loads or part-oxcart loads might it typically take to fill a floor?"

"That depended on how many rocks and stones you had to fill in between the logs, you see. I don't want to mislead you. Inside the house they had flattened logs attached to the sills all the way through the whole width of the house. Between them they would put down field rocks. Then they'd fill in sections with clay. Because if they just dumped the clay into the wide open space, they had no control. But with sections, they could pour it in one section at a time, then smooth it off like you do cement. And as the clay dried, they could still use the rest of the house or do whatever they wanted to do."

"Was the floor ground level, or did you have to step up?"

"Had to make a step, yes [raise the inside of the house above ground level]. Because had it not been for the step up, the water would run off the house and back into the house."[29]

Hard dirt floors were found in homes of other black families throughout the South. For example, the musician and composer W. C. Handy wrote in his autobiography: "I was born in a log cabin [in Alabama] that my grandfather had built. The logs were evenly hewn. Our first kitchen had a dirt floor which my father [an ex-slave] had beat down so that it looked like asphalt."[30]

Earthen floors were colder than plank ones. James Scriber referred to them as evidence of the hardiness of the "old-time people": "Oh yeh! It'd be colder, but people in them days, you know, you'd get used to it."[31]

Houses of white families also had kitchens and other rooms with earthen floors. For example, the kitchen of the "Old Stone House" in Georgetown, D.C., now on public exhibit by the National Park Service, originally had a dirt floor. It is said that the smooth, seamless earthen floor was easier to sweep and keep clean than the present-day brick floor, because kitchen waste is trapped in the joints between the bricks. Though dirt floors may be commonly perceived as primitive, they had practical advantages.[32]

The quality of these earthen floors was a result of the continuation of skills commonly practiced in preindustrial England and Africa, where dirt floors were commonplace. In seventeenth-, eighteenth-, and even nineteenth-century English farmhouses and cottages, the "floors downstairs were usually of earth, even in better houses. It had been discovered long ago that clay mixed with ox blood and ashes made a hard floor which might even be polished," according to the English architectural historian, M. W. Barley. To make the floor harder, lime, chalk, or animal bones might be added. Some English builders mixed in cow dung, since its "excellent setting properties" were well known and its use in plaster for earthen walls was "old and widespread."[33]

In West Africa, hard earthen floors were commonplace and were obtained by evenly tamping a claylike mud with a wooden beater while it was setting. To make the floor more cohesive and to prevent cracks, Africans mixed the mud with either charcoal, ashes, cow dung, or lime at the outset, or repeatedly plastered the floor with a light mixture of water and one of these cohesive agents after it had set. The lime was made by grinding shells found along the rivers. Though post–Civil-War oral informants did not know of these specific techniques, it is significant that different observers have characterized the earthen floors in African, English, Anglo-American, and Afro-American houses in the same words: "hard as cement" or "like cement." As with the construction of wattle frames, earthen walls, and thatched roofs, the traditional building skills of Anglo-Americans and Afro-Americans dovetailed. The extent to which they shared their traditional knowledge is a relatively unexplored question, but it is clear now that some blacks continued to employ this knowledge on their own, apparently out of preference. As one ex-slave from Alabama declared, "My ma never would have no board floor like the rest of 'em, on 'count she was a African—only dirt."[34]

It should be pointed out that some log slave houses, such as the one at Sotterley, originally had wooden floors. Some consisted of planks laid over log joists, while others were simply logs whose top surfaces were flattened and smoothed by a foot adz. Such logs, known as "puncheons," were not uncommon in early America. William Diggs recalled that log houses in low, flat places where standing water was a problem were raised above the ground on stone or log piers and had wooden floors. Houses with earthen floors were usually located, he says, either on a knoll or on a gentle slope, with a shallow trench dug around the house to carry water away.[35]

In regard to windows, sons of former slaves in southern Maryland—McKinley Gantt, "Hopsie" Johnson, Albert Johnson, and Benjamin Ross—recalled that log slave quarters rarely had windows with glass panes, and some had no windows at all, such as those at Blair's Purchase and Sotterley* and the log house of Frederick Doug-

---

*According to James Scriber, who knew the Sotterley house in the late 1880's, it originally had no windows downstairs; inspection of the windows confirms that they are later additions.

Figure 35
House of a black family in rural Virginia, 1898. Courtesy
Virginia Historical Society.

---

lass's grandparents in Talbot County. Wood shutters were typically used in place of glass (figure 35). Richard Macks said his parents' log house had a window but "no glass," and Eugene Genovese in his study of slave life concurred: "Most cabins had windows with shutters but no panes." These wood shutters consisted of short planks vertically aligned, crossed with wider boards to join them. Benjamin Ross and William Diggs said they were attached to the log walls by homemade hinges made of "anything that would hold," such as wire or thick strips of leather from harnesses or old shoe soles.[36]

The windows were small, as illustrated by those in figures 19 and 22. The dimensions of the two windows in the River View slave house may be typical, 1'10" x 1'6" and 1'6" x 1'3", as well as the one in the slave/tenant house on the Collison Farm, 1'4" x 1'6". As a result, the interiors were dark, especially if not whitewashed, and were lit only by the fire in the hearth, homemade candles and lamps, and, in good weather, by sunlight through open doors. William Diggs recalled that blacks stored animal grease, especially from game such as raccoons and opossums, and burned it as lamp oil in a small container into which they placed a wick. Such darkened interiors were not unlike those of peasant houses of Africa and preindustrial Europe. For example, according to an eighteenth-century account from the Congo, "The houses receive no other light than that which comes through the door. There are no windows." An advantage in having no windows or only small ones was that the heat did not escape, explained "Hopsie" Johnson.[37]

As in most American houses built before the late 1800's, the houses of black families in nineteenth-century Maryland did not have wire screens. William Diggs said some families placed tobacco-bed netting (like muslin) in the window to serve as a screen, as shown in figure 35. According to James Scriber, most "old-time families" in log houses "had nothing but a grass sack hanging up in the window." Insects were a part of household life. The plight of Maryland families was similar to that of former slave Margaret Nillum of Texas, who found plank shutters impractical. The windows "let flies in durin' de summer," she said. "But if you shuts dat window, it shuts out de light." Or as Savilla Burrell of South Carolina remarked: "Dere was plenty to eat sich as it was, but in the summertime before us get dere to eat, de flies would be all over de food, and some was swimming in de gravy and milk pots."[38]

Informants born in the nineteenth century in southern Maryland—such as Nellie and Benjamin Ross, "Hopsie" Johnson, James Scriber, William Dyson, Clem Dyson, and McKinley Gantt, all children of freed slaves—said that chimneys on the "old-time slave houses" were usually made of wood and clay.* In fact, the first four of these informants actually lived in log houses with wooden chimneys. Their recollections are confirmed by the testimony of former slaves: "Our house had a log chimney on the outside," said James V. Deane from Charles County. The grandparents of Frederick Douglass had a "dirt chimney." Since wood and clay chimneys were gradually destroyed by erosion and natural decay or were replaced by brick or stone chimneys if the house was later improved, it is not surprising that none remain in Maryland today.[39]

---

*Informants recall that there was no difference between the log chimneys on their houses in the late 1800's and those on the slave houses that were still standing in their youth. Thus, in the absence of detailed descriptions from conventional written sources and the ex-slave narratives of Maryland, recollections from these informants can give us important insights into the construction and use of these log chimneys and the life of the informants' slave parents.

Figures 19, 22, 23, 35, and 36 illustrate the common types of wood chimneys.* In general, they consisted of a rectangular base made of hewn logs about three or four feet in length, notched and overlapped at the corners like the walls of a log house. The most common type of chimney stack was built of smaller logs, gradually diminishing in length and width near the top (figure 19). Another type was made of flat boards overlapped at the corners (figure 36). Some chimneys consisted of a frame of four tall upright poles with shorter sticks or poles placed horizontally between and tenoned into the uprights. In all wooden chimneys the spaces between the wood members were chinked with mud, like the walls of the house, and the interior was thickly plastered with several layers of mud to insulate the logs from the heat. Benjamin Ross added that some "old-time" log chimneys were topped with empty flour barrels to make them higher and to prevent the wind from blowing the smoke back into the house. Also, the higher the flue, the stronger the draft, which meant an easier-starting and hotter-burning fire. Furthermore, the higher flue prevented sparks, which the upward draft would carry through the barrel without igniting it, from landing on the flammable roof covering of shingles, boards, or thatch. Though the chimney tops of some houses were below the peak of the gable roof (figure 22), William Diggs said this was unusual, at least in Charles County, due to the danger of sparks igniting the roof.[40]

The type of fire that could be burned in these wooden log chimneys depended upon the quality of the firebox. If the walls were well insulated, the firebox could withstand a fire that "would keep you real warm—seven feet away or more." To shield the chimney logs from such hot fires, the interior of the firebox was lined with large, "smooth-looking stones." Special efforts had to be made to gather them in the coastal plain region of southern Maryland, where large stones were not plentiful. Ross recalled that if his family or neighbors were going to town and saw appropiate stones along the roadside, they would note the location and, on their return trip, load them into the wagon. William Diggs said that watermen and boatmen who plied the river (among them was his grandfather) carried home flat, smooth rocks they found along the river banks. Those families who

*Houses of Southern white families also had wooden chimneys. The main house of a Georgia plantation with at least a score of slaves was described thus: "Two chimneys, one upon each end; built of turfs, sticks, blocks of wood, and occasionally a brick plastered over with clay, ornamented the outside of the house" (Emily Burke, *Pleasure and Pain: Reminiscences of Georgia in the 1840's* [Savannah, Georgia: Beehive Press, 1978], p. 327).

Figure 36
Log house, North Carolina, 1903. Photo: Underwood and
Underwood. Courtesy Library of Congress.

did not obtain stones simply lined their fireplaces with thick layers of mud plaster. Such fireplaces were, of course, more flammable, and slaves, who did not have as much mobility as freedmen, probably suffered more from house fires.[41]

Regardless of the quality of the hearth, wooden chimneys threatened all houses with fire. James Scriber (figure 37), who was reared in a "slavery-time cabin" with a "dirt chimney," and who visited

Figure 37
James Scriber, born in 1878, St. Mary's County. When
asked what had changed most during his hundred years, his answers
were clear: "Me! I've changed. Can't do the things I used to." And
next, "It's not just one thing that's changing. It's everything. And
things are changing faster, too." Photo: author.

friends living in former slave houses with similar chimneys, had this to say after examining a photograph of a house with a log chimney (figure 19):

"Well, it [the chimney] was something like it . . . that's the way it was built . . . like you build a hog pen."

"With the logs there, notched over one another?"

"Yes, that's right."

"And then plastered with mud on the inside and outside?"

"That's right. Well, it's cut into, you know, on the ends so it'd fit down tight. Course if it wouldn't go together, that's the reason they had to plaster it with clay in between, you know, the logs."

"I noticed that it is leaning a lot . . . ."

"It did lean in them days too, sometimes they'd fall. The wind would blow them down, the whole top of them you know."

"I guess you'd be in a hell of a mess then, wouldn't you?"

"Damn right. . . . Cold night, oh, what you talking about . . . it'd catch afire sometimes, the chimney, you had to run out in the cold. I mean the chimney would catch afire, them logs, you see. . . . Then they had the next day in building that up, you know, gettin' people to come and help one another. In those days, people helped one another. You wouldn't charge one another, just would help, you know. They didn't charge because they didn't have nothing to pay at all."[42]

According to William Diggs, slaves developed practical methods to lessen the danger of fires. Log chimneys, he said, were deliberately constructed to lean away from the house, so in the event of a chimney fire, the house itself would be protected, as shown in figure 19. However, some chimneys tilted so precariously that they had to be propped up by poles (figure 22); and, according to Luther Stuckey, the son of a former slave who was reared in a log house with log chimney in South Carolina in the late 1800's, the slanting chimney was not deliberate: "It just seemed the house went one way, and the chimney went the other." But Diggs characterized tilting chimneys such as the one in figure 22 as the result of "sloppy carpentry." The general good fit of the rest of the houses observed and the nearly universal "lean" of the wood chimneys in the old photographs suggest that this was deliberate; but the testimony of oral informants does not confirm this.[43]

To combat chimney fires, families customarily kept a ladder near the chimney, as in figures 19 and 36, along with one or more rain barrels full of water. Figure 38 shows a rain barrel hollowed from a log by William Jordan, grandfather of William Diggs, for such a pur-

Figure 38
Log rain barrel. According to William Diggs, his grandfather, William
Jordan, carved this log rain barrel in the years after his emancipation. Such homemade
barrels were once common around the houses of black families. Photo: author.

pose. Diggs said that children loved to scamper up the ladder and jump down from the chimney to the ground, but this was forbidden by parents since they could loosen the logs in the chimney, increase the risk of a chimney fire, and threaten the safety of the household. But "quite naturally, children would love to try, especially if their parents weren't strict with them."[44]

Diggs recounted the methods Jordan and his brethren used to fight chimney fires. "In that day, they had no fire insurance or fire engines. They had no way to put out a chimney fire other than the ladder and that rain barrel. If the chimney caught fire, they'd run up the ladder, put their back against the house, and push the stack to the ground with their feet. Then they'd dip up a bucket of water from the barrel, and pour that in [on the burning logs in the remaining portion of the chimney]." Ex-slaves from other states corroborate Diggs's account. For example, Richard Carruthers from Texas remembered, "Many the time we have to get up at midnight and push the chimney away from the house to keep the house from burning up."[45]

To lessen the danger of chimney fires, Diggs said that "the people" charred their firewood first. "They didn't have the fires you're thinking of. The wood they used inside wooden fireplaces was charred wood. The black people in the fall of the year would cut down hickory, white oak, and red oak wood. They'd bring that up and make big fires on the outside and burn the wood down to charcoal, and then store it into brush barns [light shed frames covered with pine branches], sheds, or whatever. Then they would bring that into the house and burn it. Quite naturally, they didn't blaze up like wood or paper."[46]

Upon entering a log slave house, a visitor would have seen that the log walls and chinking were usually left bare and were rarely sheathed with board siding. To brighten the interior, some houses were whitewashed. According to one historian, in the last decades of the slave era, due to the increased awareness of and concern for the health and living conditions of the slaves, "more and more slaveholders arranged springtime whitewashing parties in the quarters. The slave women sometimes did this work while the men cut firewood." Lime for whitewashing was readily available in southern Maryland, since it could be purchased or extracted by grinding or burning oyster shells. Oral informants, such as James Scriber and Clem Dyson, said that whitewashing was typical in the "old-time houses" and was applied by a homemade brush of broom straw. Dyson recalled that the traditional-minded landowner at Blair's Purchase, where he was born in 1890, always had all her buildings, including the quarters, whitewashed at least once a year. Nonetheless, the impetus did not necessarily come from the white family. Former slaves in the 1870's and afterward are known to have whitewashed their houses apart from any supervision of whites. The rationale was simple: whitewashing brightened an otherwise dark interior, created the appearance of a larger room, deterred insect infestation, and protected the wood and chinking inside and out.[47]

The downstairs rooms of most slave houses, whether of log or frame construction, were not ceiled by boards or lath and plaster. Instead, the floorboards of the upstairs chamber, crossed underneath by the hewn log joists, provided the "ceiling." William Diggs and William Dyson said that in Charles County this practice was chosen because it permitted heat to ascend from the downstairs into the unheated upstairs chamber. However, the extra costs of ceiling material may have been prohibitive. Unceiled rooms were not unique to slave houses; many eighteenth- and early nineteenth-century houses of whites were unceiled, as were most farm tenant houses of whites and blacks that were surveyed in the 1930's in Georgia.[48]

The upstairs of most log slave houses consisted of one room, usually called a "loft," that was typically used as sleeping quarters for children. Frederick Douglass recalled sleeping in the loft as a child. In some log houses a partition separated the chamber into two rooms, as in the slave houses at Sotterley and the Collison Farm. James Scriber agreed that the upstairs of most old log houses was one open room, but added that some families did try to create more privacy by building "some kind of partition with boys on one side and girls on the other. Sometimes they had an old blanket stretched across so you couldn't look right in." According to one historian, such partitions, though inadequate for complete privacy, were in keeping with the efforts of slaves to create as much privacy as possible in the crowded circumstances. Furthermore, like many white families on the frontier who lived in one- and two-room houses, slaves may have been rather relaxed in regard to privacy within the circle of the family.[49]

Homemade ladders, that led through an open hole in the floor above typically served as stairways in log and frame slave houses in southern Maryland, as in the slave quarters at Blair's Purchase and at Grasslands. Not only was a ladder cheap and easy to make, but it was practical in small, crowded spaces because it could be moved about or pulled upstairs, whereas a fixed stairway occupied a considerable portion of living space. In some slave houses the stairs were enclosed with planks in a corner, forming a closet underneath the steps and insulating the downstairs from cold drafts from the unheated upstairs.

Such stairs, however, were not common in slave houses, but became widespread in the small houses of black families built after emancipation. Ladder stairs, as well as boxed stairways, were also commonly found in small houses of whites in the mid-Atlantic region and the Appalachian Mountains. Ladder stairs were also used in the multistory dwellings of West Africa, such as those of the Dogon in West Africa.[50]

In addition to a stairway opening, some slave houses apparently had a trap door in the upstairs floor, which poses an intriguing puzzle. The only extant example is in the restored slave house at Sotterley, where it is located above the hearth and diagonally opposite from the stairwell. According to James Scriber, two other slave dwellings at Sotterley, now destroyed, along with other slave houses that he visited in St. Mary's County, had a trap door in addition to the stairway opening. There are several possible explanations. First, the trap door might have served to allow warm air to ascend from the hearth below to the upper chamber. Second, there may have been a partition with no doors across the middle of the upstairs, requiring two separate means of access. There is evidence of such a partition in the Sotterley slave house, but it cannot be determined if there was a door, since almost all of the partition has been removed. Third, the trap door might originally have been an opening for a simple ladder stair located near the hearth. Then, in later years, another ladder stair was added on the opposite side of the room because the stairway took up work space around the hearth needed for cooking. Last, it could have served as a means of escape: slaves trapped upstairs could jump down and escape raiding patrollers as they were coming up the stairs. At one point, Scriber vaguely implied that they might have been related to an escape from "haints" (haunts, or ghosts), but he would not elaborate.

All of these explanations are mere speculation, because apparently even James Scriber, born in the nineteenth century, does not know or is not telling. When asked to explain the trap doors, Scriber was evasive, and his response indicates his view toward the customs of the "old people."

"Old-time people, you know, they had their way of doing."

"I wonder why they had the trap doors."

"I don't know. They had it for a reason. They had it."

"Would it be to get away?"

"I don't know why they had it, but they did have it. All those old houses had it . . . a switchover. Oh, they had their different ways of doing, foolish ways, but that was their way of doing, so that's all there is to it, their way of doing."

Thus, trap doors to the upstairs of old-time slave houses must remain simply "their way of doing."[51]

The roof is a log house's thinnest skin; it is more vulnerable to cold, heat, rain, and driving winds than are thick log walls. So the type of roofing materials used in these houses is an indication of the living conditions within. Log slave houses in Maryland were covered with three kinds of material: wood shingles, planks, or thatch (which in southern Maryland was marsh grass and possibly straw). No slave houses were found with tile roofs, such as those on the brick slave quarters at Boone Hall near Mount Pleasant, South Carolina.

Wood shingles were split, or rived, by hand with a froe, Scriber and "Hopsie" Johnson said. Red oak and cedar were preferred because they split easier: "Minute you hit it, it would come right on out," explained William Diggs. Figures 19 and 35 show examples of well-rived shingles, tightly fitted into place. The roof in figure 19, which had nineteen courses of overlapping shingles, provided superior insulation to the one in figure 35, which only had five. Though the roof with more shingles required more time and work to make and install, residents would have suffered far less discomfort when its smaller shingles loosened or cracked, as any shingle eventually would due to weathering and winds.

Plank roofs consisted of long adjoining boards vertically aligned down the slope of the roof, with the cracks between them lapped by planks (figures 22 and 36). They took less time and trouble to build, but were far less practical than shingle roofs. Because of their length, the planks eventually warped and tore away from their fastening nails, creating leaks and drafts. William Diggs explained further that the board roof was inferior to the shingled "because all along the cracks there, dust and dirt would collect, and wherever dust and dirt collect, termites start in . . . then the board starts rotting. . . . Sometimes it would disappear or slide down, if it didn't have enough nails in it. . . . Then the crack would fill up with dirt and other debris, and then vegetation, grass, and anything would start growing into that. Quite naturally, that would bring up red ants and black ants. Those of you who have never been plagued with red ants or black ants, it's just a terrible thing because once they get in there, it's very difficult to get them out."[52]

The quality of the roofs therefore seriously affected the living conditions of the residents. As this quality ranged from excellent (figure

Figure 39
William Diggs reaping marsh grass with his grandfather's scythe. Photo: author.

19) to poor (figure 23), we see that there was considerable variety in the care of construction and maintenance among even humble log houses.

Lacking heat and insulation, the southern Maryland log houses' upstairs rooms were cold in the winter. They were not ceiled underneath the rafters or inside the frames of the gable end, or boxed in along the eaves with boards. To provide a measure of insulation in the upstairs, post–Civil-War tenant families living in the log houses stuffed rags in cracks along the eaves, as at the Cusic-Medley house discussed in Chapter IV. If slaves were able to acquire surplus cloth, they may have done this too.[53]

What was it like sleeping in a cold upstairs, unheated by fireplace or stove? Since it was a part of day-to-day living, a cold upstairs was probably accepted as inevitable, and the solution was to make warm blankets or quilts and to sleep completely covered by them. Residents spent as little time as possible upstairs, using that room primarily as sleeping quarters, with family life going on downstairs. James Scriber gives us a glimpse into these living conditions:

"Several nights I remember when I was a little fellow, I woke up, I thought there was somebody layin' on me. Snow layin' on top of the bed, been there all night long . . . . shifted through there [wood shingles]. Wind blown . . . . You didn't get cold."

"You *didn't* get cold?"

"No indeed. You see, we all had some old grass sack blankets and things over us, you didn't know you had snow until we'd poke our heads from underneath the blankets. Sleep with our heads covered up. Oh, that was a long time ago. Even in my days it was rough. All had to go through the same things, wasn't just one person. Everyone, you know, had the same pill to take."[54] Since slaves lived in similar unceiled rooms or worse, they endured similar situations.

Like peasant houses in Europe and Africa, some "old-time slave houses" in southern Maryland had thatched roofs that continued in use after emancipation. For example, William Diggs was told that slaves used to thatch their homes. A few years after "freedom" his grandfather, William Jordan, covered the kitchen attached to his house with thatch (in this case, marsh grass), and re-covered it every two to four years into the 1920's. Other freed slaves in Charles County did likewise. Animal shelters with thatched roofs, which Diggs called "brush barns," were still common to small farms in Charles County through the first quarter of the twentieth century. Documents of the mid-1820's show that thatch was also used to cover tobacco barns, known as "pen houses" in St. Mary's County,

Figure 40
William Diggs thatching a makeshift roof. Photo: author.

and William Diggs and Clem Dyson remembered that the practice continued into the twentieth century.[55]

Fortunately, William Diggs learned to thatch from his grandfather and his uncle, making him perhaps the only person still living in southern Maryland who can describe and demonstrate the age-old methods from personal experience. Diggs covered a makeshift lean-to with marsh grass to demonstrate the craft, and according to him, his are the same methods his ancestors used (figures 39, 40, 41). Instead of straw, the slaves, freedmen, and, later, Diggs used the tall marsh grass that flourished along the rivers and tidal creeks of southern Maryland. The grass had to be gathered when it was green, Diggs said. "You have to get the marsh grass in June because it's very waxy then. Very waxy. If you get it before June, it's not long enough. And in June you can bend it any way you want. If you get it after June, then it will break, and then it doesn't have the wax into it. The wax within the straw is the thing that turns the water."[56]

The preparation and installation of a thatched roof was a matter of serious concern, and great care was taken. "It was something you

1. Gathering marsh grass with a scythe

2. Chopping off the coarse stalks

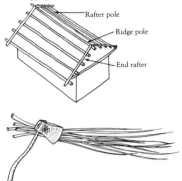

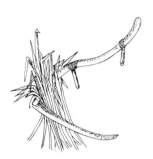

3. Thatching the first pole
   A. Lay a handful of grass over the pole
   B. Bend it over the pole (as a towel on a rack)
   C. Tighten it and push it to the end of the pole

4. Ending of first row

Last batch wraps around rafter
(A holding board will hold it in
place until it dries)

5. Thatching the second and succeeding rows*
   A. Lay a bunch of grass over the pole
   B. Twist and pull it tight
   C. Force both ends up and lay it down flat
*The thatching of each pole alternates from left to right

6. Thatching the ridge pole

First bunch—simply laid
over ridge pole

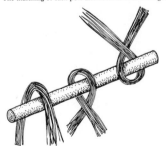

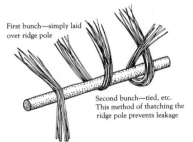

Second bunch—tied, etc.
This method of thatching the
ridge pole prevents leakage

Figure 41
Traditional methods of thatching roofs.

didn't play around with." Furthermore, each resident thatched his own roof, unlike the building of the log house, which was a community affair. "You know a leaky house is a terrible thing, so they felt that if the house were to leak, they wanted to be the ones to have made it leak." Diggs says that his grandfather and family reaped the marsh grass with sickles, scythes, or corn knives, making sure that the stalks fell straight so they could be properly aligned in bundles, like sheaves of wheat, for treatment later. The bundles were then loaded on "bull carts" and carried to the site. Many loads were needed because the grass was applied as thickly as possible to prevent damage from wind, snow, and hail. The lower and stiffer portions of the reeds were cut off, leaving the upper portion of pliable stems and blades about two and a half to three feet long.[57]

The frame of the thatched roof consisted of two rafters at each gable end, with straight poles made from trimmed saplings, called "roof poles," laid horizontally about nine inches apart along the slope of the roof up to the top pole at the apex. The poles were fastened to the rafters by nails, or, in "old-time days," by whittled pegs. Beginning at one side of the roof, bunches of marsh grass about four to six inches thick were draped over the second pole from the bottom, like a towel over a rack. The two ends were tightly twisted in a half knot against the "roof pole," and then pulled up and laid over the lowest pole so the ends of the grass descended about eight to ten inches over the eave. It was imperative to pull down on the grass and smooth it to make the surface as flat and dense as possible to shed water. The uneven ends of the grass hanging over the eaves were trimmed so the house would not look "ragged."[58]

The process was repeated along the next pole up, but beginning at the other end so the thatching alternated from left to right. At the gable ends the bundles were wrapped around the end of the pole extending over the rafter, tied in a special knot, and, after the thatching was completed, a "holding board" was nailed over the gable end to secure the marsh grass in place. At the peak of the roof, bundles of grass were first loosely laid over the ridge pole with each half descending each opposite slope. Another set of bundles was then pushed between them, draped over the ridge pole, twisted in a half knot as the others had been, and pulled back up, with one end laid over one slope of the roof, and the other over the opposite. According to Diggs, this method of thatching the ridge pole prevented leakage.

Thatching was a family affair. The father and oldest sons applied the thatch, while the mother and children carefully gathered it in straight bundles that they handed up to the men, who were on ladders. In ways such as this, the home could become a source of family pride.[59]

Slave houses elsewhere in the South had thatched roofs, though the material and methods of application differed. In nineteenth-century Georgia, the slave Okra thatched his African-style house, as did the Bakongo slave in South Carolina (figure 17). In the early nineteenth century, the brick slave houses on the Mulberry Plantation in South Carolina were thatched. Thatched roofs were not uncommon to simple dwellings in seventeenth-century Maryland, Virginia, and New England, and they may well have been used for early slave houses too. As discussed in Chapter I, first-generation African immigrants were already skilled in the crafts of their homeland. However, the methods of William Jordan and other former slaves in Charles County were substantially different, in that they wrapped pliable grass blades instead of sewing mats of stiff straw or palmetto. Whether their methods were a continuation of an as-yet undocumented African technique, or a development indigenous to southern Maryland, or an adaptation to Maryland circumstances of an African or European tradition, is not known at this point. Given the fact that Diggs knows only his ancestors' techniques, and not their origins, it is likely that we will never know.[60]

Thatched roofs were used because they required virtually no money and were made from locally plentiful material—marsh grass in southern Maryland, palmetto leaves in South Carolina and Florida. If thickly and tightly applied, thatching may have insulated as well as unceiled layers of wood shingles, and probably better than loose boards. The thatch lasted longer if a fire was used in the room covered by the thatch, since the soot that accumulated on the underside and the pungent odor of smoke deterred insect infestation. Perhaps this is one reason why William Jordan covered the kitchen wing of his house with thatch, but the main block with shingles.[61]

However, certain drawbacks eventually resulted in the demise of thatching. Grass deteriorates more quickly than wood, and, as Diggs related, "crows and blackbirds would have a wonderful time in the spring gathering dry material for nests, and snakes would have a wonderful time too. Quite naturally, you know, mice and rats would have a lovely time. So therefore this wood shingled roof would be much better. And that thatch roof, you'd have to change the straw on it about every two years, where [a good wood shingled] roof would last indefinitely and very seldom would leak. But the old thatch roof, if you had a very heavy storm it would leak." Furthermore, thatched roofs came to symbolize poor living conditions. In St. Mary's County, thatch was relegated to tobacco barns, and throughout southern Maryland it was replaced as soon as economically possible. With thatch, a connection through craft to Africa and the ancient world has disappeared.[62]

Of course, not all slave houses were of the typical log construction. Southern Maryland contains exceptional examples of frame, stone, and brick construction, and of two-room floor plans. Frame houses were less common than log ones, probably because they required more commercially made materials, making them more costly than log houses, which were built almost entirely of naturally available materials. Brick and stone houses were also more expensive and time-consuming to build, and stone buildings of any kind were rare in southern Maryland. Documents such as valuations, indentures, and assessments establish that slave houses of these kinds were uncommon. Only one of the ex-slaves from southern Maryland interviewed by the WPA mentioned a dwelling that was probably frame. None cited brick or stone dwellings. Today's oral informants agree that slave houses built of anything but logs were the exception. It is essential to note their comparative rarity, because they have been considered more suitable candidates for rehabilitation and preservation than log houses, especially when the latter had the typical wood chimneys and earthen floors. Thus, portraying slave houses based on the proportion of extant examples means that a disproportionate number of better-built houses would be included, and an inaccurate picture of slave life conveyed.*

Frame, stone, and brick houses represented the "top of the line" in housing for slaves and for the rural poor in general. In fact, one of the distinctions between the houses of slaves and of ante-bellum tenants was that tenants' homes were typically frame and included far more brick examples than did those of slaves (table 2). Since frame slave dwellings were more costly than log ones, they were more likely to be found on plantations of the wealthy. For example, the 1790 and 1800 censuses of St. Mary's County show that half of the slave quarters on wealthy plantations were of frame construction and half of log, in contrast to the smaller, more typical plantations, where almost all the quarters were log.[63]

These houses of frame, stone, or brick may have been a reward for favored slaves. Like the finer homes mill owners allotted to suc-

---

*Of the thirty-seven dwellings I surveyed that were definitely or possibly slave houses, twenty were frame, thirteen log, three brick, and one stone.

cessful foremen, such houses might have been offered to preferred slaves as an added incentive to separate themselves from the majority, who lived in cruder log houses, and thereby provide better living conditions for their families. From the little that we know about the identity of specific residents of the houses surveyed, it appears that at least one of the adult residents, if not both, was a house servant or perhaps an artisan working near the main house, rather than a field hand.

Of the exceptional types of slave houses, the frame dwelling was the most common. Like log houses, frame homes were single-unit, one-story structures with a chimney exterior to one gable end, resembling the tidewater-type houses traditional to the area. Though they typically consisted of only one room, they usually had more floor space, were more "finished" in appearance, and in general provided more comfortable living conditions than the log houses (figure 42). They were more likely to have brick or stone chimneys. With few exceptions, they had plank floors rather than earthen ones, and customarily had larger windows with glass panes that provided more light inside and more control over ventilation than wood shutters. Even during inclement weather, residents were not sealed off from the outside world. One example is the frame house at Essex (figure 43), which has one sash window with six over six panes in a gable end and two similar windows in the back length. Among the extant examples, the interiors were lathed and plastered, insulating the walls and giving a more improved appearance to the room than did exposed logs.* Some frame slave houses, as at Grasslands, were partially insulated with brick fill between the studs.† For these reasons, many preferred frame houses to log houses. Also, weatherboards on frame houses "just looked nicer" than "rough-looking" log walls and

---

*Some slave frame houses may not have been sheathed inside. For example, according to J. Spence Howard, the former owner of Brome Farm and direct descendant of the ante-bellum owners, the frame slave house there was covered only by weatherboards with bevelled edges outside. There was no cladding inside. The interior must have been bitter cold during the winter. Similar houses owned and occupied by white families have been cited in northern Virginia and Georgia in the antebellum nineteenth century. See Emily Burke, *Pleasure and Pain: Reminiscences of Georgia in the 1840's* (Savannah, Georgia: Beehive Press, 1978), p. 32.

†Slave houses with brick nogging were very rare in southern Maryland and throughout the South. In addition to the one I located in southern Maryland at Grasslands, there are a few other examples, such as three sets of slave quarters on the Stagville-Fairntosh Plantation in Durham County, North Carolina.

Figure 42
*Facade of a slave or tenant house at Cedar
Park, Anne Arundel County, built before or just
after emancipation. Photo: author.*

mud chinking, explained "Hopsie" Johnson, Albert Johnson, Mc-
Kinley Gantt, and other sons of former slaves.[64]

A few slave houses in southern Maryland were constructed of
stone. They were located in areas where large outcroppings made
stone readily available, as in Anne Arundel County northwest of
Annapolis, northern Maryland, and northern Virginia. The stone
slave house at Basil Smith's farm in Anne Arundel County is perhaps
the only surviving example in southern Maryland, and is probably
typical (figure 44). Though doubled in size in the twentieth century,
its original rectangular form, floor plan of one room down and one
up, and original exterior dimensions (18' x 16') were similar to those

Figure 43
Frame slave house at Essex, Anne Arundel County.
Located approximately one hundred yards behind the main
house, this single-unit house illustrates the type that some house
servants, though not all, occupied. The porch is a replacement
of an earlier one of similar design. Photo: author.

of other single-unit slave houses. According to Basil Smith, descendant of the ante-bellum owners, slaves quarried the massive stones from outcroppings on the farm, trimmed them into shape, and laid them in place. The thick walls and stone chimney provided living conditions markedly superior to those offered by log or even frame houses. From an early twentieth-century photograph of the farm, Smith identified a log slave house that stood near this building. Thus not all slaves benefited from the more comfortable living conditions provided by stone houses, but no records exist to distinguish which slave families occupied the stone house, and Basil Smith does not know.[65]

Although slaves fired bricks and constructed brick houses both as

Figure 44
Stone slave house on Basil Smith's farm, Anne Arundel
County. The half of the house with the door and one window comprised
the original single-unit house. One of the few remaining
examples of the masonry skills of slaves. Photo: author.

common laborers and as "expert brick layers," brick slave quarters
were the rarest type of all, for brick was more expensive than wood
or even stone, which were available from nature.* Of the three examples found in southern Maryland, two are no longer standing: the
two-room brick dwelling on the Northampton Plantation in Prince
George's County (figure 45), and a large two-story building at Mulberry Fields in St. Mary's, allegedly used as a "slave dormitory." The

---

*None of the black oral informants located in southern Maryland mentioned brick
slave quarters, nor did former slaves interviewed by the WPA. In fact, throughout
the nineteenth century, brick houses were the most uncommon type for black
families, including prosperous black landowners (and white landowners too). In my
study of over two hundred houses of black families in southern Maryland and
rural Montgomery County, not one brick house built before 1930 was found, other
than those that had once been slave houses or dependencies. This scarcity of brick
houses explains why older black people today proudly point to the upward mobility
of a son by saying, "He's got himself a nice brick house."

Figure 45
Slave quarters at Northampton, Prince George's
County, photographed in 1936. Photo: John O. Brostrup.
Courtesy Library of Congress.

sole surviving example is not really a "slave quarters," but rather a one-story dependency, located near the main house at Mulberry Fields (figures 46, 47). The Janssons, who own Mulberry Fields, said they were told that servants lived in the upstairs, while the downstairs served as the laundry for the plantation or as the loom house or spinning room, where the silk was spun, since the landowners in the ante-bellum era cultivated mulberry trees and attempted to produce silk.[66]

In keeping with the Georgian architecture of the main house, the facade of this dependency, as well as of the kitchen dependency opposite it in the courtyard, is symmetrical: a central door flanked by two windows acccented by flat arches. The dependencies, however, were not contemporary to the main house, which was built in 1755, as the 1798 federal tax list for St. Mary's County does not identify two brick houses of this type. They were probably built in the early 1800's as a stylistic improvement. The date is suggested by the architectural style and by a brick found in the wall of the kitchen dependency that was inscribed with the date 1807. Furthermore, an ad-

Figure 46
Facade of dependency, Mulberry Fields, St. Mary's County. Photo: author.

vertisement for the plantation of 1814 cites a large brick kitchen and a brick weaving house, most likely these two dependencies.

This brick dependency provided living conditions superior to those of log or frame houses. Both downstairs and upstairs were heated by brick fireplaces; thirteen-inch brick walls offered fine insulation; and sash windows with six over six panes provided adequate light and controlled ventilation for the interior. Furthermore, the dependency was larger than other slave houses, measuring 22'3" in length and 27'4" in width.[*][67]

It is important to remember that not all slaves lived in separate slave houses. Twenty percent lived on farms with fewer than five slaves and probably lived in the farm house or an outbuilding. Also, house servants, cooks, maids, and personal attendants on larger plantations commonly lived in the main house, perhaps in the attic,

---

[*]This brick dependency and slave-related artifacts at Mulberry Fields are described and illustrated in further detail in Chapter III.

Figure 47
Facade of the main house of Mulberry Fields, overlooking the
Potomac. According to plantation tradition, slaves fired the bricks on the
plantation and helped build this house in the mid-eighteenth century.
The Greek Revival portico was added later. Photo: author.

basement, or above the kitchen. Caroline Hammond, a former slave from Anne Arundel County, recalled, "All the [slaves] lived in small huts with the exception of the household help who ate and slept in the manor house." An ex-slave from Virginia said, "In the attic slept the house servants and coachmen." Julia Harris, an elderly teacher, remembers that her grandmother shared the bedroom with her "young missus" and slept on a trundle bed. An example of quarters in the main house was at Indian Range in Anne Arundel County, where slaves occupied the two rooms above the kitchen, which both measured approximately 16'4" x 16'3" (figure 48). Their walls were of frame construction and insulated by lath and plaster, and the rooms were well lit by tall dormer windows with double sashes. In terms of physical living conditions, such quarters were a decided improvement over the log dwellings of most slaves. However, the slaves had to submit to living almost continually in the environment of whites and under their surveillance.[68]

Figure 48
Servants' quarters at Indian Range, Anne Arundel County. The kitchen
was in the downstairs of this wing, and the two upstairs rooms were quarters
for the house servants and cooks. Photo: author.

Former slaves and their descendants, such as William Diggs and
James Scriber, agree that single-unit slave dwellings were the standard type, but there did exist a few examples of "double quarters,"
two identical single units on either side of a central chimney of brick,
log, and frame construction. These were at Northampton Plantation
(figure 45), Bushwood Manor (figures 49, 50), Brome Farm (figure
51), White Hall Overseer's Quarters, and Gresham. A valuation of
Sotterley in 1803 identified one double quarter, and the caretaker,
Edward Knott, remembers two more, none of which remain.

As a rule, a stairway in each unit led to that unit's upper chamber,
which was separated by a partition from the other. Although no oral
or written evidence describing residency in double quarters in Maryland during slavery has been found, their floor plan strongly suggests
that they were occupied by two families, like duplexes today. This
possibility is strengthened by the fact that Frederick Law Olmsted
described two-family slave houses in South Carolina that resembled

Figure 49
Rear length of abandoned double quarters at
Bushwood Manor, St. Mary's County. The house is
made with massive framing timbers, wide weatherboards,
and lathed and plastered interior walls. Along the opposite length
extended a front porch, overlooking the Wicomico and
Potomac Rivers, which join in the distance. The
house is destined for demolition. Photo: author.

the double quarters in Maryland. Also, double quarters excavated on the Couper Plantation on a Georgia sea island were thought to have been occupied by two families. (This was the plantation where the slave Okra built his African-style house.)[69]

Multifamily dwellings were apparently not well accepted by black families in rural southern Maryland, because they did not continue as part of the traditional way of life after emancipation. It appears that after emancipation, double quarters were occupied exclusively by one family. For example, only James Scriber's family lived in the double quarters at Sotterley. At Brome Farm, Alex Milford, who was raised in the double quarters there in the early 1900's, said that only one family lived in the house, and that it had been his mother's child-

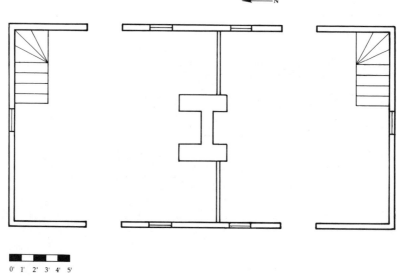

Figure 50
Floor plan of Bushwood Manor slave house.

hood home in the late 1800's (though he could not be sure about its occupancy during slavery). Clem Dyson, born in the double quarters at Blair's Purchase, recalled that only his family lived in it, with one half serving as their living quarters and the other half as the kitchen for the farm. Also, he said that the double quarters at Bushwood Manor (probably built in the 1840's) had been occupied by "Aunt Rose," a former slave, and her family at least since the late 1800's. Finally, the most telling evidence for the unpopularity of double quarters among black families was that after emancipation none of the black landowners—families who had control over their housing—are known to have built them.[70]

Slaves lived in a variety of houses: from crudely built shacks to more finished frame houses to stylish brick dependencies. Yet all of the slave houses lacked the "added-on" kitchens, bedrooms, or porches so common among black landowners' houses after emancipation. The absence of additions, of growth, among so many slave houses expresses the common burden of slavery, which circumscribed the houses and lives of black people whether they resided in a handsome brick dependency or a small, earthen-floored log house. This shared condition of bondage was a controlling factor in the develop-

Figure 51
West length of double quarters at Brome Farm, St. Mary's County. Built in
the 1840's, this house originally had dirt floors. The scaffolding in front and the paint
on the weatherboards and trims are the result of remodeling. Photo: author.

ment of slave houses, as becomes evident when they are compared
to the landowners' houses built after emancipation (Chapter V).

But there is more to the story. "Slave cabin," like the term "shack"
used by some to categorize the tenant house at the Smithsonian, is a
dismissive term; it limits our field of vision and hinders our seeing
that such houses required skills to construct and warrant a history.
Most historians of houses in America have ignored slave houses alto-
gether. Until recently, when historians of Afro-American and
Southern history did describe them, many limited themselves to that
narrow vision of slave houses as "shacks." While the existence of
exceptional, better-built houses was acknowledged, too often slave
houses were characterized as "rude, drafty, leaky, clapboard shacks,"
"crudely built one-room cabins with dirt floors," or "dark, dank holes
built flat on the ground."[71]

There is of course the risk of characterizing slave houses as too
well built and comfortable, of romanticizing slaves' housing and liv-

ing conditions, especially for exhibit purposes. We must remember that some slave houses were indeed "dingy hovels." On the other hand, it appears that many slaves—and it is not possible at this point to say how many—did not simply submit to a completely passive role. Instead, it appears that they used their repertoire of traditional skills, a synthesis of African, European, and American techniques, to construct log houses that required a substantial measure of expertise to erect. While most of their houses did have dirt floors, there was variety in the quality, as in log construction. Some could be as "miry as a pigsty," while others might be carefully laid, using traditional skills to render them as "hard as cement." Log chimneys, stone and mud fireplaces, shingled roofs, thatched roofs, windows—all provided opportunities and choices for residents to influence their environment, to "make do" with materials at hand, and to improve their situation.

These choices and the skills necessary to carry them out, as well as the limitations bondage imposed upon slaves, could be conveyed in exhibits of slave houses in our museums and parks. People like William Diggs or others could actually describe or demonstrate some of the skills, if not in person, then in videotapes or films. Such exhibits could show that ordinary slave men and women were not merely passive participants, but rather helped to build their houses, the main house, and plantation farm buildings—all of the physical stage where they acted out their lives—by drawing upon the skills of the past. Such exhibits could spark discussion of other historical issues to encourage the public to reconsider the deep-rooted stereotypes of Afro-American and American history.

CHAPTER III
Making Do: "They Didn't Have Much, But They Made Do. Yes, Indeed"

It is sometimes helpful, when attempting to characterize the spirit of a people, to quote the people directly; and although our records of slaves are far too few, their expressions are numerous and rich. In this chapter, we examine their houses as more than structural elements, and seek to find out what made them homes. "Oh, it was rough," said James Scriber, and his sentiments are echoed by other descendants of slaves, who remember the hard times endured by their ancestors and respect their efforts to provide for themselves. "They didn't have much," Amanda Nelson of St. Mary's County recalled, "but they made do. Yes, indeed."[1]

Yet rural black Marylanders did more than make do, for their very styles of making do became a part of the inheritance handed down the generations. Collectively, their ways of survival under slavery the rigors of the post–Civil-War tenancy system and to sustain an important sense of self worth. This inheritance enabled a significant minority of black Marylanders to break the chains of tenancy and emerge as landowners. Thus the story of survival under slavery tells of quite a bit more than simply making do. It is imperative that we examine how these slaves, who may seem anonymous to us at this far distance of time and place, made their houses into homes, and earned for themselves individual identity within the context of community and family.

The standard slave house floor plan was one room down and one up, so southern Maryland slave families lived in small, crowded spaces. Were they able to organize that one room as a center for family life and maintain a semblance of household order? Was there a systematic arrangement of objects and a consistent use of areas for specific functions that would have been identifiable to an outsider?*

---

*The organization of space in the downstairs for multiple uses is described and illustrated in detail in the discussion of the Ross and Cusic-Medley households in Chapter IV.

Unfortunately, no records of what outsiders saw in nineteenth-century southern Maryland slave houses have been found, and only one former slave from Maryland described the overall appearance of his home interior. Nonetheless, the WPA narratives, ex-slave autobiographies and other written sources, and the recollections of slaves' descendants who observed traditional practices continued after emancipation, do enable us to piece together composite sketches of slave house interiors and of domestic ways of life. Rather than being conclusive, these sketches are intended to be suggestive and to encourage others to relate artifacts to lifestyles.

Long hours of toil in the fields, physical punishment, sale and dispersal of family members, and the despair of being a slave were severe pressures against maintaining an ordered arrangement of objects and living areas in slave houses. We cannot know how many slaves, individuals and families, lived "like cattle," as described by Josiah Henson. "We lodged in log huts. . . . In a single room were huddled like cattle, ten or a dozen persons, men, women, and children. All ideas of refinement and decency were, of course, out of the question. There were neither bedsteads, nor furniture, of any description. . . . The floor was as miry as a pigsty. . . . In these wretched hovels were we penned at night, and fed by day; here the children born and the sick neglected."[2]

Other slaves experienced more fortunate conditions, and were able to shape their houses into more of a center of family life. Most family activities took place in the downstairs, which served as kitchen, dining room, bedroom, bathing room, and sitting room. As one former slave recalled of the one room in which he, his parents, and his three brothers lived, "We et, slep, an' done everything in jus dat one room." James Scriber and Benjamin Ross said that after emancipation, the typical arrangement in one-room houses was that the parents and infants slept downstairs, while the children slept upstairs, until the girls reached puberty, and then they slept downstairs too. Elderly informants throughout southern Maryland concurred with this description. This organization of household space was probably common during slavery.[3]

How did slaves care for and maintain their homes? Given the paucity of evidence describing the upkeep of houses, and the fact that there were thousands of slave houses in nineteenth-century southern Maryland, definitive conclusions are impossible, especially since practices and perceptions of household order and cleanliness vary greatly from family to family even within the same social class or ethnic group. None of the former slaves from Maryland interviewed by the WPA described the upkeep of their homes. Qualifying Josiah Henson's description of "wretched hovels" is the broad observation of historian Eugene Genovese:

> By and large, . . . the slaves fussed no more over the appearance of their cabins than did, say, French or Balkan peasants. With cabins cramped, with the physical demands of daily labor so pressing, with insects impossible to control, and with poultry and small animals virtually part of the household, clean, neat, well-ordered cabins required herculean effort and an improbable degree of concern. . . . The slaves, like so many traditional agriculturalists, did not draw a sharp line between house and yard and highly value household regularity and order.[4]

Descriptions from older blacks today who remember the ways of life of former slaves in the late 1800's show that at least some were highly attentive to their houses. As a youth, McKinley Gantt, born in 1893, visited log slave houses with dirt floors occupied by freed slaves and said the "old-time slave women" used to sweep the hard-packed floors "just as nice and clean every morning with homemade straw brooms." James Scriber told similar stories, and the house of the freed slaves, the Harrods, was also well ordered, as sketched in Chapter V. Howard Lyles from Montgomery County said that his grandmother, Virginia Robinson, who was a young girl during slavery, kept her log house spotless throughout her adult years, even though it was plain and the family had little money. In addition, she was a strict disciplinarian: "When she asked you to do something, it was not 'I'll do it later,' it was 'you do it now.'" Since such values are customarily acquired at home during childhood, it is probable that they were a continuation of her parents' practices during slavery. Her family practices represented the opposite extreme from those of Henson's household; probably the average degree of order and disorder lay somewhere between.[5]

Furnishings in slave houses were sparse and, for the most part, plantation-made and utilitarian (figures 52, 53). They were usually fashioned by the families themselves, by fellow slave artisans, or even by overseers. "In the quarters, we had furniture made by the overseer and colored carpenters; they would make the tables, benches, and bedsteads for everybody." Slaves also made everyday and finer objects for the main house. For example, the set of dining chairs in the Chippendale style at Mulberry Fields are thought to have been made by slave artisans (figure 54).[6]

Figure 52
Interior of the restored slave house at Sotterley. Like many museum exhibits,
some of its furnishings, such as the chairs, are too "high style," and the room lacks
the range of objects that would appear during actual residency. Photo: author.

Figure 53
Refurnished interior of the slave house at Sotterley. The
more fortunate slaves did have rope bedsteads somewhat similar to
this one, with a plain frame but without turned bedposts. Few slaves
would have manufactured tables, settees, or ceramic toilet articles
as included in this exhibit. Photo: author.

Figure 54
Dining chair, Mulberry Fields. Photo: author.

Bedsteads in slave houses, usually made by slaves, typically consisted of a plank frame with a plank or rope bottom. Richard Macks from Charles County said that his father made the beds, and his mother and sister made the mattresses. Bedsteads in the slave house of James Deane were also homemade, and his mother sewed the quilts. Another ex-slave added, "Our beds were ticking filled with straw, and [our] cover made of anything we could get." William Diggs remembered how these "bed ticks" were made:

". . . The children slept on pallets made up of the shucks of corn."

"Stuffed into something?"

"They were stuffed into what we called a bed tick. . . . Just like a mattress, but it would have the shucks stuffed into it. If there wasn't shucks, they would have hay into it, after they had threshed the wheat."

"Would you do anything to prepare the corn shucks beforehand, to make them softer? Did you or did you know anyone who would take a fork and shred them or 'rag them out'?"

"No, the only thing about the corn shuck, the part that was attached to the cob, that little part, you took that off. That's very woody . . . but that other part was soft enough. Because it would all clutter to one end, and you had to keep shuffling it around."[7]

In the absence of specific testimony, we must assume that Maryland slaves' bed-covers were probably similar to those of slaves in Virginia and further south, where blankets and quilts, almost always homemade, were used. The blankets were spun from wool, cotton, or flax, and woven by slave women specially trained for the purpose, or perhaps those too infirm to work in the fields. During their free time, and especially during winter nights, female slaves gathered together in quilting parties. As one ex-slave reported, "the women could quilt better if they gets a parcel of them together." As well as providing for the needs of the slave families, these parties were social occasions uniquely for women. Like other traditional domestic crafts, quilting also gave women a means of creative expression and the opportunity to earn community recognition for their handicraft.[8]

According to William Diggs, the slave-made quilts that he saw were not the "dainty quilts with fine stitches and small, pretty pieces of cloth like you see today. Black women back then didn't have time to fool around with that." Instead, their quilts were usually made of large sections of heavy cloth from "old worn-out coats, overcoats, blankets, clothes, or anything they could get their hands on, preferably woolen." Slaves acquired this material second-hand from their owners, Diggs explained, or swapped worn-out blankets and thick cloth among themselves, or traded with slaves on other plantations. The principal colors were "green, black, brown, and red," the red usually being flannel. The quilts were thick, durable, and warm, consisting of large blocks of cloth laid out in rectangular patterns across the backing. There were probably other variations of slave-made quilts that exhibited the more precise sewing skills of slave women, as did examples found in Georgia and elsewhere. A study of the historical quilts of black women in Maryland is now underway, and it may locate such examples and identify patterns that express an Afro-American sense of composition and aesthetics.[9]

Quilts, bed ticks without frames, or both usually served as children's beds in slave houses. They were called "pallets" and were laid on the earthen or plank floor. James Scriber described sleeping on pallets as a child and gave us some insight into the sleeping conditions of slave children, as well as of some adults.

"Now, would they [the children] have . . . a bed frame that you would sleep on?"

"No, indeed. Nothing. Right down there on the floor."

"You'd just put your bag of corn shucks down and sleep right on that?"

"Right on the floor. Right on the floor. . . . Now the older people might've had, you know, some kind of bedstead. But all the children up to around thirteen or fourteen years old slept right down on the floor. And some of the old people slept the same way. It wasn't like it is now. But some of the people were more able than some of the others, you know—having things, I mean. And that was it."

"And you said you'd pull your beds up next to the fire at night?"

"That's right, at nights."

"And during the day?"

"Move 'em out, roll 'em up, move 'em back in the corner, until the next night again."[10]

Some slaves did not have even the comfort of a bed tick. William Green, a fugitive slave from Maryland, said that some women slept in beds if they were "fortunate," but men simply slept on one or two boards, one end of which they set on a box or bench, and the other on the floor. For cover they used a jacket or sheepskin. "In this manner twenty-five or thirty men, women, and children sleep."[11] More fortunate slaves on some farms were able to buy furnishings with money they earned by hiring themselves out or by raising and selling garden produce: "As to the furniture of this rude dwelling, it was procured by the slaves themselves, who were occasionally permitted to earn a little money after their day's toil was done.

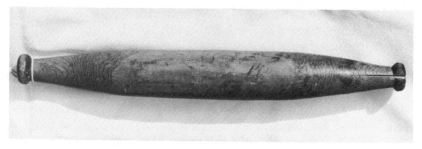

Figure 55
Rolling pin made by William Golder. One of
the few slave-made objects to have been preserved
in southern Maryland. Photo: author.

I never knew Capt. H. to furnish his slaves with household utensils of any description."[12]

Most household utensils were produced by slaves, yet only a very few have been preserved. The rolling pin shown in figure 55 was made by William Golder, a slave from Calvert County, and is in the possession of his great-granddaughter, Blanche Wilson. According to her, this was among the many things that Golder made for his family, as he was "quite good with his hands." Like other slaves throughout the South, he wove baskets, and he taught the craft to his son, Charles Golder, also born during slavery. The basket in figure 56 is an example of Charles Golder's work. Dried gourds were another commonplace artifact in slave houses, and were used for a variety of purposes, as William Diggs explained. "Those old folks believed in gourds. Them old things could hold lard, butter, milk, water, pins and needles, and every kind of thing they wanted to put in that thing. They'd put them outside and have birds building in them. At Christmas we'd paint them old things up [using a dye from walnut bark] and put a stone in them and rattle them. Have the grandest time!" The use of gourds, customarily suspended from trees on poles in a cluster, was a common practice of rural blacks and whites throughout the South. Their primary purpose was to attract nesting colonies of purple martins, which would drive crows from the farm and consume large quantities of mosquitoes and other insects. At the moment, the origin of the use in Maryland of the gourd as a rattle is unknown. A small hole was cut into the gourd to insert the stones, and it was then sealed or stoppered, Diggs explained.[13]

He also said that the "old-time people" used to cut the end of the

Figure 56
Basket woven by Charles Golder, son of William
Golder, Calvert County. Photo: author.

stem and use the gourds as water buckets. "You go to the spring and submerge it and get the whole thing full of water and come on back. Little children, five or six years old, could bring water. And that thing wouldn't leak either!"[14]

In addition to gourds, wooden water buckets and crocks were used to fetch and store water and would have been a part of the furnishings in slave houses (figure 57).

"The posture of these people [in figure 57] seems to be very erect, more so than of people in our own time. Did the older black people stand particularly straight, and was there any reason for it?"

"Well, the only explanation I can give is when I was a child, they would carry water, or any other heavy object on their head. And by carrying a bucket of water on your head and two in your hands, quite naturally, you couldn't stoop over . . . ."

"When was the last time you saw somebody carrying something on their head?"

". . . in 1925. That was at Chicamuxen [Diggs's home town]. My grandmother, we had to go down to the spring to get water, a spring is a flowing hole where the water would just flow forever. We'd go down and dip up the water and fill it, the buckets up. And then she'd put it on her head and have two in her hands, and we children would carry our buckets along with her, at that time."[15]

In the absence of written testimony from the ex-slaves or other sources in Maryland, we turn again to William Diggs for descriptions of lighting devices that may have been found in slave houses. He said that his ancestors saved the grease from "any animal that was fat—raccoons, 'possums, or whatever." They did not use pork lard, since that was necessary for cooking and they "didn't want to burn it up for light." The grease was first heated to drive out the water, then poured into a container in which a string was placed. His grandfather, who became a waterman after emancipation, saved conch shells, and he and other freed families used them as lamps. Others made small clay pots "about the size of an old-fashioned coffee mug" (approximately three to four inches high and three inches in diameter). A few had candle molds. Though Diggs's descriptions are of the post–Civil-War era, it is most likely that his ancestors' practices of using materials at hand for lighting were continuations from their experience during slavery.[16]

Slaves also made much of their own clothing. "We all wore home-made clothes, the material woven on the looms in the clothes house," said one ex-slave, and another specified, "The old women weaved clothes." Richard Macks gave further details: "During hot weather we wore thin woolen clothes, the material being made on the farm from the wool of our sheep. In the winter we wore thicker clothes made on the farm by slaves." The slave women gathered extra scraps of cloth and sewed them into quilts for the family, a

Figure 57
Scene at a well. Crocks of this type may have been
used by slaves and were definitely used by blacks in the late
1800's, when this photograph was taken. Springs, not enclosed
wells, were typical for slave quarters. Photo: Rudolf Eickemeyer. Reproduced
with permission from Ronald Killian and Charles Waller, eds.,
Slavery Time When I Was Chillun Down on Master's
Plantation (*Savannah, Georgia: Beehive Press, 1973*).

necessity on cold winter nights. After emancipation, former slaves are known to have gathered and braided scraps of cloth into rugs, which enhanced the appearance of the rooms as well as the family's physical comfort in the winter when the floor, whether earthen or plank, was cold.[17]

Clothes were commonly drab, displaying little variety in color or design that would otherwise express the individual tastes and identity of the wearer. According to Josiah Henson:

> Our dress was of tow-cloth; for the children nothing but a shirt. For the older ones there was a pair of pantaloons or a gown in addition, according to the sex. Besides these in the winter, a round jacket or overcoat, a wool hat once in two or three years, for the males, and a pair of coarse shoes once a year.[18]

"Parson" Rezin Williams said that men and boys wore rather similar, plain clothes. "The men and boys wore home-spun, three quarter striped pants and sometimes a large funnel-shaped straw hat. Some wore only a shirt as a covering for their body." At St. Inigoes Manor in St. Mary's County, male slaves were given "two shirts, a pair of trousers, shoes and stockings, and a coat, all made of wool, cotton, and flax grown on the Manor." Women received "two shifts and a 'habit' for summer, and a pair of shoes and short gown for winter." As after emancipation, some slaves probably made clothes from sack-cloth and patched them again and again, as described later by James Scriber: "[Our clothes] were made of grass sacks. And years ago, people'd patch a pants or dress or something [so much], you wouldn't know what the first piece was made of. Patchin', patchin', and keep patchin'."[19]

Children went barefoot during much of the year; when shoes were available, they rarely fit. "Parson" Rezin Williams explained, "In winter, oxhide shoes were worn, much too large, and the soles contained several layers of paper. We called them 'program' shoes, because the paper used for stuffin', consisted of discarded programs." Richard Macks recalled how shoes were ordered for slaves:

> For shoes, measures were taken of each slave with a stick, they were brought to Baltimore by the old mistress at the beginning of each season. If she or the one who did the measuring got the shoes too short or too small, you had to wear it or go barefooted.[20]

Because of the scarcity of clothing, slaves suffered in cold weather:

> My master gave me one pair of shoes, one pair of stockings,
> one hat, one jacket of coarse cloth, two coarse shirts, and two
> pair of trousers, yearly. He allowed me no other clothes. In the
> winter time I often suffered very much from the cold.[21]

Since slaves had little clothing, slave houses would have had little, if any, furniture for storing clothes, such as trunks, chests, or
bureaus. Extra clothes were probably hung on the walls from pegs or
nails, as they were in the documented homes of black families after
emancipation. Extra clothes would have mostly been for special occasions and Sundays. "On Sunday we wore the clothes given to us at
Christmas time and shoes likewise," said one ex-slave.[22]

Favored slaves, especially house servants, were given better
clothes, some of them being "hand-me-downs" from the white family. "My master gave me a child's frock, belonging to one of his own
children," recalled Charles Ball. Clothes also served to identify the
higher station of house servants: "The table was waited on by Uncle
Billie, dressed in a uniform, decorated with brass buttons, braid, and
a fancy vest, his hands incased in white gloves. I can see him now,
standing at the door." More comfortable and fashionable clothes also
reinforced aspirations of upward mobility and served as tangible in-
ducements to "behave":

> My master gave me better clothes than the little slaves of my
> age generally received in Calvert [County], and often told me
> that he intended to make me his waiter, and that if I behaved
> well I should become his overseer in time. These stations of
> waiter and overseer appeared to me to be the highest points of
> honor and greatness in the whole world.[23]

A few former slaves give us a glimpse of some of the children's
playthings that would have been found among the contents of slave
houses. Marbles, "mumble pegs," tops, and other "toys that poor
children had" were cited. What games children played cannot be
determined by artifacts alone, since many required only imagination
and a few materials close at hand. "I played . . . a game called
skinny, a game played on trees and grape vines," said one former
slave, while others recalled running races, jumping contests, and
dancing. William Diggs was told by his grandmother (who he said
was the "daily television show") that young slaves made dolls and
hand puppets from old cloth and played "make-believe." She also
said adults in the slave quarters used the "play" conversation among

dolls and hand puppets to clandestinely spread news that they did not want their owners to learn about (a practice described in detail in the Epilogue).[24]

Because music and dance were integral to the slaves' social life, musical instruments were also among the items in slave houses. "After work was done, the slaves would smoke, sing, tell ghost stories and tales, [have] dances, music, [play] home-made fiddles," remembered James Deane. Another former slave concurred, "At nights the slaves would go from one cabin to the other, talk, dance or play the fiddle or sing." Music was the highlight of special occasions: "At corn shucking all the slaves from other plantations would come to the barn, the fiddler would sit on top of the highest barrel of corn, and play all kinds of songs. . . . Dance would start after the corn was stored, we danced until daybreak." In addition to the fiddle, other instruments were cited, such as the jew's-harp and banjo. Some, like the conch shell, were not musical instruments as such: "When we wanted to meet at night, we had an old conk [conch], we blew that. We would all meet on the bank of the Potomac River and sing across the river to the slaves in Virginia, and they would sing back to us."[25]

With rations at a subsistence level, there was little food in slave houses, and hence few objects for storing it. As the types of food varied little, few cooking utensils were required. "Our food consisted of bread, hominy, black strap molasses, and a red herring a day," recalled one ex-slave, who added, "Our food was very plain, such as fat hog meat, fish, and vegetables raised on the farm and corn bread made up with salt and water." At St. Inigoes Manor in St. Mary's County, adult slaves received "two pounds of meat (pork, bacon, or beef) and one peck of meal per week." Each family cultivated a garden with at least "cabbages, cotton, and sweet potatoes" and raised chickens, which they sold for twenty-five cents, as well as eggs. After comparing the diets of the slave and free populations in St. Mary's County, historian Bayly Marks has concluded that the diet of slaves was "probably similar" to that of the poorest farmers.[26]

While no doubt some plantations in southern Maryland, as in other states, had kitchens or mess halls where slaves ate together, evidence indicates that the more common method was to distribute rations to each family for them to cook in their houses. This method is illustrated in William Diggs's recollection of stories told him by his grandparents.

"Now the question would be how did they all get fed at one time and go out into the field. You know it would take some doing to feed one hundred people at one time. Or even forty people. . . . Well, each person that was on the farm had to go to the master's store house, and they would pass out his ration for that week. Fifteen sorted herrings, and so many pounds of fat meat, so many pounds of flour, so many pounds of cornmeal, or whatever. It was all of them went to that store house and got that, and they went back to their little cabins and kept the food in the cabin. If you ate it all up in one day, that was your problem. But that's how they would do it, and when it was time for them to go in the field, they were supposed to have been up in time and cooked the food and be ready for the field. The master didn't cook for the slaves. The slaves cooked for themselves."[27]

James Scriber described the diet of his family and neighbors during food shortages in the 1880's and 1890's. As his parents and other older members of his community were freed slaves, their use of the husks of ground corn was probably a continuation of slave practices: ". . . meal husk bread. You get short sometime, get caught in a hard time when you couldn't get to a mill, and you'd have to eat it until you can get to that mill. I've had it, not a whole lot of it. Stop from starving, anything to stop from starving. Not only me either, plenty of them have had it."[28]

This plain fare, based on corn in one form or another as the staple, was prepared over the open fireplace and tested the skills of slave women, who customarily did the cooking. One method was to bake the corn bread in a "spider with legs," a large heavy skillet on three legs (also known as a Dutch oven). They pulled hot coals from the fireplace onto the hearth and set the "spider" over them. A heavy lid sealed the top, and coals were placed on it so the bread would bake through on both sides. A good cook produced corn bread that was moist and knew when it was "just right" without, of course, referring to clocks, timers, or thermometers. Some families may have added cracklings, or pork rinds, to the corn bread, which gave it a different flavor and added a measure of protein.[29]

"Hoecakes" and "ashcakes" were two other common forms of corn bread in southern Maryland and the South. A hoecake was a thin patty of corn meal, salt, and water, fried in a skillet or on a griddle at the hearth. When out at work in the fields, slaves are said to have placed the patty on a hoe held over a fire; hence the name. Ashcake was a patty of corn meal, salt, and water "about the thickness of a bun," said Jessie Beulah Kinard. It was placed in an area of the firebox swept clean of ashes, she explained, sometimes wrapped in a wet corn shuck or cabbage leaf, and covered with hot ashes until done.

Even if the patty was not wrapped in a leaf, the ashes could easily be brushed off, according to Howard Young and his wife in St. Mary's County, whose parents continued to make ashcakes on a regular basis into the early twentieth century. As the Youngs said, properly made hoecakes and ashcakes tasted quite good. Hoecakes entered into the mainstream of Southern cooking and are still enjoyed by more traditional-minded Southerners, both black and white.[30]

Just as their African ancestors had utilized the natural resources of the homeland, so too did the slaves of southern Maryland. To add meat to their plain fare of carbohydrates, they hunted, fished, and trapped. The broad Potomac and Patuxent rivers, their many tributaries, and the Chesapeake Bay, North America's largest estuary, were the spawning and feeding grounds for a rich variety of fish. An 1866 atlas of Maryland reported that "the waters of the Chesapeake and Patuxent abound in the finest fish and oysters." And of Charles County along the Potomac, "fish and oysters abound along these shores." Herring, shad, rock perch, and other fish annually migrated up the rivers to be caught by slaves. Herring, a staple in the diet of slaves, were captured in seines.[31]

Fortunately, Amanda Nelson, from St. Mary's County, remembers the traditional methods of preserving and preparing herring, a critical activity since herring was a source of essential protein year round and provided needed calories and fat. She learned the methods from her mother, born in 1867, who in turn learned them from former slaves. Other descendants of former slaves in Maryland have confirmed her account of traditional methods.

"You cut off the head, but don't scale them. Take out the entrails, and be sure to get that vein down the back and get that blood out. Then wash them real good. Then they'd pack them down in a barrel with salt, not real heavy, and lay them belly up, sideways. All the way to the top. Then in about three weeks, they'd be ready, maybe less. They'd take up the salt and make a brine. You could take some out then if you wanted to, or leave them in a long time because of that brine, don't you know. Whenever they wanted them, they'd take them out and soak them in water to get all that salt out. Then scale them. Some people would put them on a stick with branches and let them dry. Put them on the porch or in the meat house, somewhere where flies wouldn't get to them. But it was much nicer if you didn't [dry them]. Just wipe them off with a rag. They were much softer. Then you just roll them in meal—not a batter—and fry them. And they were delicious." According to Mrs. Nelson, herring was the only fish cured in this way, and smoking fish was not an old-time method that she knew of in her area of southern Maryland.[32]

The vast reaches of shallow water and the deep channels of the rivers and the bay were excellent habitat for oysters, clams, and crabs, also gathered by slaves. "My choice food was fish and crabs cooked in all styles by my mother," one former slave said. After freedom, former slaves—such as Albert Gantt, James Wilson, James Harrod from Calvert County, and Samuel Carroll and Christopher Butler from St. Mary's County—used skills learned during slavery to gain a livelihood as watermen, gathering and selling fish, crabs, oysters, and clams. As a youth James Scriber tonged in "boatloads" of oysters from "Oyster Bay" in the Patuxent River near Sotterley Plantation—a skill taught him by former slaves.[33]

Slaves also supplemented their diet by hunting and trapping. The streams, marshes, swamps, and rivers abounded with wild game. "I have hunted o'possums and coons," remembered James Deane. "Parson" Rezin Williams said most slaves preferred "possum to rabbits" in the hierarchy of wild game, though "some liked fish best." Richard Macks described hunting coons, rabbits, and opossum with his father's "fine dogs." William Jordan and other former slaves in Charles County trapped muskrats, locally known as "marsh rabbits," during slavery. In 1980, they continue to be trapped and eaten as a delicacy in black communities.[34]

Slaves made extra efforts to raise food for their families by cultivating gardens, sometimes at night after working all day. "We had a section of the farm that the slaves were allowed to farm for themselves—my mistress would let them raise extra food for their own use at nights." Another former slave agreed, "Slaves had small gardens which they worked by moonlight." In nearby Virginia, an ex-slave added, "each family had a garden, we raised what we wanted."[35]

Whether slaves caught their own food or cultivated it, their practices of "making do" had important personal and psychological benefits. They provided welcome additions to a plain diet, enriched the slaves' nutrition, and sustained their health. For example, the high amounts of protein in the game and fish complemented the carbohydrates in corn bread and molasses, while vegetables furnished needed vitamins. Furthermore, these efforts to obtain and prepare their own food, even with such limited means, provided slaves with opportunities to exercise their own skills and win more recognition from their families and the plantation community. Such efforts were important in assisting slaves to preserve their individual identity.[36]

Folk medicine was central to making do. While some owners hired physicians for slaves, especially in cases of serious or contagious diseases, it was more common for slaves to treat themselves. Said one former slave, "The colored doctored themselves with herbs, teas, and salves made by themselves." Another recalled, "The slaves had herbs of their own and made their own salves." Their African ancestors had been well versed in the use of medicinal herbs, leaves, and roots that cured specific ailments. While the flora were different in North America, the basic techniques of preparation and administration still applied, once the medicinal characteristics of local plants had been tested and learned. They passed this knowledge on to their children, and numerous descendants of slaves in Maryland, Virginia, and North Carolina concur: "The old people could read the woods just like a book. Whenever you were sick, they could go out and pick something, and you'd get well." "We gathered herbs from which we made medicine, snake root and sassafras bark being a great remedy for many ailments." Other herbs included "life-everlasting boneset and woodditney, from each of which we made a tea." The herbs, roots, and other natural substances used in folk medicine undoubtedly would have been among the contents of slave houses.[37]

In the context of today's highly technological medical establishment, such folk remedies appear quaint, if not pure quackery. However, we should consider that some natural materials, such as penicillin or the bark of quinine trees, are scientifically proven medicines, while others are currently being studied by folklorists and medical scientists. In addition, some folk remedies may have helped effect cures through a placebo effect. That is, the medicine contained no demonstrably effective substances, but it somehow relieved pain or helped promote a cure. Recent scientific studies have found that placebos are effective as pain relievers in as many as one out of three patients, and that their effectiveness may be caused by substances known as endorphins. Produced by the pituitary gland and the hypothalamus, endorphins attach themselves to the pain receptors of the nervous system and block their transmissions in the same way as morphine. It is thought that, because of their action, we may not feel terrible pain immediately after suffering a severe burn, wound, or other traumatic injury. Endorphins are also produced in low levels during pregnancy and in higher amounts during childbirth, probably engendering a sense of quietude in the fetus and helping the mother to relax and lessening her pain. When activated in extremely high amounts, endorphins can induce an overall sense of repose, even serenity, and a diminution in muscular and gastrointestinal activity, similar to the physiological response to opium.[38]

While specific substances in some folk remedies, such as digitalis in the plant foxglove, may explain the success of some remedies, the success of others may be interpreted as the result of the body's response to placebos. First, the anticipation of a remedy could have helped create a more hopeful environment for the patient, and administering the remedy enabled the family and community "doctor" to "do something," showing they cared. Faith in most remedies was based upon the authority of community tradition and was heightened by prayers and rituals integral to the remedy. All of this reinforced the patient's belief in the remedy and could prompt him to believe he was going to get better. This encouraged the patient to take the necessary nourishment and perform bodily functions and could strengthen the patient's will to live. Furthermore, a person with special status whom the patient trusted customarily administered the folk remedy. All of these factors helped to allay the anxiety of the people surrounding the patient and calmed the patient's mind and body. Last, the lessening of pain caused by the placebo effect, or by endorphins in particular, facilitated the effectiveness of the body's defensive and healing mechanisms, much more than if the patient was in a state of agitation. We do not know the success rate of folk remedies years ago, but they were most likely more effective than no remedy at all.

Popular faith in community doctors and in even their most repugnant remedies is clear from the vivid account of W. C. Handy, the son of former slaves:

> She was very dark, proudly handsome, and walked like an Ethiopian queen. She was the family physician, who could cure a fever with the juice of peach leaves, which she gathered and mashed. Mullein tea and Jimson weeds were remedies for swellings, sassafras tea for thinning blood, catnip tea for hives, and the marrow of hog jowls for the mumps. Some of her doses were hard ones. I remember when I had a bad sore throat bordering on croup she made me gargle with my own urine, and when we had the measles she gave us tea made from sheep manure. But we never questioned her remedies and we all lived.[39]

Community doctors and midwives—known variously as "old mama" or "granny lady," depending upon the region—were among the most highly respected and most knowledgeable members of the community. Typically, a slave midwife used "herbs and salves, and home liniments" to deliver babies. "Very seldom" were white doctors ever called in by the masters, though they did employ wives of overseers for the purpose. In fact, midwifery was the "most usual woman's occupation" in ante-bellum St. Mary's County. The relationships among these slave and free midwives and comparisons of their techniques call for future scholarly study.[40]

In caring for their patients, black community doctors eclectically blended treatments from their own traditions, the practices of white doctors, and prayer. The types of treatments and the doctors' leadership position is illustrated by Thomas Foote's story about his mother, a free Negro in Baltimore County, Maryland. Employed by a homeopathic medical doctor, she learned the different herbs and roots that he used to compound his medicine, and then used them herself for commercial purposes, treating slaves and free blacks. They called her the "doctor woman." She also served as a midwife and delivered babies of poor whites as well as of blacks. Like her patients, she was very religious and always preceded her treatment with prayer. But while the homeopathic doctor was allowed to use roots and herbs freely, whites suspected her of "voodooism." Specifically, she was accused of giving slaves charmed roots that encouraged them to escape, and was forced to flee Baltimore County and seek asylum in Pennsylvania. It is not known if she was, in fact, encouraging them to run away, but since black people confided in her all "their ills and their troubles," it is highly likely that she tried to help cure them not only of specific maladies, but of the more deep-seated disease, slavery.[41]

Specific recollections about midwives shed light upon some of the home remedies of these unsung doctors in black American history. One of the most knowledgeable sources in Maryland is William Diggs, whose grandmother, Amanda Diggs, trained to be a midwife during slavery, taught him some of her practices, such as the preparation of snake oil (figure 58).

Snake oil is a clear, light liquid, finer in consistency than castor oil. While today snake oil is associated with quackery, it was genuinely helpful, especially in lubricating the birth canal during childbirth. It was made from the melted fat, or tallow, of a carefully preserved and dried snake. Figure 59 shows a black snake that Diggs prepared himself and from which he made oil. He said that large snakes were preferred because they had a lot of fat. After the snake was eviscerated, its rib cage was propped open with short sticks, and it was left outside to dry. In order to keep flies, maggots, and other insects from the carcass, it was rubbed thoroughly with "Adam and Eve root." This was gathered in the woods and placed in windows, in the kitchen, and around babies' cribs to repel insects. After the snake's carcass had dried, it was stored inside the house. It is nearly odorless,

Figure 58
Amanda Diggs. Copy photograph reproduced through
the courtesy of William Diggs.

Figure 59
Dried snake prepared by William Diggs, Charles County. Photo: author.

except for a light and not unpleasant aroma. When oil was needed, pieces of fat were pinched off and melted in a pan over the fire, which also helped sterilize the oil. The product was a fine-textured lubricant. In addition to assisting women in delivery, it was used, Diggs said, to soften dry and cracked skin and to heal chapped lips. To prevent the irritating poison ivy rash, people working outdoors rubbed it on their hands and legs. Thus, many households might have had snake oil.[42]

In southern Maryland, as elsewhere in the South, "root doctors" or "conjurers" were important members of slave communities. In some respects they resembled African priest-doctors, because they treated physical as well as spiritual pains. Today, "conjurers" are often solely associated with quackery and with putting a "root" (a hex) on someone, leading to malicious actions usually associated with sex or violence. Indeed, tragic love affairs have been explained as the result of a root doctor putting "the root" on one or both parties. But root doctors may also have provided beneficial services. In a world without professional mental health specialists, they served as community psychiatrists and helped to cure psychological problems.

The possible effectiveness of their remedies is suggested by a recent multicultural study by the World Health Organization, which found that schizophrenia is cured at a remarkably higher rate in Africa and India, where traditional remedies are administered by local priest-doctors, than in modern Western nations. Though the reasons for this have not yet been determined, they may stem from the belief systems of patients and their communities—their faith—rather than from the medicine itself.[43]

Though former slaves from Maryland did not describe the practices of root doctors, they did mention the everyday charms used by slaves, which may have had the positive effects of placebos. For example, according to ex-slave James Deane, slaves wore charms made of bones, which may have made them feel better, more immune to the traumas of slavery and other sources of stress. Another former slave said that his longevity and good health resulted from the rabbit's foot that he wore. Again, it may have been that wearing this charm made him feel stronger and healthier, kept him more physically and mentally active, and thereby slowed the aging process. Such charms or other specific substances given out by root doctors would have been among the items found in many slaves' houses.[44]

It should be pointed out that objects of a more formal religious character would rarely have been found in slave houses; instead, the slaves' strong religious faith was intangibly expressed in verbal, musical, and silent expressions of belief. Severe restrictions limited slaves' religious activities, especially from the 1830's and 1840's onwards, when stringent laws were passed prohibiting slaves from gathering to worship without the owner's supervision. According to a free black in ante-bellum Maryland, "Some cruel masters believed that Negroes had no souls." Others did permit slaves to attend their church, where there might be special galleries for slaves. Slaves also worshiped at religious services conducted on the farm by the owner or by a minister in his place, who might be another slave or a free black. Since most slaves were prohibited from learning to read, Bibles and prayer books would have been absent from most homes, except perhaps those of slave preachers. Perhaps some Roman Catholic slaves would have a crucifix or a symbol of the Virgin Mary or a saint in their houses, as did some freed families after emancipation, but neither these nor any other religious objects were cited by former slaves from Maryland.[45]

However, as one former slave declared, "Dey law us out of church, but dey couldn't law 'way Christ," and the slaves worshiped on their own without benefit of specifically religious objects. Instead, they used ordinary things and endowed some of them with special qualities. Among the most universal was a wash pot turned upside down to "catch the sound" when the slaves worshiped in secret, so their master could not hear them. It was placed inside the door of the house, or, if they were meeting outdoors, the slaves gathered around it. Significantly, slaves throughout the South described the same object in the same religious context, used for the same purpose. Perhaps this may be explained culturally by the suggestion that the practice was once common to West Africa, and a part of a "ritual designed to sanctify the ground." But using the pot to "catch sound" was evidently an American transformation. It seems strange that such a ritual could be developed and sustained by so many generations, in so many parts of the South, with minimal contact among slaves to sustain both the ritual and the exact same explanation for it, unless in some way the practice achieved its stated purpose. But sound waves travel from their source in all directions, and while a kettle might perhaps trap those in the lower planes, most would pass over it, and sound waves cannot be attracted to an object. Hanging quilts on the walls or from overhead joists would muffle sound far more effectively, but such alternative methods were never cited by former slaves. It seems that there should be a kernel of truth to the kettle's purported purpose, as there seems to have been with folk remedies, but at the moment we lack a complete explanation for why this particular ritual—and not others—became and stayed widespread.[46]

Like early Christians in Rome, slaves gathered secretly in their homes to express their faith in prayer, fellowship, and song. Though they might not have a copy of the Bible, they knew its stories and identified with the Israelites in bondage in Egypt. They also perceived their own "trials and tribulations" as similar to Jesus's life and suffering, and found meaning and hope in his love for all mankind and in his promise of salvation. All would be brought to judgment, slaves and slaveowners alike. These feelings were expressed in the old slave spiritual:

> O brothers, don't get weary
> O brothers, don't get weary
> O brothers, don't get weary
> We're waiting for the Lord
> We'll land on Canaan's shore,
> We'll land on Canaan's shore,
> When we land on Canaan's shore,
> We'll meet forever more.[47]

Such spirituals were central to the religious life of slaves, because they expressed their belief in an ultimate purpose to life and their hope for reunion in the love of Jesus. The spirituals served too as a clandestine method of communication among slaves, with religious lyrics serving as code. For example, in the verses cited above, Canaan could represent the free North or Canada to runaway slaves. Furthermore, as recent historians have observed, the spirituals heightened the slaves' sense of self worth by creating a sense of sacred time in which the present was extended back, so that characters and events from the Old and New Testaments became a part of the life of slaves. The spirituals also connected this world to the world to come. Whether sung a cappella or with the musical instruments described earlier in this chapter, the spirituals were as much a part of the historical character of slave houses as their furnishings, and could be appropriately included as part of the interpretation of a museum exhibit.[48]

The clandestine worship services in slave houses were briefly described by Dennis Simms:

> We would, unbeknown to our master, assemble in a cabin and sing songs and spirituals. Our favorite spirituals were—*Bringing in de sheaves, De Stars am shining for us all, Hear de Angels callin'*, and *the Debel has no place here*. The singing was usually to the accompaniment of a Jew's Harp, or banjo.[49]

The story of William Jordan, born William Tubman, illustrates the traditional use of the home as a church and the extent to which slaves identified with spirituals (figure 60). According to his grandson and namesake, William Diggs, Tubman was born a slave in Charles County, the son of William Tubman, also a slave. The Tubman family and others used to gather secretly in their homes to worship. As a youth, Tubman's favorite spiritual was "Roll, Jordan, Roll," which he and his fellow slaves sang in the fields and in their homes. When emancipation came in 1864, Tubman memorialized

Figure 60

William (Tubman) Jordan, *originally named after his father,*
William Tubman. His family was of no known relationship to Harriet
Tubman. While Tubman elected to remain in America, his brothers emigrated to
Liberia when freedom came; they are ancestors of W. V. S. Tubman,
president of Liberia from 1943 to 1971. Copy photograph
reproduced through the courtesy of William Diggs.

Figure 61
Alexandria United Methodist Church, originally the Jordan
Chapel, Chicamuxen, Maryland. Photo: author.

the moment by changing his surname to Jordan in honor of that spiritual. With "freedom," he felt he had crossed over the river Jordan and received his deliverance.[50]

In 1866, Jordan managed to purchase a small tract of land and build a log house on it. Continuing the tradition begun during slavery, Jordan, his family, and other freed families gathered in his house to worship, no longer clandestinely. The congregation soon grew too large, so Jordan purchased and donated an acre of land for a church site. It was named the Jordan Memorial Chapel. First they built a small log church, rather similar to a slave house. Later a new frame church was built, and more recently another one at a more convenient location (figure 61). The burying ground remains on the original site, and the congregation exists to this day, over a hundred years after its official founding. As with other black churches, its heritage extends back much further.[51]

This saga of the Tubman/Jordan family and the Jordan Memorial Chapel reflects what folklorists John Vlach and Barry Lee Pearson found to be a primary characteristic of Afro-American culture: improvisation. Techniques of improvisation are woven through black music in the blues, jazz, and spirituals, and through the decorative arts traditions of quilting, blacksmithing, wood carving, and basketry. We see improvisation too in the slaves' abilities to "make do" in the hostile economic and social environment of slavery. They used creatively what was at hand to make slave houses into more than just structures: they became homes and churches and hospitals. This strategy of "making do" enabled slaves to survive the rigors of bondage. Exhibits of slave houses in historical museums or parks that show them as lifeless shelters therefore distort black history. Though in a somewhat different fashion from the tenant house at the Smithsonian, such slave houses are "backwards" too.[52]

CHAPTER IV
Houses of the Landless:
"On Canaan's Bright Shore"

Never before had black people
in the South found any reason
to view the future with
more hope or expectation than in
the 1860's.
Leon F. Litwack[1]

O h, it was a great day," said
McKinley Gantt, the son of former slaves, "a great day when Abraham Lincoln freed the colored folks." "A great day," he softly repeated to himself, nodding his head in remembrance, as if he too had been there. And in a way he had been, because Gantt, like other descendants of slaves I interviewed in southern Maryland, was speaking not only of episodes he had read about, but of personal experiences told to him by his father and mother, his uncles and aunts, and his neighbors, all former slaves. A "great day," for emancipation had brought his people the promise of a new life, in the words of the old spiritual, "across the river Jordan, on Canaan's bright shore."[2]

With freedom came the hope of new opportunities to work as one wished, to live where one wished, to vote, to go to school, to own property and a family home, and to worship and pray freely, alone and in the open fellowship of one's community. For us, this event raises the question of whether black material culture and houses reflected the rights gained immediately after emancipation. Indeed, what real opportunities did blacks have to get better jobs, to obtain an education, and to improve their way of life?

There were changes, to be sure, but they were severely limited. Slavery had been abolished, but neither blacks nor whites could start anew in an economically democratic society. In place of slavery, another economic system developed that kept most blacks impov-

Table 3

Population of Southern Maryland, by Race and by County, 1866

County	Whites	Blacks	% Black
Anne Arundel	11,704	12,196	51
Calvert	3,997	6,450	62
Charles	5,796	10,721	65
Prince George's	9,650	13,677	59
St. Mary's	6,798	8,415	55
Total	37,945	51,459	58

Source: Simon J. Martinet, *Map of Maryland: Atlas Edition* (Baltimore: Simon J. Martinet, 1866).

erished—wage tenancy and sharecropping. Though blacks constituted the majority of the population in southern Maryland, they never gained political power, and so after emancipation they remained unable to press for and obtain their rights as free Americans (table 3). The problems Maryland blacks faced were noted by one black leader, who reported that "his people would have been further advanced, had the State seceded and shared the fate of the more Southern states." Without Reconstruction assistance, rural Maryland blacks had little with which to support themselves that was independent of white control. As former chattels, they had virtually no capital to buy land, work animals, farm equipment, and supplies in order to start their own farms. There were no official efforts to divide the large plantations among former slaves. Unlike their Deep South counterparts, the wealthy landowners and political leaders of southern Maryland did not lose their citizenship and could still vote and organize and lead local political groups. The result was that they maintained control. No blacks from rural southern Maryland were elected to federal or state offices. In fact, even in Charles County, where the 1870 voter registration lists showed a black majority, no blacks were elected to political office. Furthermore, state law permitted only whites to practice law before the Maryland state bar until 1885, a restriction that in effect prevented blacks from being lawyers, not to mention judges, in the state.[3]

The economy was also controlled by whites. The freedmen who left the farms in search of jobs in the city found skilled positions closed to them due to racial prejudice and the increased number of white immigrant laborers. Blacks had held a near monopoly on the busy ship-caulking trade in the port of Baltimore. Frederick Douglass had been hired as a ship caulker before his escape. In the years following the Civil War, jobs in this trade and others were lost to white laborers, especially Irish and Germans. The result was that there were ever fewer skilled jobs for blacks, who were relegated more and more to menial, low-paying jobs with little hope of advancement, or to jobs that almost exclusively served the black community. This situation closed off a source of good-paying jobs with advancement from rural blacks—jobs that could have brought blacks more economic and political power in the state. In the rural counties of southern Maryland, blacks had few alternatives: to work the land, to work the water, or to work for whites as domestics.[4]

An examination of Freedmen's Bureau work contracts between former slaves and their employers reveals the economic plight of the freedmen and the conditions under which they began. The alleged purpose of the contracts (figure 62) was to secure jobs for freed men and women and to prevent unscrupulous employers from firing them without pay. To ensure that these contracts were not broken, the employer put up a bond, usually of one hundred dollars. The advantage to employers was that the contracts assured a steady source of low-cost labor. Fifty-three contracts for southern Maryland have survived, in which 102 former slaves were contracted for work. The tenure was usually from a specific month in the fall of the year to the same month in the next year, and most of the freed men and women (54 of the 102) were hired at eight to ten dollars a month. One freedman, highly skilled in a trade or in negotiations, was able to bargain for thirty dollars a month, but that was extremely unusual. Though the lowest wage was two dollars a month, several wives of farm hands, their children, and one elderly mother (totaling fourteen) were paid nothing and given only living quarters and fuel; two were to be given clothes in addition. Such low wages explain why houses remained the same for black families in the years following emancipation, especially since the employer kept a fourth of each month's wages to be paid at the satisfactory completion of the contract. It may well be that even these wages were higher than those received by farm hands whose employers refused to sign contracts.[5]

The tenants' contracts also reveal the broad powers that landowners had over farm hands. In addition to wages, laborers were to be furnished with "quarters, fuel, full and substantial rations, and all necessary medical attendance and supplies in case of sickness." But it was in the employer's power to decide when rations were "full sub-

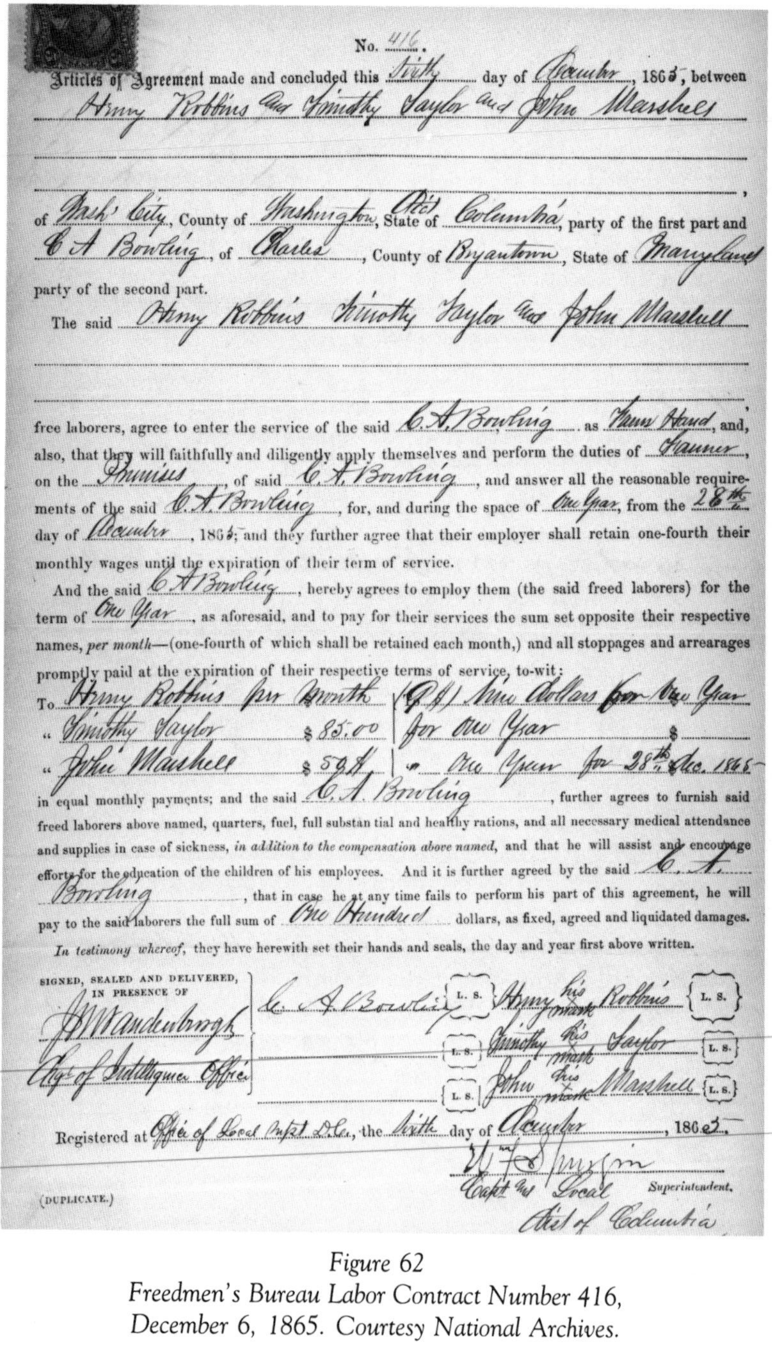

No. 416.

Articles of Agreement made and concluded this Sixth day of December, 1865, between Henry Robbins and Timothy Taylor and John Marshall

of Wash. City, County of Washington, State of Dist. Columbia, party of the first part and C A Bowling, of Charles, County of Bryantown, State of Maryland party of the second part.

The said Henry Robbins Timothy Taylor and John Marshall

free laborers, agree to enter the service of the said C. A. Bowling as Farm Hand, and, also, that they will faithfully and diligently apply themselves and perform the duties of Farmer, on the Premises, of said C. A. Bowling, and answer all the reasonable requirements of the said C. A. Bowling, for, and during the space of One Year, from the 28th day of December, 1865; and they further agree that their employer shall retain one-fourth their monthly wages until the expiration of their term of service.

And the said C A Bowling, hereby agrees to employ them (the said freed laborers) for the term of One Year, as aforesaid, and to pay for their services the sum set opposite their respective names, *per month*—(one-fourth of which shall be retained each month,) and all stoppages and arrearages promptly paid at the expiration of their respective terms of service, to-wit:

To Henry Robbins per month (Off) Nine Dollars for One Year
" Timothy Taylor $ 85.00 for One Year $
" John Marshall $ 50 " One Year for 28th Dec. 1865

in equal monthly payments; and the said C. A. Bowling, further agrees to furnish said freed laborers above named, quarters, fuel, full substan tial and healthy rations, and all necessary medical attendance and supplies in case of sickness, *in addition to the compensation above named*, and that he will assist and encourage efforts for the education of the children of his employees. And it is further agreed by the said C. A. Bowling, that in case he at any time fails to perform his part of this agreement, he will pay to the said laborers the full sum of One Hundred dollars, as fixed, agreed and liquidated damages.

In testimony whereof, they have herewith set their hands and seals, the day and year first above written.

SIGNED, SEALED AND DELIVERED, IN PRESENCE OF

J. M. Vandenburgh
Agt. of Intelligence Office

C. A. Bowling [L. S.] Henry his mark Robbins [L. S.]
[L. S.] Timothy his mark Taylor [L. S.]
[L. S.] John his mark Marshall [L. S.]

Registered at Office of Local Supt. D.C., the Sixth day of December, 1865.

W. F. Spurgin
Capt. and Local Superintendent,
Dist. of Columbia

(DUPLICATE.)

Figure 62
Freedmen's Bureau Labor Contract Number 416, December 6, 1865. Courtesy National Archives.

stantial and healthy" and when medical attendance was "necessary." Since it was the owner's responsibility to supply the quarters, many of the old slave houses were used. With money scarce, the farm laborers did not spend their meager income on improving houses they did not own.[6]

The contracts did make the landowners bear a large measure of responsibility for the education of the tenant farmers' children. For example, one clause specified that the landowner "assist and encourage efforts for the education of the children of his employees." However, little commitment was made to such efforts. Most of the elderly sharecroppers from the post-bellum period of the nineteenth century that I interviewed attended only a few years of school, because they had to go to work on the farms to help support their families and themselves. The primary schools that they did attend were inadequate. Although there were a few private black high schools and colleges in Maryland, most blacks could not afford to attend them. Furthermore, there were only two public high schools available to Maryland blacks before the 1920's, one in Baltimore and the other in Washington, D.C. With educational opportunities so limited for the majority, it is not hard to see why it was difficult for black farm laborers to move ahead and secure better-paying jobs in the country.[7]

Because of the lack of educational, political, and economic opportunities for advancement after emancipation, most houses of freed families did not differ substantially from slave cabins. Small, one-room log houses remained the predominant type; in fact, freed families often continued to inhabit slave cabins. Structural investigation thus far of houses in southern Maryland has produced no evidence to differentiate a slave house of the 1850's from a tenant house of the 1870's. This continuity in housing was in keeping with the trend further south. As W. E. B. Du Bois found in his survey of homes of rural freedmen in the South near the turn of the century, "Emancipation meant more or less of a change in home life for the freedmen, but not a violent change. . . . One and two-room cabins still prevail," and "at least one-third of the Negroes of the land live in one-room houses." Another study agreed that "the housing conditions of the negro farmer have not changed since slavery nearly so much as . . . one might reasonably expect. I have travelled through the country in almost every section of the South, and the negro farm houses consist usually of one, two, or three rooms." A study of homes of rural blacks in Alabama in the 1890's described houses similar to slave dwellings. "In the country practically all the Negroes live in cabins, generally built of logs, with only one or at most two rooms

and log chimneys were typical. Numerous photographs, stereographs, and prints of rural homes of black families taken in the late 1800's and early 1900's show that many blacks lived in small, single-unit houses with log chimneys in Florida, Georgia, South Carolina, North Carolina, and Virginia. Oral informant Luther Stuckey, born in 1894 and the son of former slaves, was reared in a single-unit log tenant house of this type in tidewater South Carolina, and when asked to characterize the tenant house at the Smithsonian during his visit, his response was emphatic: "This house is high style!"[8]

However, as a comparison of the Smithsonian tenant house with others suggests, not all tenant houses were the same, and they did change over time, albeit at a slow pace. In general, the changes among southern Maryland tenant houses were the transition from log to frame construction, from dirt floors to plank floors, from no windows or shuttered windows to glass-paned windows, from floor plans of one room down and one up to plans of two down, two up, or even more rooms, often including, but not limited to, the addition of shed kitchens or bedrooms. Du Bois found a similar evolution in freedmen's houses: "In the course of decades however a change was noticeable. The dirt-floor has practically disappeared, and fully half the log cabins have been replaced by frame buildings, and glass windows have appeared here and there."[9]

This trend proceeded at different rates in different regions. Usually, the closer a house was to an urban center and its network of transportation and distribution of goods, the faster it changed. For example, tenant houses of the type at the Smithsonian replaced the traditional one-room log house in southern Maryland first in Prince George's County, the county closest to Baltimore and Washington, perhaps in the 1880's, and had become common by the 1890's. But in the more isolated counties of Charles, St. Mary's, and Calvert, this type did not begin to appear until the 1890's, and did not become common until the early 1900's, when, as Clem Dyson recalled, "Times were getting a little better for the colored people." By the teens and twenties, the tenant houses that were typically being constructed were small, two- or three-bay structures of lightweight frame construction with two rooms down and two up, or two rooms down and one or two attached to the rear length in an L or T floor plan.[10]

This transition in southern Maryland tenant house types coincided with the shift from the open fireplace to wood stoves, which provided a welcome improvement in living conditions. Since the stove consumed less wood, less time had to be spent in gathering, sawing, splitting, and hauling wood. Also, the wood stove heated a room far

more efficiently and continued to do so throughout the night, if it was damped down properly. Furthermore, the wood stove, in comparison to the fireplace, lessened the work load on the mother and daughters, who traditionally did the cooking. They could cook standing up, rather than bending over the hearth or hot fire, and did not have to stoop to lift heavy iron pots and pans. All of this relieved the strain on their bodies, especially their backs, and was a special relief for pregnant women and for elderly women, who suffered most from back ailments and stiff, painful joints.[11]

In order to illustrate the houses of the landless farm families and the ways of life within them, I have selected two tenant houses from a surveyed sample of twenty-five that represent the continuity and changes in tenant houses. These two can be presented as more than structures, because knowledgeable oral informants who either lived in or visited them have been located. Their descriptions of furnishings and family life allow us to see what continued from slavery days in the way of furnishings and family activities, and to see how tenant houses may have looked when families resided in them. More than a general discussion of house types, these two case studies allow us to see up close the life that black people created for themselves and the life to which they were confined. We see the persistent struggle to "make do" from slavery through tenancy, and the effort to go beyond making do. Furthermore, one example, the Cusic-Medley tenant house, was occupied by white and black families, thereby providing a biracial perspective on houses of the landless after slavery. The result—a blend of material culture and social history—can help to place the tenant house at the Smithsonian in its historical context and can provide significant useful ideas for researching and interpreting, in museums and elsewhere, the history of the people through their houses and material culture.

The Ross House

The plain, one-story log structure we know as the Ross house has importance in three principal areas of material culture: as a house type, as a furnished home of a tenant family, and as a picture of black family home life after emancipation. In the 1880's it was the home of the former slave and veteran of the Union Army, Joseph Ross, whose son Benjamin was born there in 1883. Though the Ross family moved a few years later, Benjamin Ross remembered the house well, because he continued to visit it throughout his youth (figure

Figure 63
Benjamin and Nellie Elizabeth Ross, Charles County, 1975.
In 1978 they celebrated their seventy-second wedding anniversary;
in 1979 Benjamin Ross passed away. Photo: author.

63). His wife, Nellie, who was born nearby in 1888, also recalled the home's appearance, as did William Diggs, whose aunt lived there in the twentieth century. He visited the house frequently during her residency. By combining these three informants' recollections of this house and of similar ones that they lived in and visited, we can create informative sketches of the furnishings of and family life in log tenant houses in the late nineteenth and early twentieth centuries.[12]

The Rosses' small log dwelling was a rectangular single-unit house with one room down and one up, a gable-end chimney, and a central front door—the same house type that had been used for slave houses and that continued to be standard for most landless black families until the turn of the century. Like the vast majority of these homes, it is no longer standing, and no photographs of it have been found. When shown pictures of old log houses, Benjamin and Nellie Ross agreed that their house resembled those in figures 19 and 22, and added, "Everybody pretty much lived in log houses back then. There were very few frame houses, and let me tell you, white and colored lived in log houses."[13]

It is difficult to uncover the early history of the Ross house. The occupants were farm tenants who did not own land, and tenant houses of little monetary value were not customarily recorded, much less individually identified, in landowners' wills, tax records, or deeds. As a result, no written records identify its significance or its date of construction. No remnants exist above ground to date the house by structural evidence. It may have been built as a slave house, since Benjamin Ross recalled that it was considered an old house in the 1880's. On the other hand, it may have been built soon after slavery, weathered quickly, and, since it resembled a slave house, been labeled as such. It is known that the structure was used as a post-bellum tenant house on the farm of a white family, the Hancocks, who owned large tracts of land in the area. Benjamin Ross and his wife agreed that it was located at a place known as Trap Hill, but the farmland, old roads, and farm lanes are grown up in woods today, so it is impossible for the Rosses to pinpoint the exact location. There are ruins of a log house at Trap Hill on a wooded slope that may be this house, but the Rosses said it was located on the summit of the hill, rather than on its slopes. The testimony of the Rosses and William Diggs conflict on this point. Nonetheless, the ruins of the rectangular log block do give us an idea of the Ross tenant house (figure 64).[14]

Like most slave houses, the Ross tenant house had a log chimney. "I know a whole lot of people who didn't have no chimney but a dirt chimney," declared Benjamin Ross, and, referring to a photograph (figure 19), he said that the chimney on his parents' tenant house was "just like that." He pointed out that some families in the county completely covered the outside of the chimney with mud plaster in order to lessen the damage caused by weather and erosion (figure 65). According to Benjamin Ross, the plaster on the outside was the same as the chinking between the logs, and both were made of clay, sand, lime, water, and animal hair (to serve as a binding agent),

Figure 64
William Diggs at the ruins of a log tenant house on the Hancock
Farm in Charles County. It was William Diggs who led me to this site and
and who introduced me to Benjamin and Nellie Ross. Photo: author.

which were mixed thoroughly with a garden hoe and then applied to the chimney with a trowel. This was done periodically, perhaps once a year, depending on the condition of the chimney.[15]

As in earlier slave houses, the floor of the Ross home was earthen. Ross characterized it as "just as hard as cement," the same words used by James Scriber and McKinley Gantt to describe earthen floors. Throughout the nineteenth century, such floors were commonplace in log houses of black families, but Ross remembered no log houses of white families with them near the turn of the century. Evidently, dirt floors were a distinguishing factor between the log houses of white and black families. Probably whites were better off economically and so they could afford plank floors, or perhaps white landowners provided them with more improved houses.[16]

Black families tried to improve upon their dirt floors by covering them with homemade rugs. Just as they had saved extra bits of cloth for quilts during slavery, they also gathered pieces of material and wove them into rugs. William Diggs said that his grandfather, a waterman who eventually purchased and captained his own schooner,

Figure 65
Log house with chimney plastered with mud, 1895, Kentucky. Photo:
Strohmeyer and Wyman. Courtesy Library of Congress.

used to bring to his home and community second-hand clothes, blankets, and even military overcoats from Washington, D.C., that his family cut into strips and plaited into rugs. Benjamin Ross added that the poorest families used grass sacks or seed bags, if there was nothing else.[17]

Descriptions of the ways of life of families in this and other log tenant houses show further continuities in the lifestyles of black families from slavery. As in slave houses, the fireplace was the "center" of the downstairs room. It was the source of light and heat, served as the stove, and was the place where people gathered to socialize (figure 66). Ross said that during his childhood in the 1880's, rural

Figure 66
Interior of the home of a black family, probably in Virginia,
around 1900 or earlier. Elderly persons from southern Maryland
cited features in this photograph as typical of their "old-time" homes:
pot suspended over the open fireplace, stoneware plates, plank table with
drop leaves, and a wide assortment of paper from seed catalogues, magazines,
and newspapers to insulate and decorate the walls. The most colorful pages were
placed around the center of the room, the mantelpiece. Quilts cover the
spool bed. Nellie Ross of Charles County says of this photograph:
"It looks so natural," like her aunt's home in Charles County
near the turn of the century. Photo: Huestis Cook. Valentine
Museum, Richmond, Virginia.

black families did not have wood-burning stoves. As in the days of slavery, the fireplace "was the only place we had to cook," and the skills associated with cooking were carryovers from earlier times (Chapter III). Pots were customarily suspended over the fireplace,

Figure 67
Interior of the home of a black couple in Virginia in the 1890's. Luther Stuckey,
born in 1896 in South Carolina, recalls, "My mother wore long dresses and aprons
just like those." Photo: Frances D. Johnston. Courtesy Library of Congress.

either from iron cranes descending from the stack or from iron or wooden bars across the fire (figures 66, 67). Nellie Ross immediately recognized the pot suspended over the fire in figure 66 as being similar to the cooking arrangement in her aunt's house in Charles County, where she lived in the early 1900's. Benjamin Ross added that coals were occasionally pulled out onto the bricks in front of the fireplace so that cooking could be done there also. For example, bread (probably hoecake) was cooked on long, smooth griddles placed over the coals, turned with a knife (because the "griddles were so smooth"), and browned on both sides.[18]

While tenant families did have matches, they were rarely used for starting fires because, as during slavery, the fire was rarely extinguished. When the family went away, the coals were banked with ashes; when uncovered, the coals were still hot enough to ignite kindling.

In hot weather, cooking was done outside. Sometimes there was a separate kitchen, called a summer kitchen, but more usually the cooking was done over an open fire, preferably in the shade of a tree. The basic elements of cooking over an open fire remained the same indoors or out. These cooking situations were like those of the slaves earlier, and were even somewhat similar to those of African peasants.

The cooking and eating utensils of tenant families were plain, inexpensive, and functional. Most families used tin plates, granite ware, or both. Diggs said that it was not until the 1920's that he saw "china plates" in use in homes of black families. However, photographs of interiors of black family homes of the turn of the twentieth century in Virginia (figures 66, 67) do show that those families had thick white ceramic plates, and probably families in Maryland did too. Earthenware and stoneware jugs, tin cans, and pails were used to store liquids (figure 67). The knives and forks that Diggs and Benjamin Ross described resembled those in figure 66. They were plain, sturdy, and made of steel, and the forks were often so well used that the tines became worn and sharp. Ross recalled that pots and pans, which became heavily sooted from cooking over the open fire, were cleaned with soap and scoured with fine river sand that was stored in a bucket for the purpose. The table, which served as both the kitchen work space and the dining table, was customarily homemade of pine, walnut, or "of anything you could get that would hew down smooth," Ross added, and was scoured with river sand. Ross explained that the person had to be sure to use a rag to protect his or her hands, because the sand would cut.[19]

Like the other furnishings, bedding was plain, homemade, and functional, but included some purchased objects. The bedsteads themselves were rectangular boxes with slats and no springs. For a mattress, a bed tick was filled each year with thoroughly dried corn shucks or threshed wheat straw. Those families that were "well-off," according to William Diggs, had feather mattresses, which were preferred because they did not have to be refilled each year. Straw or shucks, unlike feathers, piled up unevenly inside the ticking: "You couldn't make the bed up, and then you sink down in them holes." Pillows were more comfortable because they were filled with feathers. Pillowcases and sheets were made of yellow muslin. William Diggs and Benjamin Ross did not remember black families in Charles County who sewed together flour sacks, but this practice was common among tenant families in the Deep South and elsewhere in southern Maryland. While the parents always slept in beds, many children, especially those in large families, slept on pallets on the floor, as they had during slavery time.[20]

Life was not all work for these families. At the end of the work day, or on Saturday or Sunday, they would get together for entertainment. Children had homemade dolls and played games. Music was essential. Preston Williams, who was born in 1894 in Doncaster, Maryland, and whose father operated the country store there, recalled that they sold guitars, fiddles, banjos, and other common musical instruments to black families in the area. Ross remembered that some of his childhood friends played jew's-harps and mouth organs. Even in his old age, he loved to imitate how one of his best friends used to create new sounds and entertain his friends by blowing his harmonica through his nose. "I can still hear him now."[21]

Since these families had little money for food, they had to furnish it for themselves, as slaves had earlier. In addition to gardening and raising their own chickens and hogs, some raised cows, and almost all hunted, fished, and trapped. Such efforts could be dangerous, and the results show the precarious situation in which these families lived. For example, Nellie Ross's father, a former slave, drowned while fishing for shad in Nanjemoy Creek when she was a child, and her mother had to move the family to Washington to find a living as a domestic, since she could not work the farm by herself. As a girl, Mrs. Ross returned periodically to her home community to visit her aunt.[22]

Benjamin Ross recalled that his father was an excellent hunter and always had a gun in his house, as did most blacks, whether sharecroppers or landowners. Ross and Diggs remembered that game abounded. Blacks trapped muskrats, or "marsh rabbits," and considered their meat a delicacy. The woods, marshes, swamps, and river bottoms were open to all hunters, black and white, tenant and landowner. "You could hunt anywhere you pleased, and there was no [legal] limit to what you could get. If you were smart enough to get it, you could have it."[23]

These stretches of uncultivated land, open to use by the entire community, including tenant farmers, were called the "commons," Ross said. Just as the widespread presence of log houses reflected the frontier condition of this area, so too did the free use of the commons. It was essential to the survival of the landless, as it had been for the slaves. Since it provided many materials that were either not available in stores or beyond their means, black families shaped these raw materials into things necessary to their life. One essential raw material the commons provided was wood. It was burned for heat and light, and fashioned into shelters for humans and animals and into household and farm objects. Describing the former abundance of wood, Benjamin Ross stated, "In them days there was plenty of wood. You could cut anything you wanted as long as it wasn't expensive, no matter where you were." Ross explained "expensive woods" as those prized as timber, and cited tall white oaks and virgin pines as examples. "Smaller pines, red oak, black oak, locust, you could have all of that you wanted." There was so much that "you never planted the trees back."[24]

Black families in southern Maryland, like whites and blacks elsewhere in the South, gathered lighter knots, which were pine stumps in which the resin is concentrated, to throw on the fire for illumination. Nellie Ross remembered reading her lessons in her aunt's log house in Charles County in the 1890's by such light.[25]

Nineteenth-century Maryland blacks were skilled in making household and farm objects from wood. Black farmers made their own log houses, log chimneys, log corncribs, log tobacco barns, shelters for farm animals (made of upright pine poles with a lean-to roof interlaced with pine boughs and called a "brush barn"), chicken coops, hog pens, and fence rails. Using a foot adz, Benjamin Ross's father hewed out a water trough for his livestock from a log about eight feet long and three or four feet wide. From another wide log he hollowed out a large rain barrel that he kept near the chimney under the eaves to collect water in case of fire. Ross's father also felled small oak saplings, split them into "oak splints," and wove them into baskets large and small.[26]

Perhaps it should be made clear that Ross's memories of his father's skills were from when he was older and the family had moved from this tenant house. But his father, Joseph Ross, had practiced these skills ever since his youth as a slave, so no doubt he used them while a tenant. Although this tenant house was a way station for Joseph Ross, his son Benjamin remembered stories about him that tell of a man's struggle from slavery through tenancy to landownership. Ross's account of his father gives an important human dimension to this history of material culture, and places this house in a broader historical context by suggesting the histories of many nineteenth-century houses that have not been recorded.

Benjamin Ross began with the story of his father's escape from slavery.

"You see, the people were slaves. My father worked on the farm of a man named Joe Price, and worked for a blacksmith named Dennis Toyer [or Tara]. He runned away from his boss man. He wasn't drafted. He runned away. You see, if you could get away and change your name and get into the camp [Union Army camp], change your clothes and everything, and no matter how well your master knew you, he couldn't get you. Whatever name you say you was, that was your name. That was the decision.

"Well, there were about a half dozen or more of them. And they made a plot to meet at a certain place. They had to come out close to the boss man's house, about as close as that house over there [about seventy-five yards]. And they had to be quiet. The first time they caught them. The boss man got to the camp before they did, and they carried them back. He made them promise that if he carried them back, they would stay there and behave themselves. Papa told them he would, but he didn't. First chance he got, he got away that time. Got his clothes all changed and everything ready if his master come along. [Union officers] asked him what was his name and he said 'Henry Washington.' He got his pension by Henry Washington. And then his boss man arrived, and said, 'Your name isn't no Henry Washington, your name is Joseph Ross.' Papa jumped up there, 'You're a so and so liar, sir.' And they couldn't get him. He could say anything he wanted to, you know, then."[27]

While his father may have thought he was a free man in the Union Army, he soon learned otherwise. His experience may illustrate that of other soldiers.

"They [the Union Officers] would get after you. It wasn't like it is now, they wasn't taken care of much in the camp, in the army. You'd lay out on a blanket on the ground. If it snowed, you'd get covered up with snow. If you got enough snow falling on you, you'd get warm. Then you'd have cover.

"He said that he could look across the battlefield and see dead men's teeth shining. The moonlight would be shining on their teeth and their guns would be in their hands where they fell. Sometimes he said there would be a whole regiment of them, you know, would be down. And they'd be stumbling over them.

"He was on his coffin to be killed once while in the army. He'd violated the law. He hit his lieutenant who made him mad about something and he hit him with a gun. And that broke the law. Abraham Lincoln was the President then. And he was put on his coffin, and a certain time they had twelve men with their guns loaded. Eleven men with their guns loaded, but they was blank, and the twelfth man had a bullet in there. And he was the one that done the shooting, but none of them knew who it was. And they couldn't do it until they got the word from the President. The President said, 'No, don't kill him.' They said, 'We got Henry Washington on the bench. We're waiting for your decision. What will we do?' He says, 'Spare all the brave men. We need them.' And they didn't kill him. He was near to it though."[28]

Benjamin Ross did not remember the names of battles his father fought in, and he remembered only fragments of the whole story. Nonetheless, his father's descriptions of the fighting, bloodshed, and the leaders were etched into his mind as a child. He described "the greatest battle I heard him speak of" in the following way. It may be a combination of several battles, told in this way by his father to compress the dramatic effect.

"And when the Yankees got there, why they had a terrible battle there and they shot and killed. Some of the men fell in the creek and filled the creek up. That was the battle that Grant was Abe Lincoln's general and Lee was Jeff Davis's. And Lee and Grant had met at a certain place and made a bargain where to meet one another the next morning, but Grant fooled Lee. Instead of meeting up on this hill by the church, Grant met him down around the river. When Lee found out, looking for Grant to be acoming this way with his regiment, why he was over there, and he filled his men all with bullets. That's why when we were children in school, we would say, 'You fool with me, and I'll do you like Grant done Lee.'"[29]

After the war, Ross's father realized that he could not move ahead as a tenant farmer, so he worked in Washington as a hod carrier for cash wages. He helped construct buildings in "South Washington" (Capitol Hill, southwest Washington, or Anacostia). At this time construction was booming in Washington due to the rapid growth of the government during the war. Later, Ross returned to Charles County, rented land from the Hancock family, and lived in the log tenant house described here. In 1887, he bought a "run-down, growed up" farm of one hundred acres for three hundred and fifty dollars, the amount recorded in the deed. At the same time his wife, Maria Ross, bought another farm of one hundred acres that was nearby, but not adjoining, for two hundred dollars. They had probably been tobacco farms that ceased operation after emancipation. Much of the surplus cash necessary for this purchase probably came from his Union Army pension, which he received until his death under his assumed name of Henry Washington. His flight to freedom rewarded him.[30]

Instead of building a common log house on his new property, Joseph Ross constructed a large frame one of the type then in style for rural landowners of moderate means. Rather than having neighbors build the house, as was traditional, Ross hired a white carpenter with three or four black assistants. They built a two-story frame house with six rooms: two down and two up in the principal block, with a central hallway on each floor. A two-story ell attached to the rear had one room on each floor. Though this house burned in the 1920's and no photographs of it remain, oral recollections of it show that it was similar to those described in Chapter V.[31]

Both the log house and the new frame one were the home of a "brave man," unsung in Maryland history, a man who said "no" to slavery and tenancy, managed to escape both, and become a land-owning farmer himself. His son says of him, "I never seen my father afraid—he never shot nobody—but they all respected him." Thus, from stories such as Ross's, we see histories of a house and its furnishings and of people's lives, histories that could be interwoven in museum exhibits.[32]

The Cusic-Medley House

Studying a house and its furnishings as used by different residents over time provides significant insights; and examining an American tenant house is historically valuable because there are few written descriptions of how they changed over the years. Those that have been photographed or sketched have usually been recorded only at one moment, and change over time is not shown. Yet houses age, just like people, and their appearance and the company they keep change, while certain basic character traits remain constant.

The Cusic-Medley tenant house in St. Mary's County is an example of a home whose aging has been recorded. Though the identity of its nineteenth-century residents is not known, I did locate both white and black former residents of the twentieth century. From their recollections, a colleague has drawn sketches of the farmstead and rooms as they appeared at different times. When I was first led to the house by James Curtis, Jim Bond, and other elderly blacks in the community, the house was still occupied by Abraham Medley, its last resident. The photographs that I took of the house and objects at that time and later visits document elements of the material culture of the rural poor today. Spending time with Medley revealed in part how he lived his daily life. With the assistance of Cary Carson, former architectural historian at the St. Mary's City Commission, I was able to understand how Medley organized the one open room downstairs into separate living areas, as families perhaps did in single-unit slave houses.

This house is especially significant because both white and black landless families inhabited it. Fortunately, one of the white families has preserved photographs of the house taken in 1918. In the absence of written descriptions, these photographs are vital historical documents. Former residents also provided plans of the house as they recalled it, and the descriptions reveal the basic similarity in living conditions among landless families, whether white or black. Furthermore, the former residents pointed out "special things"—such as a mother's colorful quilts, a father's special rocking chair, or a boy's prized BB gun. Such memories made this humble tenant house into a home.

Dating the construction of this house indicates the methods of investigating a "folk house" and the problems encountered. Since this is a tenant house, no written records, such as deeds or real estate tax records, document it. Furthermore, its plain design reveals no definitive, narrowly datable elements, so it could have been built as a slave house or as a (post–Civil-War) tenant house. The rafters and roof frame were attached with a mixture of wrought and machine-cut nails of the post-1830 type, establishing that the house was built after 1830.[33]

The problem is in determining a date after 1830. According to Abraham Medley, the house is "a thousand years old," meaning it was built "way back yonder," at a time far beyond personal or local memory. Since he was born around 1898 in the vicinity of the house, his recollections would seem to make the house at least of the 1850's or 1860's, because someone living during Medley's youth might have told him about the house, had it been built much later. His recollections were confirmed by Mrs. Nora Cusic, who moved into this sharecropper's house a few days after her wedding in December 1916, and who lived there for four years. She said the house was at that time an "old house" of an unknown date. J. Gwynn Buckler, the present owner of the farm, recalls that the house was old when he first knew it in the teens. There are large wire nails (a type developed after 1878) in the window and door frames, but those nails do not appear to be original. By combining the oral and structural evidence, the widest range of dates of construction would be from the 1830's to 1890. But more specifically, it appears to have been built during the middle of the nineteenth century, from the 1840's to the 1870's.

Whether it was originally built as a slave house or as a tenant house cannot, therefore, be determined.[34]

The house is a single-unit log dwelling one story in height with a gable roof and a stone chimney exterior to one gable end. Its stone chimney and plank floor prevent it from being fully representative of slave houses or of tenant houses before the mid-1890's in the lower counties of southern Maryland. However, no log houses with log chimneys or original dirt floors remain in the region, so this survival is one of the closest approximations. Also, it is one of the comparatively few log houses remaining in southern Maryland that have not been drastically "improved" with new additions.

The house is somewhat larger and more rectangular in shape than other log slave or tenant houses, with exterior dimensions of 19'2" long, 15'5" deep, and about 17' tall. Like other tenant houses, it is not completely underpinned; instead, the sills rest on pilings of ferrous sandstone, which was locally available. The walls are of large, hewn oak logs that measure seven to nine inches in width and four to six inches in thickness, joined by V-notches at the corners, the type common to southern Maryland. The bottom sides of the logs are only barely hewn, perhaps because they are less exposed to the weather than the top and outer sides. Also, since the mud plaster in a log wall shrinks away from the log above it as it dries, perhaps this surface was left in the rough to help the plaster adhere more firmly and to prevent cracks in the walls. The plaster, which consisted of lime, sand, and clay, with some oyster shell fragments (a mixture commonly used in southern Maryland), was applied over and between long strips of wood laid in the interstices of the logs. Weatherboards have been added over the logs and attached to vertical planks that are fastened to the logs with wire nails.[35]

The stone chimney with stone firebox and brick stack was located on the northern gable end, the coldest side of the house. In the 1960's the resident, Abraham Medley, removed the gable-end chimney and installed a brick stove flue in the center of the house for his wood stove, which would heat the house more efficiently than a fireplace. In the southern gable end were the only windows, one downstairs and one upstairs, located there probably to take advantage of the warm, sunny southern exposure. Today the two windows have glass panes in double-hung sashes of three different types that were probably reused from other houses. The board-and-batten shutters inside are most likely the original window coverings, in keeping with the traditional method used in slave houses and in pre-1890's tenant houses in the area.

The construction of this house displays some of the traditional features of log construction. In fact, it was the use of "pegs" in construction that Medley and his friends emphatically pointed to as evidence of the remarkable age of the house. They declared that pegs passed from one log down to another, but no pegs could be seen in the interstices. They were possibly used in the corners or along the top logs, or plates, as in the River View slave house. Nonetheless, it can be seen that pegs once joined the ends of logs to the original door frames, and they are still in place attaching the ends of logs in the wall to four-by-four posts framing the fireplace opening. So Medley and his friends were not just making up stories, and the house was built in an "old-time" way.[36]

Like most houses of the landless, the history of the occupancy of the dwelling was a mystery until oral informants were found who could identify the former residents. J. Gwynn Buckler, the current owner of the property, said he had heard as a boy around 1910 that the house had been occupied by the family of Delijah Thompson. They were white sharecroppers, but he did not know how long they lived there. The Thompsons were also the first occupants that Abraham Medley, who was raised in the vicinity, remembered. Thus the known history of this house begins in the early 1900's with a white landless family. Delijah Thompson and his wife have died, and their children's whereabouts are unknown.[37]

Beginning in 1916, clear descriptions of the house emerge, because it was at this time that the young newlyweds, Quincy and Nora Cusic, moved into the house and set up housekeeping (figure 68). Two years later, Nora Cusic was photographed with her infant son, Elwood, on the front porch (figure 69). Mrs. Cusic's recollections form the basis of a picture of the farmstead that shows the house as an isolated dwelling on a farm owned by an absentee landowner. The farm lane in front of the house led westward about a quarter of a mile to a country road, and the paved county road that now lies to the southwest of the house did not exist. There was no community of tenant houses, either in a row or dispersed about the farm, nor even a larger house close by. A nearby dwelling currently occupied by the landowner was built in about 1917 for Nora Cusic's brother-in-law, who was also a sharecropper on the farm. The property was then owned by Otto Hopkins, who lived in Washington, D.C., visited the farm only occasionally, and did not stay in a house on the farm.[38]

Based upon the photographs of the house in 1918 and Nora Cusic's recollections of it, specific elements of change and continuity can be seen. In general, the basic log skeleton of the house and its

Figure 68
The Cusic-Medley house, St. Mary's County, October 15, 1918.
Copy photograph, reproduced through the courtesy of Nora Cusic.

single-unit, rectangular form have remained constant, but its outward appearance has changed dramatically. In the 1918 photographs, the house is hardly recognizable as the house we see today. The logs were completely covered with weatherboards and the corners accented with trim boards, giving the appearance of a modest frame dwelling. A small shed porch sheltered the front entrance "to keep the rain from beating in through the door," according to Nora Cusic. The porch roof was supported by plain rectangular posts. The house was whitewashed on the outside, according to custom. The roof was not covered with the traditional wooden shingles, but with tar paper, a new feature at that time on folk houses. Overall, the house resembled a well-maintained cottage.

Nora Cusic remembered her family's constructing new outbuildings around the house that reflected their efforts to provide for themselves. They raised their own corn and stored it in a small frame corn house they built about fifteen yards behind the house. They fed the

Figure 69
Nora Cusic and her son, Elwood, in 1918, on the
front porch of their tenant house. Copy photograph,
reproduced through the courtesy of Nora Cusic.

corn to their livestock and poultry and carried it to the mill to be ground into meal. Like families described in the next chapter, the Cusics used outbuildings for more than one purpose. For instance, the corn house also served as the meat house, since a large barrel of salt was kept there for storing hams, shoulders, and side meat. Nora Cusic did not mention a smokehouse, so presumably the meat was carried elsewhere to be smoked. Next to the corn house was the privy, which she called the "moonlight house" because of the crescent moon on the door. Next to it was a small hen house. About seventy-five yards behind the house to the east was the spring, where the family fetched water and stored milk and butter in a cool box. There was also a vegetable garden behind the house, and produce such as turnips was stored in a vegetable kiln. Nora Cusic described this as a circular hole in the ground about two feet deep in which vegetables were stored on a bed of straw and then covered with more straw and a mound of dirt. Mrs. Cusic's parents had been tenants on a farm elsewhere in St. Mary's County, and she said that they "made lots of vegetable kilns" when she was growing up. Since numerous elderly blacks throughout Maryland also described them as part of the rural homestead, vegetable kilns must have been a common method of preserving certain foods for most rural families before the days of refrigeration.[39]

Nora Cusic's descriptions of the house's interior furnishings revealed the way of life of this family and how they organized the one open room into separate living areas. Her descriptions also told of her efforts to make this plain house into a comfortable home for her family.

The floor was of planks about eight inches wide, not of earth like other log houses of the landless. She recalled that the cracks between the planks were wide enough to sweep the dirt through; in fact, they were deliberately filled to "keep out drafts." The log walls were covered inside with tar paper like the roof, and were either painted a bright color or were whitewashed to "brighten up the place." This also created the appearance of a larger space, a basic concept of interior design. The fireplace in the northern gable end was no longer in use, Mrs. Cusic remembered; instead, it was sealed off, and two pipes for two wood stoves were set into the chimney. One was for cooking, and the other was a "sitting stove." Asked if the house was cold inside in the winter, she replied, "no colder than any place else." The tar paper siding plus the log walls effectively insulated the house.

Though it consisted of one room down and one room up, the dwelling was essentially a one-room house as the Cusics used it, since nearly all household activities took place downstairs. The upstairs was used only to store "certain odds and ends" and as sleeping quarters for overnight guests. Mrs. Cusic said she rarely went upstairs. In contrast, the downstairs served as kitchen, dining room, pantry, sitting room, and bedroom for children and parents.[40]

These uses are indicated by her arrangement of the furnishings (figure 70). Because it served a number of purposes, the simple plank table was placed near the center of the open room; it was the only flat work space in the house. On this table meals were prepared, vegetables washed and chopped, dough mixed and rolled out, meat cut, potatoes peeled, and so forth. The family ate around the table, seated in the cane-bottom chairs shown in figure 71. Mrs. Cusic kept two pie safes, which held her flatware, plates, bowls, seasonings, and food. She hung her pots, pans, and skillets on the wall by the wood cook stove as, she said, "everybody did."

The more formal social space was centered around the "small couch" along the front wall, and chairs from the table were drawn up

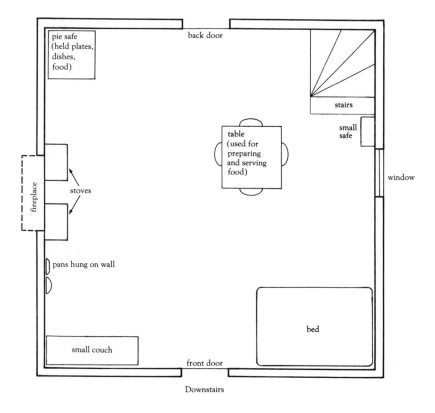

Downstairs

Not drawn to scale

Figure 70
Furnishings plan of the Cusic-Medley house during residency of the Cusic family.

when guests visited. As was common in working-class homes, furnishings were lightweight and movable and were rearranged to accommodate more people and different occasions. Since most furnishings were, like the dining chairs, unpainted, the interior was rather drab in appearance, as the interiors of tenant houses typically were in the South, and the "warmth" of the house depended primarily on the hospitality and character of the residents, rather than on the furnishings.

The entire family—husband, wife, and two infants—slept in the one bed downstairs. There was no crib or cradle. Though no other

Figure 71
Nora Cusic in 1978 with the set of chairs she brought with her when
she moved into the log house in December 1916. Photo: author.

family has been located during this survey that slept in this way, it is probable that other families in small houses also did so. Mrs. Cusic added that her oldest son, Elwood, and daughter Yvonne were born in this bed. It had a simple wooden frame with slats supporting springs and mattress. It was placed in the southwest corner, across the room from the wood stoves in what seems to have been the coldest corner of the house.

To keep the family warm, Mrs. Cusic sewed quilts that were the most colorful objects in the house. Mrs. Cusic has continued to make them, and is reported to have made as many as thirty-five in one year. Such efforts were not unusual for women, both black and white, in houses such as this; the quilts kept their families warm, added a dash of color to their homes, and provided a form of creative and artistic expression.

The life of this family was hard, but they were able to escape and become landowners because Quincy Cusic supplemented his income from sharecropping by fishing, crabbing, and oystering. Like Joseph Ross and his wife, the Cusics eventually saved enough money to buy their own land and build a modest two-story house with two rooms down and two up, a style in keeping with rural landowners' houses of the period. While Mrs. Cusic and her seven children, most of whom live in the vicinity, recalled the "old shack" with some affection, they did not consider it to be "home." Home was synonymous with ownership. In referring to the property they purchased (and still own), Mrs. Cusic said, "This is the only real home I ever had."[41]

But this was home for Abraham Medley, a black sharecropper who moved into the house shortly after the Cusics left in 1921. Not because he owned it, but because he lived there for more than fifty years, from 1921 through 1978, except for an interval of three or four years. Most of his memories of people, work, his wife, his children, and of important and mundane events were related to this house, and this, rather than ownership, made it home for him. During his adult life it was all he had for a house. Though it did change in general appearance, its small size and plain appearance remained the same throughout those years, reflecting that it continued to be the home of a tenant.

We see this house during two periods of occupancy by the Medley family. The earlier, the decade of the 1920's, is when the young Medley couple, newly married like the Cusics, moved into the house, and when their four sons were born there. Recollections of this period were provided primarily by the oldest son, Charles A. Medley, born in 1921. His mother is deceased. Age, feebleness, and a lack of dentures prevented his father from clearly articulating his recollections of this early period. Nonetheless, Abraham Medley's memory remains surprisingly sharp, and he did confirm or correct parts of his son's account of the 1920's. The more recent period of study began in 1974, when I first located, investigated, and photographed the house. Abraham Medley was then living alone there in impoverished conditions.[42]

Based upon the recollections of Abraham and Charles Medley, we can gain an approximate sketch of the farmstead during the first period of their occupancy (figure 72). If seen from above, the farmstead would have appeared as a dwelling in the midst of a small, cleanly swept dirt yard, with one small structure (the hen house) behind. There was no fence around the house. Leading up to the home was a dirt farm lane from the larger house (the landowner's), with its complex of farm buildings behind it. From one perspective, the tenant house was an extension of that complex, connected by the farm lane down which Medley came to and from work. Depending upon the

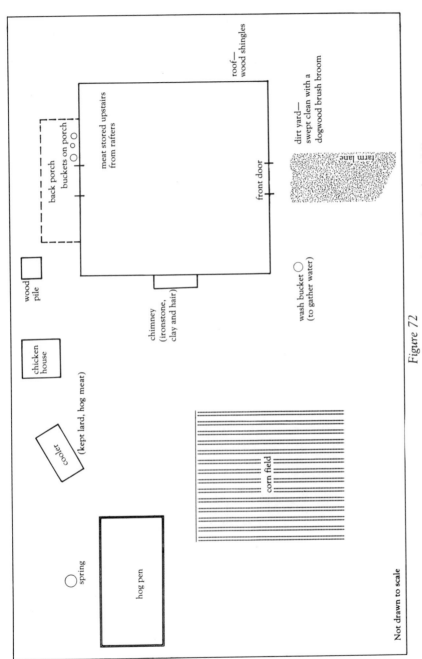

Figure 72

The Cusic-Medley farmstead during residency of the Medley family in the 1920's.

yearly choice, fields of tobacco or corn surrounded the yard of the tenant house.

Paths radiated from the yard that led to the springs, hog pens, privy, and vegetable gardens. Indeed, footpaths crisscrossed the countryside, because the Medleys and many other tenant families did not have horses, mules, or oxcarts, much less automobiles. Footpaths joined this farm to others and to the church, school, and town. When Charles Medley began walking to the school several miles away, one of the things he learned first from his father was the short-cuts along country paths. This was like teaching him the road map of the community, only parts of which could be drawn today, as new woods around the farmstead, along with new housing and roads, have virtually erased this age-old system of travel and communication.[43]

As the sociologist of the rural South, Arthur Raper, wrote, paths were to plantation workers what roads were to plantation owners. Though the rural middle class in southern Maryland did have access to the steamboat, railroad, or (in the early twentieth century) the automobile, most landless farm workers did not. They traveled by wagons drawn by oxen or horses, or simply walked. Examining the world of these people, such as Abraham Medley, leads us gradually to realize that, aside from mental pictures of such distant places as Washington, Baltimore, Africa, and Biblical lands, their world was contained within the short radius of "walking distance." The principal destinations were neighboring farms, the church, the market, and home. In a predominantly illiterate society such as this, there was little chance of a letter bridging the distance to a distant place, and most communication was oral and face-to-face. Consequently, for tenant families in this region and in other isolated rural areas of America as recently as fifty to seventy years ago, communication was still primarily by word of mouth, and everyday travel took place at a speed no faster than that available to peasants of the ancient world.[44]

A closer inspection of this traditional farm world reveals that the house and its surroundings tended to form an interrelated complex, with the houses and places of food production close by. For example, we see that one path from Medley's house led down to the bottom land north of the house, where the hog pens were located (figure 72). The land there was too wet for cultivation, and its forest provided shade and food in the form of roots, young shoots, and nuts to supplement the food given them. The moist ground provided a wallow, essential to allow hogs to cool themselves, since they do not have sweat glands. Because these vital animals provided the Medleys with most of their meat and lard, it was imperative that the hogs not only survive the hot summers, but that they stay healthy and gain weight.[45]

Hog killing was one of the big events of the fall, bringing people from all over the community to lend a hand. The hogs were butchered after several "good frosts" indicated that cold weather had come to stay; a warm spell after the hogs were butchered could make the meat spoil, and the family would face a lean winter. Usually the hogs were killed in late November. Charles Medley did not remember the different stages of hog killing or the methods by which the "hog meat" was cured, and his father's frailty prevented him from describing this autumn ritual in detail, but they probably followed the typical methods. First, the hams, shoulders, and sides were "salted down," that is, rubbed thoroughly with a mixture of salt and black pepper or sometimes red pepper, and molasses and brown sugar were added if "sugar-cured" hams were preferred. The meat was laid side by side on a shelf in the meat house for six to eight weeks, and then suspended from hooks to let the salt drip off. It was then smoked over a slow fire in a smokehouse for a few days and afterward hung somewhere for storage through the year. Charles Medley did remember that "hog meat" was kept in the "cooler," next to the chicken house in the back yard. It resembled a pie safe with "holes drilled in the front doors." He did not remember first curing the pork in salt, as the Cusics did, or smoking it in smokehouses. Abraham Medley did say that old-time people hung hams, side meat, and shoulders from the rafters of houses, where it stayed cold throughout the winter, a practice common among North Carolina tenant families. While Charles Medley did not recall this practice in this house, it is possible that his father continued with this tradition without his son's remembering it.[46]

Also located in the bottom land was the spring. There was no well. Hauling water was one of the daily chores, especially for children. In addition to providing the family with water for drinking and cooking, the spring served to refrigerate dairy products. Milk and butter were stored in jars and crocks, placed in a wooden box set into the spring, and cooled by the water.[47] Like most tenant families, the Medleys had no icebox or separate structure like a springhouse or dairy, and the open spring was not safe. During hot weather, the spring water might not have kept the unpasteurized milk sufficiently cool to deter bacterial growth. Because milk is an excellent host, bacteria entering the milk from any source—whether an infected udder, barnyard dirt, unwashed hands, an unsanitary bucket or jar, or flies—could multiply rapidly.

Diseases resulting from contaminated milk were physically debilitating and sometimes fatal: intestinal ailments such as amoebic dysentery or diarrhea, which were more likely to be fatal for babies than adults; liver disorders, such as yellow jaundice and infectious hepatitis; and typhoid fever. Typhoid might attack an entire family because the germs were passed in the stool of the afflicted. Since family members had to nurse one another and often did not wash their hands thoroughly after caring for the stricken person's bodily functions or after using the toilet themselves, the germs could quickly spread among the household via milk, drinking water, or food. The entire process, a seemingly unbreakable chain of habit with severe health consequences, was the despair of Southern doctors for generations. Though a vaccine was developed for typhoid fever by the late teens, there was still no cure once a person was afflicted until the development of antibiotics in the 1950's. The disease lasted a minimum of four to six weeks, and the stricken person had severe difficulty in eating, and might vomit what he could eat. In severe cases the intestines could hemorrhage, leading to death because of this or other malfunctions of vital organs. If several members of the family were afflicted at the same time, it might be almost impossible to plant, tend, or harvest crops and to care for farm animals.[48]

Since on the Medley homestead the hog pen was near the spring, there was also the risk of contamination of the drinking water by surface-water runoff. This practice of locating an animal pen, barnyard, or privy close to an open well or spring was common on farms of poor families in Maryland and throughout the South. While no members of the Cusic or Medley families are known to have suffered from these diseases, they lived under the daily threat of them as a result of the lack of proper sanitation and refrigeration and the layout of their farms. Since proper medical care was rarely available, and tenant families did not have surplus savings to support them in the event of catastrophic illnesses, such diseases were disastrous.[49]

One problem in retrieving the history of this house, or more generally in preserving the people's history through oral interviews, is having to rely upon memories fifty or sixty years old. For example, the Medleys did not remember the corn house and privy that Mrs. Cusic recalled, but they did recall another privy that was located about fifty yards behind the house. Moving the same privy to a different hole "every so often," after the old hole filled up, was a common practice. The only outbuilding they described was the hen house. The roof of the dwelling was no longer covered by tar paper roofing material, as seen in the 1918 photograph of the house (figure

68), but by wood shingles, a less effective type of insulation. A back porch had been added, about ten feet wide and about ten feet deep, though the front porch remained the same. Plank partitions were added to divide the downstairs and upstairs into two rooms each, creating more privacy. The tar paper that had insulated the log walls inside the house was replaced with cardboard. Since we know nothing of the brief interim between the residencies of the Cusics and the Medleys, the reasons for the changes cannot be explained. It is strange that they occurred so quickly (in about one year), and that while some may be seen as improvements, such as the back porch and the partitions downstairs and upstairs, others diminish living conditions, such as the removal of the outbuildings and of the tar paper siding on the roof and walls. No doubt there are explanations for the changes, but we simply do not have the sources, and probably never will. Most likely the changes were made by Matt Long, who purchased the farm from Otto Hopkins, the owner during the Cusic family's residency.

Like the Cusics, the residents of the tenant house at the Smithsonian, and other farm tenant families, the Medleys furnished the house sparsely. The sketches of the interior, based on Charles and Abraham Medley's descriptions (figures 73, 74), identify the larger pieces, but do not include many smaller, everyday objects. Since they had little money, most of the objects were functional. The few purely decorative objects they remembered were "pictures and things" on the mantelpiece. This is in keeping with other tenant families in Maryland and North Carolina, who recalled that their families, especially their mothers, usually had a "special something" that they purchased or that relatives, friends, or white families gave to them. In these tenant houses, as in the Medley house, the mantelpiece was where decorative objects were typically displayed.[51]

The kitchen was the center of family life. Like the Cusics, the Medleys cooked over a wood stove piped into the chimney. Next to the stove was a small wood box with a hatchet for chopping the stove wood down to size. During the year, logs and dead branches were gathered from forests around the house, carried to the wood pile behind the house, and chopped and split into stove wood.

Because the fire was going every day of the year for cooking, and because it was also necessary for heat, gathering and preparing wood was a constant process. "Chopping wood and carrying it to the house" were important daily chores, especially for boys. Like such other chores as hauling water, feeding the hogs, milking the cow, and feeding the chickens, providing firewood was essential to survival. Otherwise the food would not have been cooked, or the house heated. Children therefore provided vital services to the family. As the former sharecropper, Amanda Nelson, also of St. Mary's County, pointed out, it was essential for the family's welfare that parents instill in their children a sense of responsibility and pride in performing these daily tasks. Like the Medleys, she recalled specific incidents in which

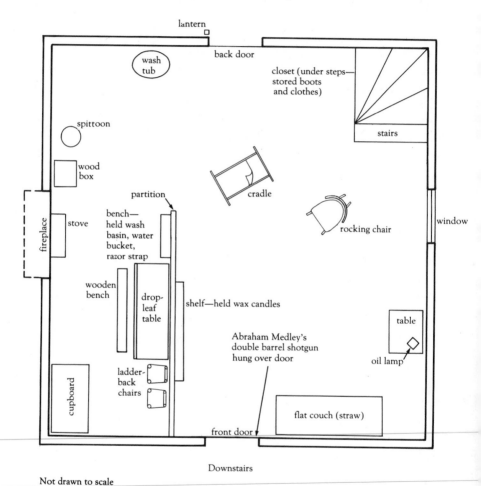

Figure 73
The downstairs of the Cusic-Medley house during
residency of the Medley family in the 1920's.

she made sure these lessons of responsibility were learned. This sense of family responsibility was common among rural black families.[52]

The other principal furnishings in the small kitchen of the Medleys were a cupboard in the front corner and a drop-leaf table across from the stove (figure 73). The cupboard contained the dishes, flatware, bowls, and certain foods, such as flour, meal, sugar, and cof-

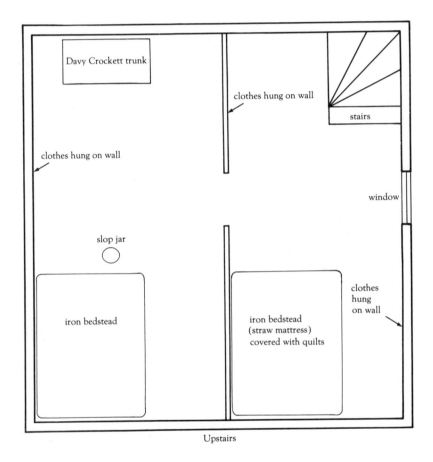

Davy Crockett trunk

clothes hung on wall

stairs

clothes hung on wall

window

slop jar

iron bedstead

iron bedstead
(straw mattress)
covered with quilts

clothes
hung
on wall

Upstairs

Not drawn to scale

Figure 74
The upstairs of the Cusic-Medley house during
residency of the Medley family in the 1920's.

fee. The Medleys recalled that their cupboard, a homemade piece of furniture, had a wooden door with wooden knobs. For obvious reasons, the drop-leaf table was common in small tenant farmhouses. Ladder back chairs with cane seats stood at each end of the table, and along each side was a wooden bench for the children. Because of the lack of other furniture and because it was the only flat surface in the kitchen, the table served as a work space for preparing food, as a dining table, and probably as a desk for the children to do their homework. Like most farm families, they probably gathered around this table for everyday family conversations and neighborly visits. Along the partition beside the table, the Medleys remembered, was a wooden bench on which they kept a wash basin, water buckets, and razor strap. They washed their dishes here and their hands and faces in the morning and evening. Their father shaved here. They drank water from a coconut shell dipper, set into the water bucket on the bench, and presumably a mirror hung on the wall. Thus, this small partitioned room served as kitchen, dining room, wash room, and family room.[53]

Unlike the Cusics, the Medleys did not use the downstairs as a bedroom, as reflected by the furnishings in the room opposite the kitchen. Along the front wall was a straw couch. Charles Medley remembered that the couch was never used as a bed, which seems unusual in a family of four children, but that it was only used for sleeping if someone took a nap during the daytime. Next to the couch was a small table on which an oil lamp was placed. Beside the table and in front of the window was a rocking chair. Charles Medley remembered that this rocker was his father's special chair. "We had one rocker, I remember that one, yes, because I couldn't sit in that one. That was Daddy's seat." There may have been a few more ladder back chairs, or perhaps those in the kitchen were brought into the living room to seat everyone. There were no rugs for insulation and decoration, or curtains, only a blue pull shade over the window. Along the partition in the living room was a shelf on which the Medleys kept their wax candles. This could also have been a place where special family things might have been kept. On a rack above the front door was one of Abraham Medley's prized possessions, a double-barreled shotgun. One might think that this was his most cherished object, but when I asked Medley what he would have tried to save from his house in case of fire, he replied, "the little bit of money that I had," which he kept in his pocket. As Medley put it, he would reach for his pants in case of fire.[54]

Most daytime family life went on downstairs or outside around the house. Thus, babies and young children would not have been left upstairs, but they and the articles associated with them would have been near where their mother worked. For example, Charles Medley recalled that during the day his mother kept the baby near her in a cradle in the living room or kitchen; at night the baby was taken from the cradle to the parents' bed. Other former share-croppers recalled that some families used a bureau drawer, set down upon the floor, in place of a crib. Amanda Nelson remembered that when she had to leave the house for a short while, she used to tie her baby's ankle to the table leg so he could not crawl to the stove and burn himself.

In the southeast corner of the living room was a boxed stairway. Underneath it was a closet in which boots, shoes, children's clothes, and other household goods were stored. Like most houses of this size, the steps were necessarily narrow and steep to allow for more living space. To keep cold drafts from descending into the downstairs, the stairway was enclosed with vertical planks and sealed by a plank door.

Like the downstairs, the upstairs was divided into two rooms (fig-ure 74). The stairway opened into the children's bedroom. It was stark. There were no rugs, and the window had a blue pull shade like the one downstairs. The iron bedstead, which was pushed against the partition wall, had a straw mattress covered with homemade quilts. Charles Medley said that there was no other furniture in the chil-dren's room, not even a trunk. They hung their clothes on the wall. The children all slept in the same bed, except during hot weather, when some slept on quilts or pallets. "'A pallet on the floor,' that was our motto," recalled Charles Medley. While he was reminiscing about his childhood, I asked him if he remembered any special toy. He recalled fondly a lever-action BB gun. "It was the only toy my father ever bought me, and I always kept it with me, even carried it to bed."[55]

The parents' bedroom contained an iron bed with a straw mattress covered with quilts. As with the Cusic family, quilt-making was a common household activity in which otherwise throw-away pieces of material were reused to create something functional and decora-tive. The parents' bedroom also contained a washstand, water pitcher, basin, towel, and slop jar. As in the children's room, clothes were hung on the wall. There was a metal trunk, with leather straps, called a "Davy Crockett trunk." Charles Medley did not recall what was kept in the trunk, but other sharecroppers from Maryland, South Carolina, and North Carolina remembered that the parents' finer clothes ("Sunday clothes"), along with important

objects such as the family Bible, the marriage license, and money
were stored in a trunk for safe keeping.[56]

During this period, the four rooms of the Medley house were divided according to family use. Although there are no photographs to
document the house at this time, Charles Medley was able with the
help of his father to reconstruct a picture of family life in the 1920's.
A long period follows that the Medleys were reluctant to discuss, so
our next picture is of Abraham Medley living alone in this house in
his old age in the 1970's.

By this time the house had deteriorated and the outbuildings and
gardens around the house were no longer present, their absence reflecting the fact that Medley depended on others for food and income, and that he received little of both (figure 75, 76). The yard
around the house, which had been swept clear when his family lived
there, was grown up in grass. He kept no chickens, and the hen
house had been torn down. While Medley continued to raise hogs in
the bottom lands, the cooler for storing hog meat was gone, and presumably someone kept the pork from his hogs for him, since there
were no storage facilities. The spring in the bottom land was no
longer in use; instead, a path led to another spring in the woods
behind the house. This one served only as a water source, not as a
cooler for milk and butter. The privy was also gone. Lacking sanitary
facilities, like traditional peasants throughout the world and like
many sharecroppers in the Deep South until recent times, Medley
simply went into the woods or fields. In his later years, Medley suffered from serious "bladder problems," probably prostate trouble, and
complained that he had to "squat like a hog to pass water."[57]

Age was not kind to the Cusic-Medley house; without a supportive
family, the house deteriorated from its appearance in 1918. By 1976
(figures 75–80), the front and back porches were gone. The weatherboards seen in the 1918 photograph of the house were loose, and
some were missing, revealing the logs underneath. The roof was covered with tar paper accented with broad white stripes across the top
of the dwelling; presumably this patterning was an accident of the
particular pieces of tar paper available for the cheapest repair of the
roof. The chimney had been removed from the north gable end, and
the Medleys had built a brick stove flue in the center of the upstairs.
It carried the smoke from a tin heat stove added to the south side of
the room, and from the cook stove in the old former "kitchen,"
through pipes from the two wood stoves. It was supported by the
overhead joists upstairs and did not extend into the room below.

The back yard was the principal living and work space outside,

Figure 75
*West length (facade) of the Cusic-Medley house
in 1974; compare figure 68. Photo: author.*

and the front yard not used at all. Because the back yard contained the wood pile and the path to the spring, the back door was used for practical reasons. Medley used the front door strictly for social purposes, and eventually sealed it over inside with cardboard to further insulate the house. Figures 77 and 78 show Medley at work in his back yard, "bustin' wood" near his wood pile. Close by was his homemade saw horse, on which he cut logs to stove length; inside the house was a large two-man crosscut saw for the purpose. Probably either a relative or a friend helped him saw the wood. Also in his back yard were a large galvanized tub, two empty twenty-gallon cans, and a wooden ladder leaned up against the back wall. As was common in rural houses without enclosed foundations, yard implements were kept underneath the house.

Among the other artifacts in the back yard were homemade wooden objects, showing that Medley, like Joseph Ross earlier and other tenant farmers, knew the basics of woodworking and used those skills to provide for himself. For example, leaning against the wall of

Figure 76
View of the east length (rear) of the Cusic-Medley
house, March 1976. All of the outbuildings described
by the Cusics and Medleys are gone. Photo: author.

Figure 77
Abraham Medley at age 78, March 1976. Photo: author.

the house was an oak maul that Medley had fashioned for driving wedges to split logs (figures 79, 80). In earlier years, he cut cord wood and hewed logs for railroad ties, houses, and barns to supplement his farm income, and made mauls for the trade. Next to the oak maul was a grubbing hoe, whose handle Medley had made from a sapling that he had debarked and smoothed with a draw knife. During one of my visits, Medley was in the process of shaping a six-inch log into a cylinder for a well windlass, which he probably sold or bartered, since he had no well.

Modern artifacts also appeared in the back yard. For example, an empty metal milk crate served as a chair for visitors. Next to it was an empty plastic Wonder bread wrapper—no longer were biscuits or corn bread made in his house. Next to the door was a massive, thickly padded vinyl armchair (figure 78). As the rocker by the window in the living room had been his special chair when his family was living with him, this was his special chair in his old age. He kept it in his back yard, facing the woods and fields behind the house. Its orientation reveals the extent to which Medley had separated himself from

Figure 78
*Abraham Medley in his back yard. The back length of the house
retains the small weatherboards of 1918. Photo: author.*

Figure 79
Abraham Medley's back yard. Photo: author.

the world about him. Its cheap, mass-produced quality may at first appear to be out of keeping with the traditional and homemade things around it; but synthetic, mass-produced objects like this chair, and food like Wonder bread, are now integrated into the material culture of the "folk," having replaced certain traditional elements.

The interior of Abraham Medley's home is that of an elderly person who, lacking employment, money, and means of transportation or communication, has created a world of his own. In years past, Medley had worked outdoors, while housekeeping was the responsibility of his wife and children. At that time the house was carefully maintained. "You ought to have seen it when my wife was alive," Medley said. The walls were customarily whitewashed, but now the walls, ceiling, and floorboards were blackened by soot from the wood stoves. Modern communication technology—telephone, radio, television—was absent from Medley's world. Since there was still no electricity in 1976, the house was lit only by sunlight through the glass window, which was closed by a wood shutter during the winter to keep out cold drafts. The kerosene lamp's globe was sooty, so it

Figure 80
Detail of artifacts, Abraham Medley's back yard. Photo: author.

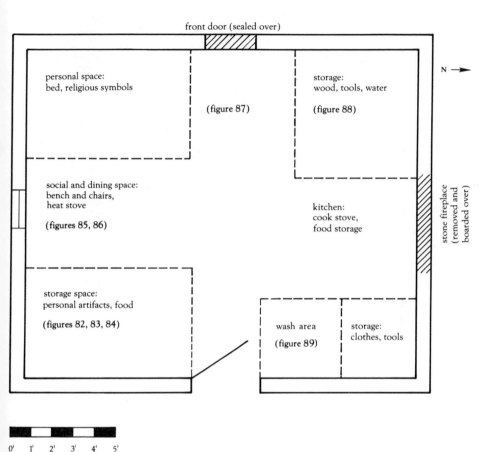

Figure 81
The downstairs of the Cusic-Medley house during
residency of Abraham Medley in the 1970's.

provided only dim light. Living alone, unable to read, and without a job, Medley had little need for light at night except to see his way around the house and to go to bed by.[58]

Nonetheless, when we ask if his lifestyle might have a discernible organization to it, we begin to perceive an order to the arrangement and use of his one-room space. This organization, partly deliberate, partly unconscious, is illustrated in the diagram in figure 81. The

Figure 82
Southeast corner, interior of Abraham Medley's house. Photo: author.

area to the left (southeast) of the back door served as storage space (figures 81–89). The corner itself was like a bin, for several bushels of white potatoes had been poured on the floor, banked on two sides by the corner of the house and on another by a piece of plywood. The front of the "bank" was left open. The potatoes were stored here because this was the darkest corner of the house, away from sunlight that would have caused the potatoes to sprout. There was no basement in which to store them. On the wall above the makeshift potato bin was nailed a wooden crate with a door that was used as a kind of cupboard or cabinet. Figure 83 shows its contents: two boxes of Lipton tea, a dirty saucepan with a rag inside it, a can of nutmeg, two bottles (perhaps of cough syrup), a comb, an empty jar of Maxwell House coffee with paper or a rag inside, another empty fruit jar with a rag, a can of poison dust that served perhaps as an insecticide, a dirty coffee cup, a paper bag, and a can of sausages. On top of the crate were a drill bit, a mousetrap, a hairbrush, a tin can, and a single set of shoelace eyes for Medley's boots.

Gradually, as we accustom our sensibilities to the information these "everyday" objects contain, it becomes clear that the way of life of

Figure 83
Crate used as a cupboard in Medley's house. Photo: author.

Figure 84
Table in southeast corner of Medley's house. Photo: author.

the American rural poor is before us, a way of life recorded by Farm
Security Administration photographers in the 1930's but rarely seen
in portrayals of American life in textbooks or historical museums.
In such houses, one object served a variety of purposes, and a clutter
of seemingly unassociated objects gave the home a lived-in quality.
For example, next to Medley's bin in the corner was a large empty
crock, in which potatoes or onions may have been stored at one
time. Mrs. Nora Cusic recalled that her husband stored dried eels,
used for crab bait, in similar crocks. Along the wall of the south
gable end was a small table covered with a sooty oilcloth (figure 84)
that held a small snap-lock box of Anacin, a can opener, a spool
of thread, a tin measuring cup, an empty jar of fruit drink, two
pocket watches (showing different times), a paper bag, a blackened
kerosene lamp, a plastic coffee cup with a tea bag and spoon in it,
a box of Domino granulated sugar, empty cans of Maryland Chief
Spinach and of Dole Pink Grapefruit Drink, and an unlabeled coffee
can with a knife stored in it. There were also tubes of Ben-Gay and
Musterole ointment and a bottle of Yager's Liniment that Medley
used for rheumatism. Above the table was a sportsman's calendar and

Figure 85
Abraham Medley inside his house. Photo: author.

a key on a string hung from the wall. Next to the table was a large empty Kaiser Gypsum Jointing Compound can that Medley used as a chamber pot.

The sitting space, directly in front of the window, consisted of a simple wooden bench (figure 86). Guests sat on the bed next to the bench in the southwest corner. A few feet across from the bench was a tin, wood-burning heat stove. Underneath the bed and within easy range of the bench was Medley's spittoon. Medley made his own chewing tobacco twists, which he sweetened with brown sugar.

Above his bed were the most personal and religious objects in the house: a snapshot of Medley on a tractor, a large crucifix, and a medallion of the Virgin Mary. Like many southern Maryland blacks, Medley was a Roman Catholic. The iron bed was in poor condition. Most of the paint had flaked off, and there were no sheets or bedspreads, only a few dirty and rumpled blankets (figure 86). At the foot of the bed and in front of the door in the western length (front door) was a short sofa. It was not used for seating visitors; instead, clothes and coats were scattered about on top of it.

Above the front door hung a single-barreled shotgun suspended by

Figure 86
Abraham Medley seated by his bed. Photo: Cary Carson.

wire loops. The one he had had in the 1920's was double-barreled.
This one had undergone several home repairs that included taping
the stock together and taping the barrel to the hand rest (figure 87).
Though the front door was sealed over with cardboard, the gun still
hung in its traditional place over the front door lintel.[59]

In the northwest corner was a plank table covered with an oilcloth
on which were kept two water buckets, one of galvanized tin and one
of enamelware (figure 88). The bottom of the latter was blackened
with smoke; it had obviously been set directly upon the stove to heat
water. In the other bucket was a metal dipper, and another dipper
hung from the wall above the table. Medley kept his old scythe
propped up against the wall between the table and sofa, its blade
turned under the table for safety. Also on the table were two bowls
and a tin can. In the corner was stacked a small pile of sawn logs
that had not been split. In the back of this wood pile was stored the
two-man crosscut saw.

Opposite the former fireplace in the northern gable end was a
wood cook stove that was rarely used. On top of it were blackened
pans, a Ball jar with either meal or powdered milk inside, a mixing

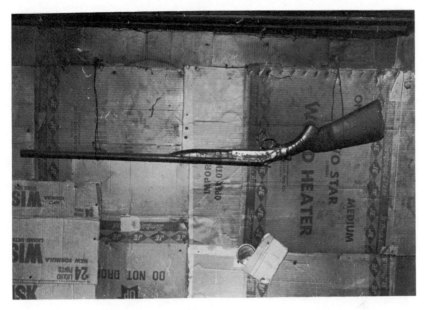

Figure 87
Abraham Medley's single-barreled, hammer-action shotgun. Photo: author.

bowl, and a jar of Jif peanut butter. The stove had not been cleaned for a long time. Medley ate mostly canned foods.

In the northeast corner of the room was a wooden box in which Medley kept some of his clothes. On the wall hung a variety of objects: a hand saw, a metal potato masher, a lunch box, a draw knife, and a spatula. Next to the back door were an axe, a broom, and a small, comparatively fancy table stand on which was placed an enamelware pan that was blackened by smoke on the bottom (figure 89). This was Medley's wash basin, where he shaved and washed up. Above the basin was an Oldsmobile rear-view mirror suspended on wire loops from the wall. Below it was a long oval herring can nailed to the wall that served as soap dish. There was also a small veneered cabinet where Medley kept his toilet articles. This area was selected as his "wash room," so to speak, probably because it was near the sunlight from the door, and the waste water could be conveniently tossed out the back door.

In comparing the house during this last period of occupancy to the house in earlier periods, we see that many household activities no longer took place, and many artifacts associated with those activities

Figure 88
Northwest corner, Abraham Medley's house. Photo: author.

were removed or stored away. The house now reflected the life of an impoverished man, living alone, no longer using the land of the farmstead for his sustenance. He used the dwelling for shelter at night, and during the day he either sat outside in the armchair, if weather permitted, or inside on his bench. Having no one to talk to, he talked to himself, and upon arriving at his house, I would occasionally hear him engaged in animated conversation. His principal activities were "bustin' wood" for fires and making things from wood like the maul, hoe handle, and cylinder for the windlass. Food, especially canned or packaged products, was provided by friends and relatives and the local country store. He may have been on welfare, though it did not seem that he received even that much money.

In 1976, the house still did not have electricity, indoor plumbing, an icebox, or running water. Though he lived alone and suffered from "bladder problems," rheumatism, and old age, Medley did not give up. He retained a remarkable memory, and still recalled specific events of my first visits several years before, even though at that time his mind had seemed clouded by senility and alcohol. Like many elderly people, his mind was much sharper than it appeared at first

Figure 89
Wash area of Abraham Medley's house. Photo: author.

meeting. His lack of dentures made articulating thoughts difficult for him, and he was also hard of hearing. Therefore, it was difficult for him to talk to people and for them to understand him, and his mind was dulled by lack of stimulation from conversation. Nonetheless, Medley was responsive to the attention I showed him during the interviews with him and later with his son, and appreciated my interest in his old house. He laughed at my interest with a mixture of bewilderment and of understanding of his house's significance. Though he was infirm, his sense of humor was intact, and he continued to enjoy life, especially the company of others.[60]

In the winter of 1977–78, Medley's advancing age, poor health, and feebleness, and the deteriorating condition of his house, made it impossible for him to live alone. He was taken to the hospital for a while, and all his possessions were removed from his home. Today Medley is more frail than several years ago, and his hearing is worse, but he is under the good care of his son, Charles, who continues to live in St. Mary's County, not far from his childhood home. Charles is patient with and attentive to Medley, whose gentleness and discipline Charles recalled with respect: "He never hit me in his life. He used to shake his finger at me and that meant business, but he never beat me." Like Benjamin Ross, Charles Medley respected his father's character.[61]

Since the Cusic-Medley house is now abandoned and is one of few log houses remaining in southern Maryland, it is a valuable example of the American people's history (figure 90). Possibly, if an interested historical organization can be found, the landowner may be willing to donate the house to it. The house could fairly easily be dismantled, moved to another site, and preserved as an example of a sharecropper's house. The vital and otherwise unavailable evidence of the recollections of its former residents and the photographs of it at different periods of occupancy could be used to reconstruct the dwelling, its outbuildings, work places, and surrounding paths. I hope this evidence can help create an educational exhibit of the life of the occupants of this house and, by implication, an exhibit of the life of other landless rural families in Maryland.

One important point is that Medley organized his home, even if loosely, into distinguishable areas for specific purposes (figure 81). A similar organization of room use also marks this house in earlier periods, the one-room Ross tenant house, and the tenant house at the Smithsonian. These are a few examples of families that succeeded in ordering their homes and in living beyond mere survival by improvising within the confines of limited space and means.

Figure 90
Back yard of the abandoned Cusic-Medley house, December 1978. Photo: author.

Some accounts describe slaves living totally without pattern. The behavior recorded in this chapter indicates how some sharecropper families, and hence probably some slaves, organized their living space into functional units and cultivated a sense of self and family that they passed on to their children. While we should not minimize poverty's disruptive effects on rural black landless families, as clearly described by W. E. B. Du Bois near the turn of the century, this chapter's case studies show that black families were not necessarily broken by their poverty.

There was a strong continuity in house types from slavery to freedom. Small log houses remained commonplace through the nineteenth century and into the twentieth, and were inhabited by black and white sharecroppers, as evidenced by the Cusic-Medley house. These houses of landless families were not as a rule expanded with additions; instead, their rectangular form remained constant, while their appearance, state of upkeep, and furnishings changed. Poverty of material things remained constant, but not poverty of spirit. And certain improvements appeared: wood floors instead of earthen floors, brick or stone chimneys instead of log chimneys, glass windows instead of wooden shutters, and wood-burning stoves instead of open fireplaces.

But such changes came slowly. Most of the photographs in Chapters II and III of houses in the late nineteenth and early twentieth centuries were remarkably similar to the dwellings described by former slaves. As McKinley Gantt said, emancipation was a "great day." It brought the promise of freedom. While that promise uplifted hearts and led to serious attempts by people like Benjamin Ross's father to stride forward, freedom was still a long way off.[62]

CHAPTER V
Houses of Landowners:
"The Colored People Want Land"

We all know that the colored people want land.
Night and day they think and dream of it.
Representative to South Carolina
Constitutional Convention, 1868[1]

Some colored people realized their dream of owning land, and their houses and material culture help complete our picture of the physical world of blacks. All too often are rural blacks stereotyped as landless tenants, to the neglect of this significant group of landowners. Their place is important in American and Afro-American history and in museum exhibits related to that history, because they usually led their communities and the local and national black organizations. More secure financially than tenants, landowners could support schools, churches, lodges, and insurance societies, the principal institutions of the rural black community. Also, they usually provided the preachers, trustees, teachers, and other leaders who directed those institutions. As one scholar of black communities in the post-bellum South concluded, "There is no doubt that the backbone of the rural Negro population is the group of successful Negro owners and renters. . . . The Negro race looks to this class for its leaders and supporters of rural institutions."[2]

Though a minority, black landowners were present throughout Maryland and the South in the post-bellum nineteenth century. There were 179,418 black farm owners in 1900 in the South, 211,087 in 1910, and 212,365 in 1920. Throughout Maryland in 1910, black families owned 12,068 homes. In southern Maryland in 1910, over a third of the black families (almost a half in Calvert County) owned their homes (table 4). This group of landowners therefore constituted a numerically important part of the population, in addition to the leadership positions it held in the community.[3]

Table 4

Homeownership of Black Families, Southern Maryland, 1910

County	Homes Owned by Blacks	Homes Rented by Blacks	No Report	Total Homes of Blacks
Anne Arundel County	775	2,025	129	2,929
Calvert County	427	488	24	939
Charles County	639	816	71	1,526
Prince George's County	833	1,199	130	2,162
St. Mary's County	554	731	50	1,335
Total in Southern Maryland	3,228	5,259	404	8,891
Total in Maryland	12,068	32,774	2,335	47,177

Source: U.S., Census Bureau, *Negro Population in the United States, 1790–1915* (New York: Arno Press), p. 486.

While several studies of black landowners in the South and Midwest have focused on their motivations and methods of acquiring land, on the communities and towns they founded, and on the institutions, businesses, and political networks they developed, scant attention has been paid to their physical domestic world. What did their houses look like? How were they built, and how did they compare to those of slaves and tenants? How did they change over time? Did black landowners live on isolated farms among whites, or did they form all-black communities? How did they lay out their farmsteads? How did they furnish their houses, and how did their houses' interiors compare with those of tenants?[4]

While some black landowners interspersed their holdings among farms owned by whites, many gathered together to form black communities with adjacent tracts of property. Examples of such communities surveyed in southern Maryland are Beachville and Abell in

St. Mary's County, the Muirkirk settlement in Prince George's, Chicamuxen in Charles, and Ball's Graveyard, Ben's Creek, and Helen's Creek in Calvert. In Montgomery County, north of Washington, I surveyed others: Sugarland, Martinsburg, Jerusalem, Jonesville, and Big Woods. The rest are listed in Appendix I. Established in the years following emancipation, these communities were important havens for black families, and the vestiges that remain, along with residents' recollections of them, enable us to visualize their houses and material culture.[5]

Freed slaves perceived landownership much like English and other European immigrants: as a sign and a safeguard of liberty. According to W. E. B. Du Bois, "by far the most pressing problem" of freed slaves was land, which was "absolutely fundamental and essential to any real emancipation of the slaves." To them, "freedom, respectability and getting ahead were inextricably associated with farming their own land," concluded historians August Meier and Elliott Rudwick, for landownership provided a critical measure of autonomy and stability. Since most freedmen were farmers by profession, they had to have land in order to control their trade and to earn a living that would enable their families and children to advance. Furthermore, the importance of landownership was ingrained in the American ideology. The sanctity of private property and of the individual's rights were basic tenets of the American creed. After observing blacks in the years after emancipation, one scholar wrote: "Every Negro who procured one of these patches saw himself at once in the light of an independent planter, placed upon an equal footing with his former master, and looking into the future, beheld himself a landed proprietor."[6]

The communities freed slaves founded followed a typically American pattern. They were founded on the basis of individual ownership, rather than as cooperatives or communes. This was somewhat contrary to the more communal African tradition. Among West African societies, the land was customarily worked by specific village groups and was not considered to be individually owned; instead, the village shared it, and each family was assigned a plot for its use. The land itself was not seen as being "owned" by the village; instead, the land belonged to the ancestors or gods, and was the village's only in usage. (It is interesting to note the substantial parallels to Native American land concepts.) Elements of communalism continued during slavery. Field labor and harvests were shared among the slaves, and while individuals may have been singled out for advancement and for better living conditions, they all remained slaves, and most lived under similar conditions. What they used and lived with was "theirs" not in ownership, but only in usage.[7]

As a concept of man's relationship to the earth, private ownership of land was essentially Western and adopted by the Africans in America. Blacks conformed to the dominant culture for practical reasons. It would have been virtually impossible to establish a community with a model of social organization that was opposite to that of the Western culture. Simply to get the land was a struggle, because it required money, equipment, hard work, good luck, and, usually, the approval of a white landowner. To found a new order was beyond the question for most. Having lived together so long as a confined group, blacks no doubt wanted at this time to have something for themselves that they could call their own. For them, as for most Americans, that was freedom.

How were blacks able to acquire land? Freed without compensation for their long years of labor, they had no money. Since Maryland did not secede from the Union, no plantations were confiscated. While the Freedmen's Bureau did establish schools in southern Maryland, it did not buy or sell land. Also, none of the communities in southern Maryland that I surveyed appear to have grown from antebellum free black communities, as did the Big Woods community in Montgomery County, which developed around the nucleus of fifty acres purchased in 1814 by a free black, or the East Towson community in Baltimore County. All of the tracts of black communities surveyed in southern Maryland were bought after the Civil War from prominent whites.[8]

The position of those white landowners in the years after the Civil War is ambiguous. According to a group of recent historians, whites were unwilling to sell land to blacks in the South, and those who were cooperative were intimidated violently by other whites who feared that landownership would put blacks on an equal footing.[9] But the presence of hundreds of black landowning families throughout southern Maryland shows that whites were willing to sell land to blacks there. It is doubtful that whites in southern Maryland were drastically different from whites further south, since they had been slaveowners and had supported the Southern cause. They certainly did not believe in racial equality. But while they continued to believe in white supremacy, they were not afraid of blacks as landowners. Of course, they were not willing to sell to all blacks. Instead, they sold to those who were "acceptable," ones whom they had known for many years in the community or who were former slaves of theirs. The sociologist, Arthur Raper, found that Georgia whites did likewise. By rewarding selected blacks, the overall system of white control was not disrupted. As in Georgia, the tracts that whites sold were those that they no longer used or that were less fertile. Some land, such as that sold for the Ben's Creek community in Calvert County, was forest that had to be cleared for settlement and cultivation. According to George Carroll, the land his ancestors purchased and settled in Beachville in St. Mary's County had been a swamp.[10]

Paternalism was another factor that prompted whites to sell to blacks. While they did not accept them as equals, white planters may have wanted to help some of their former slaves to "get on their feet." For example, Jennie Tongue Reichart recalled that her grandfather gave former slaves small tracts of land from his plantation in Calvert County.[11]

This sense of paternalism may have been quickened by the need for labor. After emancipation, plantation owners needed hands to work their tobacco fields, and, rather than risk losing their former slaves to nearby towns and cities, they would offer small holdings at modest prices to induce them to remain and work on their farms. Indeed, many black freedmen who became landowners worked as farm laborers after emancipation. Some white families may have suffered financially after emancipation, and these payments from land sales would have been an important additional source of income. One historian of Charles County has written that "with the end of the Civil War and slavery, the large tobacco plantation ceased to exist. Small farms with two to ten acres planted in tobacco were in the majority." By 1910, blacks owned 639 of these parcels in Charles County, 361 of which the U.S. Census categorized as "farm homes," that is, homes with a few acres in cultivation. To meet their payments and pay their taxes, most black landowning families had to make the most from what their land provided, and have at least two sources of income, one being an alternative to working the family farm. In the communities surveyed, only a few small farmsteads alone provided sufficient income for the families. Most men hired themselves out as farm laborers; of the 29,072 Maryland Negro males engaged in agriculture as "farmers" in the 1910 U.S. Census, 22,189 were farm laborers, and some of these laborers were small landowners.[12]

Other jobs were important, too. In the black settlement of Muirkirk, Prince George's County, begun in the 1880's, Augustus Ross (no known kin to Benjamin Ross) and his neighbors found employment in the Muirkirk Charcoal Pig Iron Foundry. They had bought land from an estate that was being divided by its heirs, and they supplemented their wages with proceeds from their small truck farms and orchards. George Carroll said his grandfather, Samuel Carroll, and the black settlers at Beachville in St. Mary's County worked three jobs. They farmed their own land for family subsistence, share-cropped on other farms, and during the winter worked as watermen on the Potomac River and Chesapeake Bay, selling oysters, crabs, and fish they caught to Washington and Baltimore markets. In Montgomery County, the former slaves who founded the Sugarland community worked as quarrymen at the Seneca Rock Quarry, which furnished the red sandstone for the rowhouses and office buildings then being constructed in Washington, Baltimore, and other cities. Joseph Ross, the former slave and veteran of the Union Army (see Chapter IV), worked as a hod carrier in Washington, earning enough money to buy a hundred-acre farm in Charles County that had been abandoned after the war. [13]

Among the most successful blacks were the full-time professional watermen. Most had probably acquired their skills during slavery, since a "considerable number of slaves" had either worked with their masters on the water or operated their masters' boats by themselves. After the war, almost 40 percent of the rivermen on the Potomac were "ex-slaves working small skiffs." One example was William Diggs's grandfather, William Jordan, who became a professional waterman after emancipation and managed to purchase a few acres. Carefully saving his earnings, he purchased a schooner and hauled freight to and from Baltimore, Washington, and towns along Maryland rivers and the bay. A skilled sailor, he even extended his trade to Haiti. Other freed black watermen founded communities along the tidal creeks and inlets, which provided safe harbors and easy access to open water. The Abell community in St. Mary's County is one example. Among the residents was Beverly Collins, who captained the *Mark Stevens*, a 54.5-foot sailing vessel, known as a "sharp sail bugeye," built in 1888. Others were Henry Stewart, who sailed the 50-foot bugeye *Eva Clarence*, built in 1887, and James Dickerson, who captained a 51.5-foot sailing craft. Luke Clark, his brother Joe Clark, Taylor Green, and Henry Branson also owned sailing vessels and had "good reputations on the river." Other blacks, such as Richard Jones, an "excellent riverman," did not have sufficient capital to buy a boat and so sailed crafts belonging to others on a sharing basis. Some of these watermen owned "fine farms on the river front," and the holdings are still in the possession of their descendants. All of these people constitute a compelling story of black enterprise. [14]

The houses they built are important elements of the black histor-

Figure 91
*Oscar Crump in front of the home of his mother, Sadie Crump, in the Muirkirk
community, Prince George's County, Maryland. Photo: author.*

ical experience, for, as W. E. B. Du Bois found, the "great impulse
toward better housing" came from these successful black landowners.
Beginning with small log dwellings and culminating in the early
twentieth century with larger frame houses, their homes reflect the
evolution of housing for black families. Now that blacks were free
and owned their homes, they could save, make improvements, and
utilize new products for house construction. These products were the
results of advances in sawmill technology that made possible fast,
efficient lumber production, while steel mills developed faster methods of manufacturing nails, and the expanding railroad system facilitated the transportation and distribution of building materials. The
result was that, in the post–Civil-War period, houses throughout
Maryland and the nation were increasingly constructed of mass-
produced, low-cost, purchased materials.[15]

While slave and tenant houses had remained constant in size, landowners' homes were larger, because these families had surplus capital and control over their houses, and so could utilize advances in
house building. They may also have hired local carpenters, who in
turn consulted builders' manuals and design books marketed on a

Figure 92
Sadie Crump, born in 1877, soon after her one hundredth birthday. Photo: author.

nationwide basis. Whatever the specific source, more and more houses of rural black landowners reflected the middle-class culture of the times. The houses had more of a variety of floor plans that featured rooms for specific functions, instead of one or two rooms shared by the entire family, changes that did not appear in new tenant houses until somewhat later. Furthermore, landowners' houses were likely to display decorative elements outside and in, such as cross-gable pediments, porches with scrollwork brackets, and paneled stairways with turned bannisters and newel posts. In the last decades of the nineteenth century, black landowners shifted from being almost exclusively producers to being consumers of house construction.[16]

Examples of such houses include the Sadie Crump house in the Muirkirk community of Prince George's County, built as a plain two-room log house in the 1880's by a freed slave, and remodeled and enlarged along the back length by Sadie Crump to resemble a more fashionable frame dwelling after she bought it in the early 1900's (figures 91, 92). Mrs. Crump weatherboarded the log walls, enlarged the windows, lathed and plastered the walls inside, and added picture moldings from which pictures were hung, as her parents, also landowners, had done in their nearby frame house where she grew up. The house of John Medley in the Beachville community in St. Mary's County, built in the 1890's of typical lightweight frame construction, illustrates one house type of black landowners in the late 1800's, this one having a floor plan of a single parlor and a side hall passage downstairs, and a two-story ell behind the parlor (figure 93).[17]

The home of Robert Collins, built in 1898 as the residence of a successful black farmer in the Abell community in St. Mary's County, is an example of a once-fine home built with a mixture of decorative elements from the popular Colonial Revival and Victorian Cottage styles (figure 94). It is more stylishly furnished than most other houses of black landowners outside and in, and featured such details as bracketed eaves, a cross-gable facade with the gable vented by a diamond window and capped by a finial, and a paneled doorway with glazed sidelights and transom. A paneled stairway with turned bannisters and newel post highlighted the entrance hallway, and decorative moldings and paneled doors accented each room.[18]

But these houses did not stand alone. Like immigrants in a new land, the freed people banded together to form communities (see Appendix I). As historical resources, these men and women provide important insights into the settlement patterns of freed slaves, along with the methods of house construction and the evolution of housing after the Civil War. Because the residents were landowners, deeds

Figure 93
Facade of John Medley's house in the Beachville community,
St. Mary's County, Maryland. Photo: author.

exist that name residents and specify the amount of land purchased, the date, and occasionally the price paid. The history of the communities is enriched by elderly oral informants' stories about the founding of the communities and their ancestors' relationships to the white landowners from whom they purchased the land and with whom they continued to coexist. By recalling the farmstead complexes and house furnishings, they make possible farmstead sketches and furnishings plans. Furthermore, the landowning families tended to have photographs of themselves made—to have their portaits painted, so to speak—and those that have been preserved allow us actually to see these men and women of the past.[19]

These communities developed by accretion; that is, the first few settlers bought small acreages, and later settlers purchased adjacent tracts. Usually the communities were parts of one or two large parcels of land sold off over a decade or so by one or two prominent white families, as illustrated by the Sugarland and Jerusalem com-

Figure 94
Facade of Robert Collins's house in Abell,
St. Mary's County, Maryland. Photo: author.

munities in Montgomery County and Ben's Creek in Calvert County. Some of the purchasers were former slaves of the white families, but most moved into the area from nearby farms or were of origins unknown to us today. They cleared the land, built the houses themselves, and over the years, as other black families arrived, developed communities whose log houses and rail-fenced fields probably resembled small frontier settlements.[20]

In regard to the settlers' family origins, the communities were rarely founded by extended families. Deeds, federal census manuscripts, and oral informants show that instances of several brothers, sisters, or other relatives buying land in the same community were the exception. Instead, communities typically began with one or more unrelated families in the late 1860's, and in the 1870's and 1880's grew larger as one family after another moved in. By the early 1900's, the children of the founders intermarried, transforming the community into a large extended family and repeating the kinship pattern that had developed in the slave quarters. Particular traditions continued, such as the taboo against first cousins marrying.[21]

The freed slave community with the richest combination of historical resources—houses, artifacts, written records, and oral descriptions—is Ben's Creek in Calvert County. The oldest extant houses in Ben's Creek were built soon after emancipation. Of these, four were still standing in 1977, along with the log ruins of three others. There are also examples of houses built in turn-of-the-century styles, reflecting the evolution of housing. Furthermore, most of the houses in Ben's Creek have been abandoned, so modern improvements have not masked their original appearance. As in many other communities, there is an oral informant in Ben's Creek who remembers its earliest history, and the use of her recollections in reconstructing this community's history can serve as an example for other historians and lay people interested in doing similar research.

Ben's Creek was located near the village of Island Creek, and together they were considered "one of the most progressive and thriving villages around"; yet today it resembles a ghost town of abandoned houses and fields. Fortunately, the sites have been identified by Blanche Wilson, born in 1903, whose grandparents, all former slaves, were among the original founders of the community in the late 1860's (figure 95). She is the only survivor of the old community who still lives there. She recalled that there were once nineteen houses in the community, sixteen of them log or partially log; the others were frame.[22]

In 1977, four log houses were still standing, more than in any other black community surveyed in southern Maryland. They constitute valuable evidence for the study of log construction by former slaves, and each is a document of early attempts at self-sufficiency by freed families, since they were made of locally available material and constructed by residents and neighbors. Together, these buildings and sites testify to the efforts of an entire community to establish itself in an independent and respected niche of society, and by implication testify to the efforts of other freed families in similar communities throughout Maryland and the South. Like the log houses American tradition associates with Daniel Boone and Abe Lincoln, these buildings tell of pioneers who played a large part in the founding of a new era in American history.

The land along Ben's Creek had been owned by the Hellen family, prominent planters in the ante-bellum era, and one of their former slaves, James Harrod, was a founder of the community. Harrod's wife, Cecilia Golder Harrod, had been a slave on the nearby Parran planta-

Figure 95
Blanche Wilson, community historian of Ben's Creek. Photo: author.

tion. Another settler, James Wilson, had been a slave of the Turners, who also lived nearby in the community of Wallville. All the black settlers were well known to the local white elite and had a so-cial status in the county that was a combination of the "inferior" status inherited from slavery and the higher rank of free landowners.[23]

Deeds show that the first freedman to settle in Ben's Creek was James Wilson, Sr., Blanche Wilson's paternal great-grandfather. He bought 34.25 acres in 1866 on Ben's Creek where it flowed into the Patuxent River. According to the 1870 census, Wilson was born in 1813, and his wife Matilda was born in 1819. He was listed as a farmer, but his great-granddaughter says he was a waterman too; he docked his boat in the cove at Ben's Creek, and from there ventured into the Patuxent River and the Chesapeake Bay. He was able to raise the astounding amount of $962.00 to meet the asking price for the property. The deed stated that the amount was "duly paid before the delivery hereof"; Wilson perhaps saved some money during slavery, and supplemented this with his earnings as a waterman and farmer. Like Joseph Ross, his son, James Wilson, Jr., had served in the Union Army during the Civil War, and after his discharge he returned to Calvert County and bought land adjacent to his father's. His father taught him how to work the rivers and the bay, and the federal census of 1880 listed his occupation as "oysterman."[24]

At the same time, other black families were settling in Ben's Creek too. Lewis Bourne purchased nine and three-quarters acres in 1869 from the Hellen family, and in 1874 acquired twenty more acres from them. In 1870, Peter Gross purchased six acres from the Hellens. In 1873, James Harrod—Blanche Wilson's maternal grandfather, born in 1840—purchased six acres for $35 per acre. However, they were already living there and had built a house by 1873, since Blanche Wilson definitely recalled that their first child was born elsewhere, but that their second child, born in 1869, was born in the log house. In 1884, Louis and Lidia Brooks purchased 3.26 acres and 29.5 acres of land from the Hellens, but, like the Harrods, the Brookses were living on the land prior to that time, in their own log house, one of the first built in the area. According to Miss Wilson, by the 1880's there was a "regular little town back here." She remembered hearing stories of a store that was located along Ben's Creek Road past the Harrod house on the west side. According to her, "you could buy anything you wanted there, even a marriage license"—apparently an exaggeration intended to make a point.[25]

The founding of this community gives us a rare glimpse into the economic situation of former slaves in post–Civil-War Maryland. As shown by such oral informants as James Scriber in St. Mary's County, and by the Freedmen's Bureau work contracts, most freed men and women were destitute and were locked into a tenant-landlord relationship that resembled peonage. However, a significant few were able to make enough money from farming, fishing, crabbing, oystering, and jobs in the cities to buy land during Reconstruction, even at high prices. This feat was accomplished without credit—deeds show that they paid the price in full and that there were no loans or mortgages.

Ben's Creek also reveals an important aspect of the relationship between blacks and whites. According to Blanche Wilson, the settlers were from the general vicinity and were known by local whites. They must have been considered "acceptable," since whites would not have sold to just any black person. James Harrod had been a slave of the Hellen family, which owned the land along Ben's Creek. His wife, born Cecilia Golder, had been a slave on the Parran plantation nearby. After emancipation, the Parrans and Cecilia Golder remained friends, and, according to Miss Wilson, the Parrans visited the Harrods frequently at their home in Ben's Creek, even in the twentieth century. Elsewhere in Calvert County, the Tongue family, owners of the Hooper's Neck Plantation, sold small tracts of land to their former slaves. In Georgia, Arthur Raper found similar incidences of whites selling to blacks whom they knew well and considered "safe." As for the sale of land to black families upsetting the racial status quo, as some have argued, it must be remembered that these blacks were buying only small parcels that did not threaten the large farms of hundreds of acres owned by the ruling whites.[26]

Like the founders of Beachville, Abell, Muirkirk, and other communities in southern Maryland, and of Sugarland and Jerusalem in Montgomery County, the founders of Ben's Creek literally had to build their community from the ground up. According to Miss Wilson, her grandparents said that they cleared the land of trees for their fields and homes, and used the timber to build their houses, outbuildings, and fences. Most of their first houses were log, because that was the type they had built during slavery and they had the necessary skills; furthermore, logs were the only inexpensive building material available. Families worked cooperatively to help one another. It was this community cooperation that impressed Miss Wilson most about the establishment of Ben's Creek. She recalled stories told her of the construction of the home of her maternal grandparents, the Harrods, with whom she was very close.

"They helped him [James Harrod] in every possible way they could. They cut logs, hewed out logs, and some of them hauled out logs with oxen or with a horse. They needed stone and mortar to fill in between the logs and to build the chimney, and anybody that found a stone around, they would haul them to the house or maybe somebody else would come around to haul them. If he was around,

Figure 96
Rear length of the original log block of the Harrod house, Ben's Creek. The logs of the house were originally exposed, the door had no window, and the roof was covered with wood shingles and had no dormer window. Photo: author.

they would come and help him. If he wasn't, they could go on and work just the same. Even when he would come home at night, someone would come and help with various jobs on the house. And something that I thought was very nice: quite often someone would send him dinner so he wouldn't have to prepare that." Miss Wilson recalled that house building was to some extent a biracial effort. "The majority of people helping him were black, but there were one or two white neighbors in the vicinity, and they had them coming in too." Figure 96 shows the log house and its stone chimney, the product of community cooperation.[27]

According to Miss Wilson, all the log houses were built more or less alike. They resembled the log slave houses illustrated in earlier chapters, though she did not recall any wooden chimneys. Everyone called them "farmhouses," she said. They were "straight up and down houses," with one room downstairs and one or two upstairs, and usually an outside kitchen. Though plain in appearance, without decorative trim or porches, the log houses were nonetheless handsome in their own way. For example, most families whitewashed their homes inside and out, using a lime and water mixture. In the

Figure 97
Brooks log house, Ben's Creek community, Calvert County,
Maryland. Originally built as one-and-a-half stories in the late 1860's
by freed slaves; heightened to two stories by a frame addition in the early
twentieth century. A one-story shed kitchen of frame construction
was added to the rear length. Demolished. Photo: author.

twentieth century they purchased lime, but Miss Wilson heard that some families in the early days burned oyster shells to extract the lime.

An especially pleasant feature of the community was that "all the houses had a view," since the land was clear of woods. "You could look from one house to another and call out to your neighbors without leaving home." Located on hilltops, the Bourne and Brooks houses commanded lovely views over fields and forests to the Patuxent River, about a mile to the south. All along Ben's Creek Road, which ended at James Wilson's farm on the Patuxent River, there were houses with picket fences, vegetable gardens, outbuildings, and fields surrounded by rail fences. Having been raised in this community when it was flourishing, Miss Wilson misses the view of other houses, and has a strong attachment to those that remain. In early December of 1978, she said she just had a funny feeling about the Brooks house (figure 97), even though she could not see it because of the woods that had grown up. When she went outside and walked over, she saw that the current owners had bulldozed the house and were burning the pile of hewn logs. Though the house had not been lived in for some years, it was one of the oldest and most important in Ben's Creek. Its massive pine log walls securely V-notched into place in the corners made it one of the best-built log houses that had survived in southern Maryland (figures 98, 99). It was a part of her community, and Blanche Wilson missed having it around. Figure 100 shows the site after demolition, illustrating the eradication of houses in Ben's Creek that Blanche Wilson has already seen, and the fate that she foresees for the remainder.[28]

Analyzing the methods of house building at Ben's Creek shows the skills of the newly freed slaves. They employed to their own advantage their tradition of making do with very little. They knew, for example, the qualities of various types of wood. For the walls of the Harrod house, chestnut was selected because, according to Miss Wilson, it grew so tall and straight. It was commonly used in Ben's Creek for log buildings, she said, and for fence rails. At the Brooks house nearby, large pine logs were selected; some were as thick as 9″ by 6″ (figures 98, 99). One hundred years later, they still remained sound. (Pine is an unusual choice in so well-made a house.) To protect logs from rot and from termite infestation, the sills were placed a foot or more above the ground on ferrous sandstone pilings. To anchor the log walls at the corners, they used a V-notch, the type most commonly found in southern Maryland among the surviving log houses of both whites and blacks. Indeed, builders throughout the mid-Atlantic region preferred this type.[29]

Though plain, the houses had modest improvements over the earlier slave houses, and careful attention was paid to insulation. For example, they had wooden floors instead of dirt floors. To insulate the space underneath the floors and to prevent cold winds from blowing up and through cracks in the floorboards, the builders filled the crawl space under the house with dirt. The houses of the Harrods and Brookses illustrate this, and William Diggs from Charles County recalled that many of the old log houses that he knew, including slave houses and the home of his grandparents, were insulated this way. To insulate the walls, the builders filled the spaces between the logs with long, flat stones that they covered with homemade mud daubing or lime mortar. The stones were laid in place diagonally so that they would support the plaster better (figure 99). The result was a warm and comfortable house.[30]

Glass panes, in either double-hung or single-hung sashes, replaced the plank shutters of slave houses. These improved the comfort of

Figure 98
V-notched corner of the Brooks log house, Ben's Creek. Compare
the cruder joints in figures 19 and 22. Photo: author.

Figure 99
Gable wall of Brooks log house, Ben's Creek. The large size of the logs,
the stone in-fill placed on a slant between the logs and plastered inside and
out show the care given to the construction of this house. Also, the window was
set deep into notches in the logs to anchor it in place. In the early 1900's the house
was covered with weatherboards and resembled a frame house in appearance.
The vertical planks served as "studs" for the weatherboards. Like other
houses at Ben's Creek, this one was whitewashed. Photo: author.

---

the residents by providing more sunlight inside the house, more control over ventilation, better retention of heat, and a visual rapport with neighbors and the outdoors during inclement weather. For enhanced appearance and insulation, the walls were lathed and plastered.[31]

Despite these improvements, the houses strongly resembled slave houses. Like the Sotterley slave house and the slave house at River View, the log house of the Harrod family measured about 17' x 15' (interior), probably for practical reasons. Miss Wilson recalled that the downstairs of the Harrod house was "hard to heat" with just one open fireplace, so any larger space would have required a second fireplace. Also like the slave houses, the first homes at Ben's Creek were unceiled. Instead of lath and plaster, the floorboards of the loft served as the downstairs "ceiling," and the hewn joists supporting the

Figure 100
Site of the Brooks log house after demolition, December
1978. Most nineteenth-century houses of rural black families
have shared, or will share, a similar fate. Photo: author.

floorboards were left exposed, giving an unfinished appearance to the interior. Thus the first-generation log houses basically resembled the traditional homes that the freedmen had left behind a few years before.[32]

Of the nineteen sites in Ben's Creek, the homestead of James and Cecilia Harrod has the most complete collection of historical resources and most clearly illustrates the effects of autonomy and landownership upon material culture. In charting the history of the place, it is clear that the Harrods were able to exercise considerable control over their living conditions and to improve them substantially. For example, the first section of the Harrod house (figure 96), built around 1869, resembled the single-unit log houses of slaves and tenants; but by the end of the century it had been enlarged into an imposing frame structure with a shed porch along the facade and a cross-gable pediment. Houses of the landless—such as the Cusic-Medley house or the tenant house at the Smithsonian—did not have such additions or decorative features.

Blanche Wilson is the oldest living person who recalls the Harrod homestead as it appeared when her grandparents lived there. Since her birth in 1903, her life has been closely associated with it. It was one of her three homes. Her father died when she was young, and her mother lived with relatives. One home was in New Jersey, another in Baltimore, and the third in Ben's Creek, close to the Harrod place. Throughout her youth, she visited her grandmother, Cecilia Harrod (figure 101), for long periods of time. In 1923 she began teaching in the district's log schoolhouse for black children and lived with her grandmother Harrod. In the 1930's her mother, Margaret Harrod Wilson, joined them and nursed the elderly Mrs. Harrod until her death in 1944. Miss Wilson and her mother then moved back into their own house in Ben's Creek and lived together until her mother's death. Miss Wilson is still there, in a house filled with artifacts and memories.[33]

Gifted with an alert and retentive mind, Miss Wilson learned the history of the farm and of Ben's Creek from her grandmother, mother, and other relatives and neighbors in the community. While the Harrod place today is an abandoned house with fields grown up in woodlands, Miss Wilson's recollections allowed us to re-create the farm's earlier appearance. The resulting reconstruction of the farmstead, the analysis of the evolution of the house over time, the sketches of the household furnishings, and descriptions of their uses, all provide insight into the fabric of black life in nineteenth-century Maryland.[34]

A farmstead resembles a small community, consisting as it does of separate, specialized, interdependent parts (figure 102). The principal components were the house, yard, outbuildings, gardens, animal shelters, work places, and fields. Paths and lanes connected this farm to others and to the market towns. At the Harrod farm, this road was Ben's Creek Road, along which stood other, similar farms. The Harrod farm stood on the west side of Ben's Creek Road and consisted of about six acres. It was developed on the edge of a plateau that dropped steeply to a creek and swamp about a hundred yards from the road. The original log house was built on high ground at the edge of this plateau and faced south. Its east gable end, to which the two-story frame addition was attached, was oriented toward Ben's Creek Road. A large stone chimney was on the west gable end, beyond which the plateau dropped down to the bottom land. A dirt drive led from Ben's Creek Road up to the house, passed by the paling fence that surrounded the house, and continued over to the complex of outbuildings located on the southwest side of the house. To the south and east of the dwelling were two fields that rotated in use, one being planted in feed corn and the other in clover or rye to serve as pasture. Behind the house (to the west) was a large

Figure 101
Cecilia Golder Harrod. Copy photograph, reproduced
through the courtesy of Blanche Wilson.

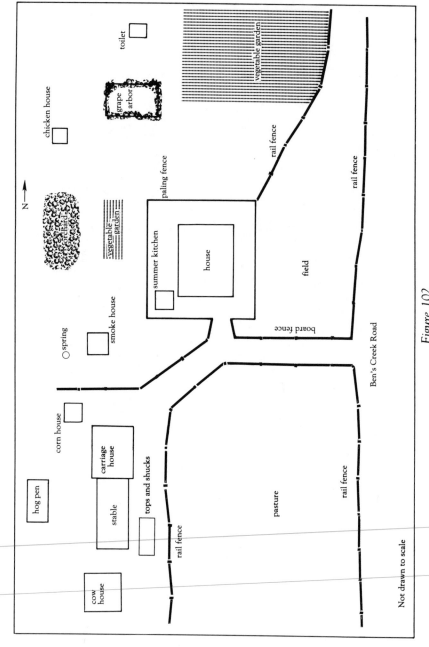

Figure 102

Farmstead of the Harrod family in the early 1900's, based on the recollections of Blanche Wilson.

garden and orchard that led back to the bottom land, which was too wet for cultivation and was left in forest.[35]

Fences surrounded the farm and defined specific areas within it, like walls in a house. They controlled the movement of farm animals and protected the crops. Rather than buy barbed wire or other types of fencing, the Harrods split chestnut rails and rived palings from white oak for the purpose. They used rail fences to border the entire farmstead and larger spaces within, such as the field and pasture, while paling fences enclosed the house yard, vegetable garden, and other small spaces. A board fence lined the drive leading up to the house.

The Harrods' outbuildings were like those of many other farm owners and were more numerous than those of tenants and wage hands, since the latter had less stock and equipment. None of the buildings remain today, but Miss Wilson recalls their approximate location, construction, and use. The principal outbuildings were the stable and carriage house, the cow house, corn house, smokehouse, chicken house, and privy. All were of frame construction. Some families, Miss Wilson recalled, had oxen instead of work horses, and those that raised tobacco had tobacco barns.[36]

Like most things on a farm, each outbuilding served many purposes. Even when an old outbuilding was dismantled, the lumber was reused to build another structure, or burned by the occupants, or, if the farm was abandoned, by neighbors. One example of the multiple use of an outbuilding was the stable and carriage house on the Harrod farm. The two-room building sheltered the buggy, harness, and other equipment on one side of the partition, and the horse on the other. In the loft underneath the gable roof were stored blades of corn used as fodder.

The Harrods raised corn and used almost the entire plant as feed for stock. They gathered it in separate stages. The tops were cut first, then the leaves (or blades) pulled, then the ear picked in the shuck. Unlike other farmers, Harrod did not chop up the stalks for fodder, but left them in the field and later cut them down and burned them in a pile. He stored other pieces of the plant separately and alternated them as part of the diet for the animals. The tops and shucks were kept in a specially constructed building that consisted of a frame of split rails placed close together and laid like rafters in a gable form, about six to seven feet tall at the apex and about fifteen feet in length. The tops of the corn were placed horizontally across the logs and then covered by another vertically aligned layer. After the ears of corn were shucked, the shucks were stored inside the shelter, which was enclosed by a paling fence. During the course of the year, the tops and shucks were fed to the stock, and the building served as a playhouse for children. "We all loved to play in those shucks," Miss Wilson recalled.

Miss Wilson added that the shucks were also used to stuff mattresses. They were "ragged out" (shredded) with a fork to make them soft, and then stuffed into bed ticking, either to make a new mattress or to thicken an existing one. "Everybody had corn shuck mattresses," she recalled, reiterating William Diggs's earlier testimony. Thus corn provided both food for animals and human comfort.[37]

After being shucked, the ears of corn were stored in the corn house, an outbuilding that measured about 10' x 15'. Like the corn house described by Nora Cusic (Chapter IV), it served a number of purposes. In addition to corn, Miss Wilson recalled that dried garden vegetables were kept there. The family raised black-eyed peas, white-eyed peas, white beans, and other legumes. After they were dried, Mrs. Harrod placed them in an old sheet or canvas and paddled them gently to make shelling easier. They were then stored in "196-pound flour barrels" in the corn house. (Such barrels of flour were advertised in the 1898 Sears, Roebuck catalog for $4.60.) Miss Wilson remembered that each barrel was about half full. Some of the beans, peas, and corn were saved as seed for the following year; the Harrods rarely bought seed.

Meat was also stored in the corn house. After the hogs were butchered, the meat was "salted down" inside the corn house, either in bins of salt or in trays of salt on plank shelves. (Miss Wilson did not know exactly which, "because we children didn't have much to do with that.") After a month or two, the meat was removed and wrapped in empty cornmeal bags, hung in the smokehouse, and smoked over a smothered fire of apple tree wood or sassafras.

Miss Wilson remembered that they saved apple tree branches especially for this purpose. After smoking, the meat was returned to the corn house and hung on hooks from the rafters. Sausage was also smoked and hung in the corn house. Thus, the corn house was like a pantry or cellar to the main house.[38]

Another farm structure was the hog pen, which was made of split rails and located southwest of the house near the bottom land. Pigs were penned here while being fattened on corn before slaughter in late November or December. Throughout most of the year they were given free range and usually stayed in the bottom land, which served as a wallow; they fed on the wide assortment of plants, roots, berries, and nuts there. They were also given slop from the kitchen.

Other outbuildings included separate houses for the chickens and turkeys. Turkeys also roosted in trees, Miss Wilson said, and ducks roosted on the ground wherever they wished. The poultry had free range during the day and fed in the field, pasture, and bottom land. Fowl was an important mainstay to the family, providing meat, eggs, and feathers for mattresses. Miss Wilson remembered that whenever chickens or ducks were killed, the feathers were saved, dried for several months, and then stuffed in bed ticking and pillows. Each bed had two mattresses, one of corn shucks and one of feathers. During the winter, the warmer feather mattress was placed on top of the corn shuck mattress, while during the summer, they were reversed. The thick mattresses provided excellent insulation for body heat and, with quilts piled on top, the residents stayed warm throughout the cold winter nights. This is another example, among many, of the family's self-sufficiency and industry.

A vegetable garden and grape arbor were planted beyond the paling fence behind (north of) the house. They raised "all sorts of vegetables": tomatoes, onions, beans, peas, turnip greens, sweet potatoes. To keep out the poultry and other animals, the garden was enclosed by a paling fence. Many of the vegetables were canned for consumption in the winter. Those that were not canned—such as root vegetables like turnips, parsnips, or "oyster plants"—were preserved in vegetable kilns similar to the ones described by Nora Cusic and by the families who lived in the sharecropper house now at the Smithsonian. The kiln was dug in the garden after the plants had been harvested and a paling fence put around it. In addition to garden vegetables, the family canned apples, peaches, and pears from their orchards. They also gathered wild berries. Miss Wilson fondly remembered that her industrious grandmother would start canning just as soon as the "blueberries jumped on the bush."

The grape arbor provided not only grapes for jams, but a place with cool shade as well. Also, a hole was dug in the ground in the grape arbor, and milk and butter were stored in crocks there, rather than in the spring. The family called this place the "cooler." When asked why they did not use the spring (as did the Cusics, the Medleys, and the families who lived in the sharecropper house at the Smithsonian), Miss Wilson could not explain and simply said, "That's the way we did it."[39]

The yards around this house, and many other farmhouses in the South, were kept clear of grass. Miss Wilson remembered, "any little clump of grass was chopped out with a hoe," and the yard swept daily with a bundle of "nice dogwood branches," selected from the woods nearby especially for the purpose. Sweeping the yard was called "scraggin' the yard," and the broom a "scrag broom." The dirt yard diminished the chances of a brush fire burning up to the house, and eliminated the grassy haven of mosquitoes, rodents, and snakes. Yet the yard was colorful with flowers. "Don't say a word about flowers," Miss Wilson said. Her grandmother loved them. She had all types: red roses, yellow roses, yellow, white, and pink chrysanthemums, and daffodils, to name a few. The former owners of Mrs. Harrod, the Parran family, frequently visited her and brought seeds, bulbs, and cuttings. "Everything the Parrans had, my grandmother had." There were also evergreens about the place, volunteer holly trees, and, of course, cedars. Flowers were not planted in the middle of the yard where "they would be in the way," but were planted along the paling fence around the house, lined the walkway up to the house, and "anywhere else Grandmother thought they would look nice." When in bloom, they were cut and used to decorate the interior. No members of sharecropper families mentioned having such a profusion of flowers around their houses.[40]

The outbuilding closest to the house was the small, frame "summer kitchen." During hot weather it contained the wood stove that was ordinarily kept in front of the fireplace in the log house. A metal stove pipe led to a ceramic chimney in the kitchen's ceiling. "We used to call chimneys like this an earthen jar." The location of the "summer kitchen" was not permanent, because they "used to move it around," though it always stayed relatively close to the house. "When they took the stove out, that was the biggest thing in there, and then they could move the building as they wanted." She did not know why they moved the kitchen, nor did she ever see how they moved it: "When I turned around, it would be moved." Miss Wilson did not know whether or not this summer kitchen was original to the log house of 1869.[41]

The construction of the Harrod house reflects the evolution of black landowners' houses in Maryland over a forty-year period (figures 103, 104). Using the house-building skills and community cooperation that they had practiced during slavery, James Harrod and his neighbors first built a one-story log house with a fieldstone chimney (figure 96). Except for the shed dormer window, board-and-batten siding, and a few other features that were added later, it resembled the log houses that they knew in slavery and later (figures 19, 22, 24). It contained one room downstairs and two upstairs. Most likely, the downstairs was originally divided into rooms without walls, like Abraham Medley's house (figure 81). The 1870 census of

Figure 103
Southeast elevation of the Harrod house, Ben's Creek. Photo: author.

Calvert County shows that the family consisted of only James and Selia [sic] Harrod and two daughters. By 1880 the family had grown to include five daughters plus Cecilia's father, William Golder.[42]

Being a self-employed farmer, Harrod was able to respond to the need for more space by adding onto the gable end of the log house a handsome two-story frame block, one bay deep (figure 103). The facade was three bays in width, with a central door flanked by windows, resulting in the tripartite, bilateral symmetry that was popular among rural landowners of moderate means in the late nineteenth and early twentieth centuries. The style of the new facade was heightened further by the wide front porch and the cross-gable pediment that accented the roof line. This addition made a strong statement to the outside world of prosperity and permanency, in contrast to the more roughly built original log houses.[43]

The new block's downstairs served as the parlor and the dining room on more formal occasions (figure 104). It consisted of one room with lathed and plastered walls and plain trim around the windows and doors. There were built-in closets, indicating the accumulation of material possessions; a framed-in chimney for a wood-burning stove; and a quarter-turn staircase with molded bannisters

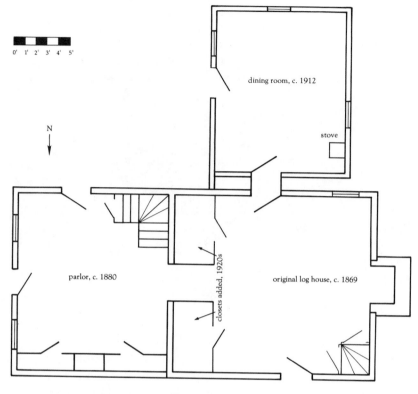

0' 1' 2' 3' 4' 5'

N

dining room, c. 1912

stove

parlor, c. 1880

closets added, 1920s

original log house, c. 1869

Figure 104
Evolution of the Harrod house, 1869–c. 1912.

and square newel post that suggest both stylistic aspirations and the money to achieve them. The large double-hung sash windows with six over three glass panes provided more interior illumination and ventilation than that provided by the small windows and doors of the original log house. The one upstairs room served as the parents' bedroom and was heated, unlike the upstairs of the log block. The frame of the new block was made entirely of commercially cut lumber and was fastened by nails, except for the primary members (the corner and center posts and sills), which were hewn and fastened by the traditional methods of mortise, tenon, and pegged joints. Thus the construction of this block of the late 1870's or early 1880's was a marriage of the old and the new.

In about 1912 ("when I was about nine years old," Miss Wilson said), another frame addition was built on to the original facade of the log house. It replaced the small "summer kitchen" and served exclusively as a dining room. The upstairs room, which was heated, was used as sleeping quarters. The walls upstairs and downstairs were lathed and plastered and whitewashed. The use of the downstairs solely as the dining room shows that yet another household activity had been given a room of its own. This is in keeping with the trend toward specialization of the uses of rooms.

The frame of this addition contained no homemade materials. All wood members were cut at a mill. They were either purchased, or sawn from the timber the Harrods felled on the property and hauled to the mill. Modern wire nails were used to attach the timbers. The addition was constructed by hired carpenters, not by the community, according to Miss Wilson. The construction of this last addition marked the final stage of the building of this house, and contrasts tellingly with the first homemade log dwelling.[44]

As the farm's layout and the house's evolution reflected the changing lifestyle of the Harrod family, so too did the interior furnishings. They illustrate the improvements in living conditions in comparison with slave and sharecropper houses, the more extensive acquisition of material things, and the more marked accumulation of fine things that would become heirlooms.

According to Miss Wilson, her grandparents' home was similar to most other landowners' homes that she visited, but was a little better appointed than most. For example, some homes had a bed in the downstairs parlor, whereas her grandparents' house did not. Despite the additions to the dwelling, the downstairs of the original log house remained the very heart of the homestead throughout the Harrod residency. Originally it served as the kitchen, dining room, and informal family gathering place. Miss Wilson recalled that the walls were whitewashed and kept clean of smoke and grime from the fireplace and stove. The plank floor, which did not have rugs, was swept daily.

The most prominent feature was the large, open fireplace. Blanche Wilson recalled seeing long rods across the fireplace. During Miss Wilson's mother's youth, her mother (Cecilia Harrod) suspended pots for cooking from these rods. In the early twentieth century, the fireplace was no longer used for cooking. Instead, it simply heated the kitchen in the early fall and late spring before the wood stove was installed for winter use. At that time, the fireplace was sealed over with a board specially designed for the purpose.

Though the tradition of cooking over the fireplace had given way to cooking on the wood stove by the early twentieth century, Miss Wilson recalled that her grandmother treated the grandchildren with "johnnycakes" baked in the fireplace. They were ashcakes, or thick patties of corn meal, that her grandmother Harrod wrapped in green poplar leaves and baked in ashes on the hearth; they were a staple of slaves (Chapter III). Blanche Wilson recalled that she and the other grandchildren enjoyed the "treat" of something different, and begged their grandmother to make some more. But ashcakes reminded her of slavery, and she replied, "No, I don't want to go back to those days." Though she may have been treated well by her owners, she was not nostalgic for days gone by.[45]

Most of the everyday things used in storing, preparing, cooking, and serving food were kept in the kitchen. Figure 105 shows the approximate arrangement of the larger pieces of furniture; the smaller details are omitted. A large pie safe, whose two doors had pierced tin panels, stood in the corner opposite the stairs. On its three shelves were stored the everyday dishes, cups, glasses, and flatware. Pots and pans were kept in a cupboard along the south wall (originally the front of the house). As in the sharecropper house at the Smithsonian Institution and in most small houses, the space underneath the stairs served as a closet. Among the large staples stored there were barrels of flour and meal, a ten-pound bag of salt, and a fifty-pound lard can of sugar. Along the east wall was a work table where the food was prepared, with shelves above. Miss Wilson said that the large closets presently built into the east wall were installed in the 1920's because the kitchen was "so large and hard to heat." Here, too, the plank floors were left bare.[46]

What we know today as the kitchen sink was located next to the back door, and consisted of a wash basin on a homemade box. Above it were two water pails on a shelf. A towel hung behind the door. The dishes were washed there, and the waste water tossed out the back door or saved as slop for hogs. A person coming in from work or washing up in the morning washed his hands and face there. Thus, the kitchen was similar in one way to the bathroom of today. Next to the back door was, of course, the most practical place to locate the washstand, which is probably why the same arrangement was found in the Medley house and in the sharecropper house in the Smithsonian.

The dining table stood in the middle of the room and was surrounded by six chairs. The sharecropper houses described earlier had only one table, in the kitchen, with two chairs and benches for the children, that doubled as the work and dining table. In this land-

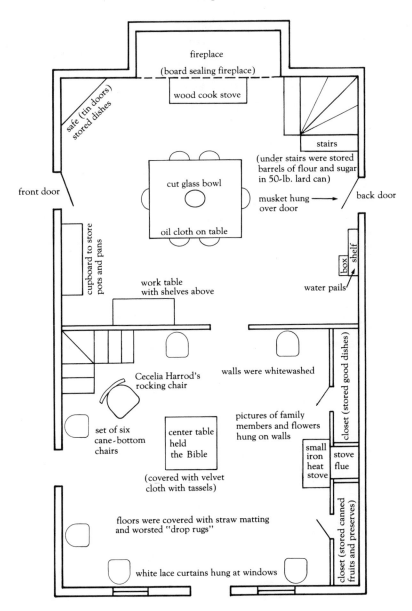

Not drawn to scale

Figure 105
Furnishings plan of the Harrod house, based on
Blanche Wilson's recollections of the early 1900's.

owner's house is our first example of a table being described solely as a "dining table." It was covered with an oilcloth that, like many things of Mrs. Harrod's, was treated with care. "Grandmother was just as particular with it as with a white cloth. You had better not put just anything on it." When asked if she remembered anything that her grandmother kept on the table, she described a "cut-glass bowl that was filled with flowers and fruit in the summer."[47]

The musket that James Harrod carried when a soldier in the Union Army hung over the door in the kitchen. He continued to use it for hunting. When asked why the gun was kept there, Miss Wilson explained, "It was not for decoration purposes like they do today, but just to get it out of the way." As in the Cusic-Medley house and other small homes with small or no closets, the walls were often used for storage.

The parlor in the downstairs of the addition of the 1880's was far more elaborately furnished than the parlors or sitting rooms of the homes of the landless. It was even higher style that those in many landowners' homes, since Miss Wilson recalled that some of those houses had beds downstairs, while others were not as nicely kept and furnished as her grandmother's. According to Miss Wilson, her grandmother had been a house servant for the Parran family during slavery, had lived with and used "nice things," and wanted to have them in her own home.

The parlor measured 13'3" x 15' inside the room. The quarter-turn stairway, with a paneled wall, molded bannisters, and newel post, that was built along the south and west walls, gave the room a formal and attractive appearance not found in houses of rural black tenants. While the walls did not have decorative cornices or chair rails, the brick stove flue was framed in, the windows and doors were trimmed with plain moldings, and the plaster was always kept neatly whitewashed and bright. The floors were made of narrow, tongue-and-groove floorboards (in contrast to the wide planks in the original log house), and were covered with straw matting and "worsted drop rugs." Placed around the room was a matching set of "six cane-bottomed oak chairs." There was no sofa. Unlike Abraham Medley, the man of the house (James Harrod) "was not particular about where he sat." It was Mrs. Harrod who had a special chair, a handsome rocker that matched the chairs in the set of six, except that it was larger and had arms. Miss Wilson still has the chair.[48]

White lace curtains and pictures on the walls added color and interest to the parlor. According to Miss Wilson, the pictures were mainly of a religious nature, but some were photographs of the family and prints of flowers. There was at least one photograph of each member of the family on view somewhere in the house. Adding to the decoration of the parlor was a circular "center table" placed in the middle of the room, in keeping with middle-class styles of the nineteenth and early twentieth centuries. "The center table," wrote American architect Andrew J. Downing in 1850, "is the emblem of the family circle." The Harrod's table was covered with a "velvet cloth with tassels," and no sharecropper house contained a table of comparable style.[49]

The large family Bible was kept on the center table. It is significant to find a religious object given such an esteemed place in a room intended for social interaction. The Bible was more than an ornament, as it was often used in family readings. Its prominent place and its use show that this family did not separate social life and religion. The faith of this family had been forged during slavery, like the faith of William Jordan (Chapter III). During that time, Miss Wilson said, her grandmother was taught by the Parrans and by her mother that, through God's grace, she "was just as good as anyone," and that it was "how you lived your life" that counted, not your social position. This faith in God was a source of strength for all the Harrods, and their respect for and daily use of the family Bible were simply a small statement of their faith.[50]

The parlor was also used for storage, which is in keeping with the tradition of giving rooms multiple uses. There were no closets in the original log house, so shelves, cupboards, and pie safes had been used. The addition of the 1880's solved the storage problem, and the walls on either side of the stove flue were boxed in and made into closets with paneled doors. Inside were stored the more precious, breakable, seldom-used objects: the set of fine dinnerware for special occasions and scores of jars of canned fruit, preserves, and vegetables that the Harrods put up for the winter, and other things.

When asked to recall her favorite thing in her grandmother's house, Miss Wilson remembered a wooden lap desk lined with velvet and inlaid with mother-of-pearl. Kept in the parlor on a side table, its hinged top covered a space for storing paper and pens. Miss Wilson thought that this was a present to her grandmother from the Parran family. No desk or piece of furniture of this quality was mentioned as part of the furnishings of any sharecropper house surveyed. Miss Wilson's childhood fascination with the lap desk indicates her early esteem for things literary and educational. When she grew up, she pursued these interests and became a schoolteacher in the community.[51]

Just as the parlor of the Harrod house was more elaborately furnished than were those of sharecropper houses, so too were the three
bedrooms upstairs, the furnishings of which also reflected the Harrods' appreciation for fine things and their ability to buy them. Most
of the furniture, Miss Wilson recalled, was purchased from firms in
Baltimore, which was "far from my grandparents, yet close," thanks
to the steamboat that stopped at nearby wharves along the Patuxent
River. Like the railroads that served other isolated rural counties, the
steamboat enabled families of some means to purchase objects of
contemporary style directly from manufacturing centers, and thus to
participate in the national material culture. Thanks to the steamboat, the Harrods did not have to rely upon themselves or local
craftsmen for furniture. Manufactured pieces were seen as a mark of
upward mobility and status, and were preferred to the more common
homemade objects.

Blanche Wilson's grandparents' bedroom was the house's most
formally furnished room (figure 106). The plastered walls were kept
brightly whitewashed, and lace window curtains added a touch of
frill. The large oak bed that stood between the two front windows
was part of a set of bedroom furniture, ordered from Baltimore, that
consisted of a bed, a bureau, a washstand with towel rack, six cane-
bottomed chairs (different from the ones downstairs), and a small
rocker. The bed dominated the room, and it seemed all the more
massive due to its two mattresses, one of corn shucks and one of
feathers. "It took something to make up that bed nice," Miss Wilson
recalled, especially for a child. In the front corner of the room near
the head of the stairs stood the oak washstand. On top of it were two
pitchers, a basin, her grandfather's shaving mug, a soap dish, and,
below, a chamber pot. Towels hung on a rack above the stand. On
the opposite side of the bed were two chairs of the set of six, which
of course were moved about the room (chairs rarely stay in one
place, though museum exhibits usually display them as if they do). In
front of the brick stove flue was a small wood-burning stove and a
wood box. This is an early example of a heated upstairs room. In the
back corner of the room was an oak bureau with a framed mirror
attached. There were no closets in the bedroom. At first, the Harrods simply hung their clothes from a long board on the wall to
which hooks were attached. Blanche Wilson recalls that during her
late childhood they added a shelf over the hooks, which they hung a
curtain from to conceal and protect the clothes. Eventually they purchased a wardrobe.

By the time Miss Wilson was a child, all of the Harrod children

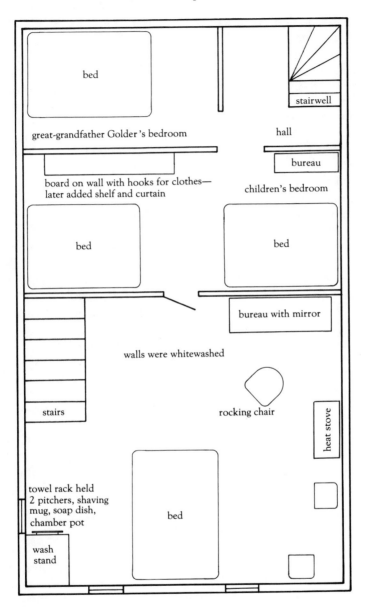

Not drawn to scale

Figure 106
Furnishings plan of upstairs of Harrod house, based on
Blanche Wilson's recollections of the early 1900's.

had grown and left home, so she did not know the house when children were growing up in it. According to her mother, one of the two rooms in the upstairs of the log house had been the bedroom of the six daughters, and the other was for their grandfather, William Golder. His room was the smaller of the two and was at the top of the stairs (figure 106). It was probably the parents' room when the log house was first built, before he moved in. After the frame block was constructed in the late 1870's or early 1880's, the parents moved into the new bedroom and gave this room to Golder, Cecilia Harrod's father. He lived there until his death in 1897.[52]

Like all the members of this family, William Golder was an intelligent and industrious person. Born in 1805, he had been a slave on the Parran farm and was a craftsman who made things to fill his family's needs, a family trait passed on to his daughter Cecilia. Among the things he made during slavery were a rolling pin and wooden bowl that Miss Wilson has preserved (figure 55). He made baskets, and taught his son Charles that craft. Miss Wilson has saved at least two of her uncle Charles's baskets (figure 56). They were "thrown down the hill" by vandals after the Harrod house was abandoned, but Miss Wilson rescued them.

The daughters' bedroom had two wooden beds, of a different style from the parents', that were also purchased from Baltimore. They stood opposite one another and took up most of the space in the room. Like the parents' bed, they each had a homemade corn-shuck mattress and a feather mattress that were reversed according to the season. The other pieces of furniture were a bureau and some chairs, probably from the same set as in the parents' bedroom. There were no closets, so hang-up clothes were kept on hooks along the walls. Unlike the upstairs of most small log or frame houses of that era, the walls were lathed and plastered, which insulated the interior, and the room was brightened by whitewashing.[53]

Because six children occupied a room that had little space except for furniture, there was little space each child could call her own. This is in contrast to today's middle-class home, which may have no more than two or three children per room. As family size decreases, it is more and more common to have one child per bedroom. This acquisition of personal space by children is one of the more important changes in housing and family life that emerges from a comparison with the past.

Blanche Wilson's descriptions of her grandparents' home could serve as an invaluable asset in the creation of a museum exhibit. But Blanche Wilson is not alone; I have cited some others—William

Diggs, Benjamin and Nellie Ross, James Scriber, and Abraham Medley—and there are many more like them throughout southern Maryland who are valuable resources for preserving the people's history. McKinley Gantt, the son of former slaves who became land-owners, provides another critical link to that history with his remarkable stories of his parents' torturous route "up from slavery." Whereas we must picture the Harrod homestead in our minds, we have photographs of the Gantt parlor as McKinley Gantt's father and mother actually furnished it in the nineteenth and early twentieth centuries that would be vital aids in creating an exhibit honoring these people's past.

Gantt's stories of his parents' lives shed light on the experiences of slaves, overseers, and planters of the ante-bellum era, and his descriptions of his family's daily life and their skills in "making do" in the post-bellum era reflect the continuity of traditional ways of life. Gantt's testimony is rich, complex, not always precise in detail, and, all things considered, one of the most vivid accounts we have of the struggle for human dignity within the presence of pervasive racial oppression.

Like Benjamin Ross, McKinley Gantt is proud of his father, and remembers his father's stories about his life as a young slave (figure 107). His father was born a slave on the plantation of Dr. John Parker at Parker's Wharf in Calvert County on the Patuxent River, and Gantt recalled hearing that, while many planters were mean to their slaves, "Dr. Parker was good to his slaves. He would feed them, and clothe them, and not work them to death like some others did." Albert Gantt was an adventuresome boy, and enjoyed going on trips within his limited world. Dr. Parker favored Gantt, and took him on his travels through Calvert County, riding "behind the carriage to open the gates." Among the houses that Dr. Parker visited was the nearby farm of Dr. Leonard Mills. It was neither elegant nor especially large, having three rooms down and three up. But in comparison to the rough log houses of the slaves and overseers, it was an impressive structure. While most log houses measured approximately 16' x 18', Dr. Mills's house was 29' x 46', and around it stood outbuildings, including an icehouse and two large tobacco barns, and slave cabins. Young slaves would have kept Albert company and exchanged news with him while he waited for Dr. Parker to finish his consultation. As they drove away, they passed fields of tobacco and corn where slaves were at work, and the forests that provided logs for the slave houses. A decade later, Albert Gantt, now a free man and a veteran of the Union Army, returned to Calvert County

Figure 107
Family photograph of Albert Gantt.

and managed to buy that farm of 150 acres. At that moment he acquired one of the largest landholdings and finest houses owned by a black farmer in southern Maryland (figure 108).[54]

How was Gantt, a freed slave, able to buy this land? There are no simple explanations, because we are involved with people who left no written evidence of their thoughts; yet we can get important clues from some stories that Albert Gantt told his son, McKinley. According to McKinley, his father said that "some of the colored people didn't want to be free because they didn't have no place to go. If the master had said, 'you gotta leave here now!' why they'd been in bad trouble. Where would they go?"[55] This was perhaps the response of elderly slaves. But Gantt was young and ambitious, personal characteristics that were major factors in his becoming a major landowner.

Rather than wait for emancipation, Gantt freed himself by joining the Union Army: "When Abe Lincoln put out the call for the colored troops to come help win the war, my father joined." Unlike Joseph Ross in Charles County, who ran away to join the Union

Figure 108
McKinley Gantt in front of the Gantt home in
Calvert County, Maryland. Photo: author.

Army, Albert Gantt was able to gain the permission of Dr. Parker, who told him that he was welcome to return after the war. Albert joined the U.S. Colored Troop, Volunteer Light Artillery Brigade, according to the commemorative citation that hangs in the living room, and fought in the critical, bloody battles in northern Virginia in the last years of the war: Bermuda Hundred, Cold Harbor, and Petersburg. In the fierce fighting at Chickahominy Swamp, Gantt's leg was broken when his horse was shot out from under him. After he recovered, he was sent to Brownsville, Texas, where he was discharged in 1866. Rather than stay in the West, and perhaps become a member of the 10th Cavalry, the famous black regiment of Indian fighters, or buy a farm in a new land where he had not been a slave, Gantt returned to Calvert County and the Parker plantation. When asked why his father made this decision, McKinley Gantt said, "Well, you know they say a chicken will come home to roost, and that's just what he did."

Upon his return, McKinley Gantt said that Dr. Parker told his father: "You can stay in this little ole house that you're living in [one of the log slave houses on the plantation]. But I tell you what I want you to do. Find yourself a boat and you oyster and fish, and you can make a living. Oysters will bring you 25¢ a bushel. Bring me oysters, fish, and things like that, and that's your rent."[56]

His father then acquired a boat, perhaps simply a rowboat or perhaps a "bugeye," a popular and efficiently designed sailing vessel used by Maryland watermen, said by one authority to have been developed in part by early African slaves in Maryland. Because the Parker plantation had a landing known as Parker's Wharf on the Patuxent River, Gantt could dock his boat near his home and work the rivers and the Bay for oysters, crabs, and fish. According to his son, he "set out hand lines with homemade bait" to catch crabs and fish. As for expenses, he had to purchase a boat and some fishing equipment, but "most of the fishing stuff, they made themselves." Thus, Albert Gantt, who had little money after slavery except his savings from Union Army pay, could make a living as a waterman with little initial capital investment.[57]

Albert Gantt worked as a waterman for about three years. Then Dr. Parker "come to Pa and say, 'You know how to work, and I got a farm I'm going to put you on.'" He stayed there for a "right smart while," then moved up to Baltimore to work for the customs house. While his son did not explain how he acquired this job, it may have been through political patronage, since Albert Gantt was a "lifelong Republican." The names of ships entering the harbor had to be registered with customs. This job was more profitable than that of waterman, and required no initial cash outlay. As for skills, they could be learned on the job by a willing student. "My father could neither read nor write, but he could print. What he saw on the boat, he would print that on a card and take it to the customs house. That paid him $300 a year. Man, he was somebody then! He stayed up there about two or three years. Then he came on back home and bought this place. He stayed there long enough to save close to a thousand dollars. This place cost $600."[58]

By working several jobs successfully, and by not remaining a farm laborer exclusively, Gantt was able to make and save enough money to buy the house. But money alone was not enough, because local whites had to be willing to sell. Had Gantt not been trusted by the white community, which knew him well through his years of work on the Parker place, it probably would not have allowed him to buy. According to McKinley, Albert was in the local store one day when he overheard Mr. Thomas Ireland, who had bought the Mills farm, saying that he wanted to sell the farm. Rather than discuss his desire to buy the farm in front of an audience, Albert Gantt did not say a

Figure 109
Family photograph of Aleitha Gantt.

word, left the store, and waited outside until Ireland left and was alone. He told Ireland that he wanted to buy the place and, when asked if he could pay the price of six hundred dollars, he replied that he could pay two hundred down and so much a year. Ireland replied that he trusted Gantt and was willing to accept the terms. Thus Gantt was able to keep a large portion of his savings from his job in Baltimore and buy a fine farm, the good qualities of which he had known since boyhood.

At first his wife, Aleitha, was alarmed by his daring to risk their savings, and refused to have any part of the purchase. But Gantt, determined to make this a joint venture, convinced her to drive with him to Prince Frederick, and together they signed the deed. Thus Gantt's ambition, hard work, and ability to make the most of his skills, plus the cooperation of a few whites in the community and

Figure 110
Side yard and back length of Mills-Ireland-Gantt
homeplace. Photograph shows the well that McKinley Gantt used
and the paling fence rived by his parents. Photo: author.

jobs that provided a cash income, all enabled him to become a land-owner.[59]

Albert and Aleitha Gantt worked as a team, and their joint efforts helped the farm prosper. They provided much of the labor in the cultivation of their cash crop, tobacco, and hired hands only when necessary. According to McKinley Gantt, his mother "worked right alongside his father" and "could do the work of any man" (figure 109). She helped her husband build one of the tobacco barns, as well as the paling fence that still surrounds the front of the house (figure 110). Its construction is indicative of their work together. They felled trees on the property and sawed them into logs with a crosscut saw, Aleitha on one end and Albert on the other. Next they split the logs and shaped them into pickets for the fence. "She had an ole axe, and he had one, and she would be on one end, and he on the other, and they'd bust it [split the log]. Then he would take his froe and go to work. Them palings are perfect, aren't they?"[60]

The outbuildings, storage places, and vegetable garden were further evidence of their self-sufficiency. In the outbuildings—the corn house, tobacco barn, smokehouse, icehouse, and chicken house—they preserved the products of their labor. To the north of the house was a large vegetable garden. Among the many types of produce that they raised was a type unknown to me: "blue head greens," which grew "about three feet high and had leaves about a foot long." They were boiled in a pot outside the house: "You never had anything nicer." They also raised "sembling gourds," which apparently resembled common gourds, since one end was bulbous and the other end was a long tube. They were left in the sun to dry, hollowed out, and used as "drinking cups." They were kept by the water buckets in the kitchen. "That was cheap," Gantt recalled. "Didn't cost them nothing."

Cabbage, which we now know to be especially rich in vitamin C, was basic to their diet and was preserved through the winter in "cabbage pens," an easily made shelter that protected the cabbage from the frost. They were commonly used by white and black families throughout Maryland, including the families who lived in the tenant house in the Smithsonian. Gantt remembered how they were made. His parents first uprooted the cabbage from the garden, dug a shallow trench, and transplanted the cabbage into the trench, covering the roots with dirt. Close to that was dug another trench, and row after row of cabbage was transplanted to form a square, which was then enclosed by a low fence of wooden rails, "like a hog pen." Logs or boards were laid across the rails, and over these were placed thick pine boughs to keep the frost off the cabbage. "They'd keep all winter. I don't care how cold it got, you could go out there and get a head of cabbage." This is one example among many of how families maintained a nutritious and varied diet before the days of refrigeration.

One of the most important outbuildings was the smokehouse. According to Gantt, "Everybody had hogs. My father used to have them, don't know how many. Used to kill them ourselves. Back then, everybody smoked their meat. . . . Man, that smoked meat was the best you ever tasted. Everything's changed. Used to smoke meat with apple tree wood, that would give it a different relish. Some would use sassafras. . . . Hang the meat up on rods with a wire running through it. Smother the fire and smoke that meat just as brown, and it would taste to death!" Unlike many black farmers, who could afford only hogs, the Gantts raised cows and slaughtered one each winter. The sides of beef were also cured in the smokehouse. "That would taste good too," Gantt recalled.[61]

Despite these times of comparative plenty, Albert and Aleitha Gantt remembered hard times when food was scarce, and told their children stories about life in bondage. Gantt recalled the stories about his mother's owner, Duke Barnes, whose farm was not far from the Gantt home.

"My mother was a slave of Duke Barnes. He was a man who just didn't care for slaves, and he just treated them like, like they were slaves. . . . I heard my father say, 'Dr. Parker was a really good man to his slaves, but Barnes treated his slaves bad.' He wouldn't feed them. Had to go, had to work, they'd better, or he'd beat the devil out of them. And land, he had land for the dogs, he had some kind of land, and he had some sort of colored people. . . .

"He had a bunch of them in there cleaning up the barn and them that he was hot with, he'd tie them up by the thumbs and put the rope across a tie pole and swing them such that their feet would touch, and then he'd get up there and whup, whup, till he got tired of whipping, then he'd go sit back and read his paper. After he rested up, he'd go back to whipping again. And slaveholders around the neighborhood would actually tell him: 'Why you whip those niggers that way?' 'Ah, I don't pay no 'count to them, they ain't no more than animals no way.' 'You hear those niggers, why ain't you feed them?' 'They're nothing.'

"Before he died, you see, people got free then. And certain ones that he treated bad and whip like that, he wanted them to come see him. They had left the place then, and he sent for them to come. Some came, and some didn't. Man, the devil came after him. He told them to drive that black ox out of the yard, he was dying. On his bed, dying, he said, 'Drive that black ox out the yard, he standing there gazing at me, and I don't want to see him.'

"Ole man Duke Barnes, he was something. My mother said, 'Wonder if he didn't see those switches that he'd been beating those men with?' Those things were haunting him."

Asked about overseers on slave plantations, Gantt recalled hearing that they too had hard times.

"Most plantations in Calvert County had overseers. Had a little better log house than slaves. You see, they'd treat the overseer bad, too. I heard my father say that he [Parker] had more colored people down on his place than were needed, and they hired him [Gantt's father] to a man over in Bowen's Neck, near Prince Frederick. This man didn't have no slaves, but he used to hire slaves and they say, he had a right good little farm.

"One day, they sent him after food, and he had an overseer there too. The overseer went with him to get his food, and coming back, one of them ole rich ones come along, riding a horse. He [his father] had a bucket in one hand and another bucket on top of his head. He

rode up there and told the overseer: 'Take that bucket off that nigger's head and put it in your hand and carry it too.' He took his
horsewhip and whipped that overseer: 'You're no more than that
nigger. If I ever come along this road, and catch you going along and
that nigger got a whole handful of food and you walking with your
hands in your pockets!' He took that whip and whipped that overseer
all across the top of his head. Overseer couldn't say anything. Better
not! So in a way, that bunch had quite a few white slaves too."[62]

Despite these experiences of insult and brutality, the Gantts were
not reduced to abject subservience, and they clearly retained a
healthy measure of self worth that their photographs reflect (figures
107, 109). Due to their cooperative work and their talents in farming,
their land prospered, and Albert Gantt was able to buy even more
acreage, until he finally owned about 250 acres.

This placed him among the top 12 percent of the black landowners in Calvert County in 1910. In addition, Gantt was one of the
trustees of the Island Creek Church and, because of his secure finan-
cial position, was a member of the building committee responsible
for the construction of the handsome neo-Gothic frame church in
1881. As a veteran of the Union Army, church leader, prominent
landowner, and successful farmer, Gantt was a leader of the black
community in Calvert County.[63]

His home illustrates his success. Unlike the Harrods, who constructed and then enlarged their home, the Gantts purchased a late
eighteenth- or early nineteenth-century plantation house. Its interior
decorative features—chair rails, cornices, and mantelpieces—reflect
that period. The furnishings illustrate how, as successful landowners,
the Gantts were able to buy into the mainstream of the material
culture popular in their day. Upon their death, their son, McKinley
Gantt, and his young wife moved into the house. They kept his
parents' furnishings more or less in place. A few years later, McKinley's wife died childless. He continued to live in the house, changing
his parents' parlor hardly at all (figure 111).

The Gantts' furniture was similar to that advertised in mail-order
catalogs, as revealed in a tour around the parlor. The upholstered
furniture closely resembled a "five piece framed upholstered parlor
suite" advertised in the 1902 Sears, Roebuck catalog for $12.45 that
consisted of a "sofa, rocker, easy chair and two parlor chairs." Perhaps the most imposing piece in the room was the pump organ with
a mirror and decorative scrollwork, similar to the "Acme Queen Parlor Organ" illustrated in the 1902 Sears, Roebuck catalog for $27.45
(figure 112). There were two varieties of parlor tables, one with

Figure 111
McKinley Gantt in the parlor of his parents furnished
around the turn of the century. Photo: author.

straight "fancy turned legs" (figure 113) and one with a "shaped top"
and curved "graceful legs" (figure 111), shown in the same catalog
for $1.15 and $6.75, respectively. Other chairs in the room included
what appeared to be one of a set of dining chairs (figure 113) advertised in the 1897 Sears, Roebuck catalog for $1.00 and described as
having a

> high back, beautifully carved and embossed panel, elegantly
> turned spindles, has a fine handwoven cane seat, fancy turned
> legs, bent braced arm pieces securely fastened to back and seat.
> It is made of the choicest kiln dried rock elm, is warranted
> to be perfectly put together and substantially finished in antique
> oak.[64]

A rattan rocker and a cane rocker also among the furnishings were
not of types illustrated in the catalogs. Against one wall was a four-
shelf bookcase with a glass door, filled with books and magazines,
and of a type somewhat similar to a bookcase advertised in the 1897
catalog for $8.00.[65]

Figure 112
Pump organ in Gantt's parlor. Photo: author.

Figure 113
Detail of Gantt's parlor. Photo: author.

Accessories included a handsome clock on the mantel, similar to the "Acme Queen Cathedral Gong Clock" adorned with a bronze figure of horse and rider. In the 1902 catalog, this "mantel clock" sold for $5.75. The oil-burning "banquet lamp" on one of the parlor tables (figure 111) could not be exactly identified, but it resembled one sold for $6.95 in the 1902 catalog and described as "delicately tinted and the decoration consists of natural color flowers, put on the globe before the last firing by free hand work." The floor was covered with a plain carpet, highlighted by an Oriental-design area rug without fringe that resembled the moquette rug that sold for $1.95 in the 1897 catalog.[66]

Piped into the fireplace, Gantt's wood stove was very much like the "Acme Air-Tight Heating Stove with hot blast draft and hot air circulating system," advertised in the 1902 catalog for $5.65. On the walls hung large framed portraits (photographs) of Albert and Aleitha Gantt, a picture of the Sacred Heart of the Virgin Mary, a framed award Albert Gantt won in an agricultural contest, numerous other prints of landscapes and flowers, and Albert Gantt's commemorative discharge from the Union Army. Above the mantel hung an embroidery with the aphorism, "What is Home Without Mother."[67]

These artifacts were more numerous, decorative, varied, and costly than the furnishings of the tenant families I surveyed. The objects in the parlor cited above for which prices were given cost $77.10. An informant named Arthur Smith, whose father was a tenant farmer in the early 1900's, said his father's wages were nine to twelve dollars per month, so the few parlor furnishings that were cited from the total of the Gantts' possessions would have represented more than six months' income of a nearby tenant farmer.[68]

In a highly transient era, this is one of the comparatively few houses in America that has been lived in by only two generations of the same family for more than a century. Its future is imperiled. Soon after his discharge from the infantry after World War I, Gantt and his bride moved into his parents' house, and he never left. He said that he was recently offered over $100,000 for his 250 acres, but he refused to sell. For years he raised tobacco and worked in the Calvert County courthouse. He lived alone in the old plantation house, living in many ways a traditional lifestyle, forsaking running water, indoor plumbing, and electricity. He lived almost exclusively in the kitchen and the adjoining dining room, which he converted into his bedroom. He slept on a cot. Modern facilities included a telephone and a transistor radio, but he still used kerosene lamps for light and wood stoves for heat. He usually cooked over a butane gas range, but from time to time he returned to the old wood stove in the kitchen, especially when baking corn bread, which "didn't dry out so bad" as when baked in the gas range: "It's that slow heat." He was concerned about the gradual deterioration of his house, but in his old age, it was too much for him to maintain alone.[69]

In the spring of 1980 McKinley Gantt died. Pending resolution of his estate, his house was locked up by court order. If none of his nephews or nieces, who are said to be his heirs, are especially interested in the place, the house will likely be torn down, the furnishings sold and dispersed, and the land developed into small home lots.[70]

Comparing black landowners' houses with those of the landless reveals that there was little difference in material circumstances immediately after emancipation. Like immigrants newly arrived in a foreign land, both groups built houses like those they had known before, and continued with traditional skills and customs, including the survival strategy of "making do." Also like immigrants, the family unit remained essential: men, women, and children worked to sustain the whole.

Gradually, however, the landowners' material environment developed marked differences. Their farmsteads resembled complete entities, with a central house supported by a network of outbuildings, gardens, and fields. Slave and tenant houses, while they might have had some outbuildings, were not the center of an entire farmstead, but were more like service buildings to the landowner's house. In landowning communities such as Ben's Creek, all the houses were more or less on an equal scale, while houses of tenants were by no means equal to the neighboring "main house." Thus, the farmsteads of black landowners were set in a community context that exhibited a greater degree of autonomy and equality. Absent were those constant reminders of lower status that tenants experienced.

In closing, the question remains whether the houses, yards, and interiors of black family homes were distinguishable from those of white families of the same social and economic class. It appears that improvisation ("making do") characterized black homes, but that is not a uniquely black activity; the Cusics also improvised. While certain threads ran through the various case studies—for example, I found multiple uses of objects and rooms, and ubiquitous religious artifacts—these are not exclusively Afro-American expressions. From this study, it appears that socioeconomic factors—that is, freedom and landownership as opposed to slavery and tenancy—most influenced the material culture of these southern Maryland families. How-

ever, this does not mean that uniquely Afro-American characteristics were not present, but only that they were not seen in this
early stage of analysis. It is hoped that treating the houses and material culture of black people as significant historical topics, and dem-
onstrating the rich resources available and the methods of investigating them, will prompt further studies. Most likely, these studies will
discern uniquely Afro-American characteristics in everyday material
culture like those found in black decorative arts. Furthermore, these
studies will compare more systematically Afro-American historical
houses and material culture with those of rural Southern whites of
the same class, as well as with those of other ethnic groups. In this
way we may be able to assess more clearly the influence of class and
ethnicity on material culture, and reflect this in our museum exhibits. These are challenges that lie ahead.

In summary, we have seen that black people, living in a racial and
economic environment hostile to their aspirations of equality and
upward mobility ever since their arrival, have had to make do to
survive, and their houses and their material culture represent both
their creative efforts and their restrictions. Even the most formal of
the black landowners' houses in southern Maryland were comparable
only to those of the rural middle class, and the furnishings of the
Gantts—one of the wealthiest black families in rural southern turn-
of-the-century Maryland—were on the level of mail-order catalog
furniture. But the homesteads that slaves, farm tenants, and landowners described show that these people were not minions to their
material environment or socioeconomic restrictions. We have seen
how, in an extreme situation, Abraham Medley organized his space
into rooms without walls. Skills were passed from one generation to
the next, enabling people to build log houses that were not just shacks,
and to make medicine, furniture, household utensils, quilts, and other
domestic articles. The land around them provided their food and
building materials. One may see only conformity in the floor plans
and designs of most of the old dwellings. But learning about the residents and their descendants demonstrates that poor and humble surroundings need not produce a poor and humble spirit. People can and
do rise above their environment.

EPILOGUE
Celebrating the People's History:
"From Somebody Who Wore the Shoe"

The sketches and the more detailed case studies of the houses and material culture presented so far are intended to help us visualize the physical, domestic world in which rural blacks lived. But the object of this study, after all, is not just to record the people's history in written descriptions and photographs, but also to encourage other ways of researching and presenting our history. Museum exhibits are one important way of doing that. As this study has shown, material culture is more than lifeless artifacts. The study of objects should lead back to the people who used them. Ideally, an exhibit should be living; there should be historical interpreters who can bring the past to life. But for many conventional museums it is virtually impossible to have interpreters with the exhibit always present, so it is an important moment in historical preservation and education when they are. The inclusion of the tenant house at the Smithsonian and of oral informants related to it in the Festival of American Folklife in 1978 was just such an occasion and will be examined as a suggestive example.

As a result of the research I had completed on the tenant house, the Office of the Folklife Program at the Smithsonian Institution contracted with me in the summer and fall of 1978 to organize sessions with participants about traditional black community life and sharecropping. The tenant house and the area around it, described in the Introduction, were to serve as the setting. Since the men and women that I had interviewed during my research on this house and in my earlier work in Maryland were quite knowledgeable about black community life and the lifestyle of tenants, I invited twenty-one of them to participate, along with the scholar Arthur Raper. The participants were divided into small, compatible groups to attend on alternating days throughout the seven-day period of the festival. There were two panel discussions daily in front of the house, open to questions from the audience (figure 114). A demonstration of butter

Figure 114
Panel discussion on sharecropping and traditional
ways of life of black families at the Festival of American
Folklife. Left to right: George McDaniel, William Diggs, Howard
Lyles, Clem Dyson, Amanda Nelson, Luther Stuckey,
George Johnson, and Charlie Sayles. Photo: Mary Sue McDaniel.

churning, one of the everyday activities in a house such as this, was set up. Each participant was asked to bring personal artifacts about which he or she could talk easily that illustrated the traditional lifestyle of black families. Tables were arranged around the house, and the objects displayed on them. Taking turns, some participants demonstrated butter churning, while others were seated at tables and informally discussed the histories of the family artifacts with small groups or individual visitors.

Each participant made significant contributions. Vivian Harley helped to educate visitors about the tenant house. Her husband, Edward Harley, grew up in it, and she had visited it in the 1960's as a social worker for the Savoy family. She stationed herself inside the house, and to scores of visitors she told of the life of her husband and of the Savoys in this house. She fascinated visitors with stories of how her husband, who was one of eight or nine children in this house, and his brothers and sisters, all slept in one of the bedrooms upstairs. "As many as could slept in one bed, and the spillover slept on pallets on the floor." She also emphasized, "Being poor did not mean you had to live in a dirty house," and explained that the residents she knew made a serious effort to keep this tenant house clean. She spoke with respect of women in houses such as this, who made do with so little.[1]

Other women associated with the tenant house—such as Elizabeth "Mamie" Johnson, Helen James, Mary Parker, and Octavia Parker Proctor—also added their recollections about life there. Rachel Diggs, mother of William Diggs and daughter of William Jordan, told of her family's rich history, portions of which have been described in previous chapters. Florence Hallman, Ida Hallman, Howard Lyles, Ora Lyles, and Evelyn Herbert explained old-time ways of life in Montgomery County, Maryland. Amanda Nelson, the wife of a former sharecropper from St. Mary's County, who had contributed to the research on the tenant house in the winter of 1978, sparked the panel discussions with her informative stories and gentle humor. Explaining a full day's work for a woman on a farm years ago, she described working in the house as well as in the fields, with her baby not far away, asleep on a quilt in a box in the shade. On one level, these stories of individual experiences were simply entertaining anecdotes; on another, they conveyed to the audience the cooperation and discipline that were integral to the lives of many black families. The story Amanda Nelson told about her son, Norman, who was in the audience, is an example.

"My mother only had to speak to me twice to get me to do something. By the third time, I knew she meant business, and I brought my children up the same way. Well, it was my two boys' responsibility to bring in the wood every night. It was a chore they didn't like, but I had to have my wood in the morning to start my fire. Well, one night it was real cold, and I asked my boys twice about bringing in the wood. They said they were going to do it, but pretty soon I heard them upstairs going to bed. I waited until they were nice and warm in the bed, don't you know, and then I called up to them, 'Boys, I'm waiting for my wood.' They had to get up, get dressed, and go out in the cold and bring in that wood, and they never forgot to bring in that wood again."[2]

To explain the raising and curing of tobacco, the Parker sisters brought several stalks of tobacco from their own tobacco barn, and Clem Dyson brought his own tobacco knife, spear, and stake and showed how tobacco stalks were cut in the field, speared, and hung to dry on stakes in barns (figure 114).

Figure 115
William Diggs telling stories to an
audience of school children, Festival of
American Folklife. Photo: author.

A born storyteller, William Diggs was highly successful in educating people about traditional black family life. He brought literally a truckload of artifacts from his private collection, and used them as the basis for some of the accounts given in Chapters II, III, and IV. Large groups of visitors gathered around him as he engaged them with a wide range of animated stories related to his artifacts (figure 115). Among the objects that he explained was a ball and chain (figure 114) that was "sawn off my great-grandfather's leg during slavery" (William Tubman, Sr.). Showing the old photograph of his grandfather, William Tubman, Jr., who was also a slave, Diggs told stories of his ancestors' life in bondage. After lifting that ball and chain, seeing the photograph of a man born in slavery, and hearing Diggs's stories, young students did not soon forget the burden of slavery.

Other artifacts that Diggs put to educational use were several homemade dolls and hand puppets. One of the hand puppets—a heavyset black "Mammy"—was used as a "newspaper during slavery," Diggs said. Since most slaves were not allowed to read or write or meet freely, they spread news by word of mouth, and information that house servants overheard in the main house was relayed to other slaves in the quarters in their games with hand puppets. An engaging actor, Diggs played the different roles with his hand puppets. For example, the stout "Mammy" puppet would excitedly relate to the other puppets, "I heard it through the grapevine that the South has just won a big victory in Virginia. The South might just win the war. What will we do, what will we do!" But in another performance, "Mammy" related the news, "I heard it through the grapevine that President Lincoln has just put out a call for colored troops. They say if you can just get to Benedict [Maryland] and join the army there, you will be free, you will be free!" (There was in fact an encampment of black Union Army soldiers at Benedict. McKinley Gantt's father, Albert Gantt, enlisted there.) Diggs heard of the use of hand puppets to spread the news as a child directly from his grandmother, great-aunts, uncles, and other former slaves.[3]

Diggs also brought a section of a log from his grandfather's log house, which was built soon after emancipation and used as an early church (Chapter II). Diggs had dismantled the house to preserve it from further decay. With his grandfather's broad ax, he showed visitors how his grandfather and other men, both black and white, hewed logs to build their houses years ago.

Since this was the Festival of American Folklife, and the Smithsonian is the national museum, it was important that this session go beyond black farm life in Maryland. In previous research, I had located Luther Stuckey, who was born near Georgetown, South Carolina, in 1894 and later moved to southern Maryland. A man of great strength and pride, and a former President of the Charles County, Maryland, chapter of the NAACP for twenty-four years, Stuckey (figure 114) intrigued the crowds that gathered around him with his vivid recollections of life in the rural South for slaves and for sharecroppers up to World War I, a way of life that was like another world to most visitors. His stories were made personal by his large photograph of his parents, taken in the late 1800's. They were both born during slavery. He told of his mother and his mother's mother, who were put up on the auction block to be sold. He described the scene as told to him: the auctioneer pulled down his grandmother's dress to display her strong shoulders and ample breasts; "They wanted a woman like her and bid on her something terrible." She was sold away from her daughter. "They never heard

Figure 116
Arthur Raper (with full beard) in the farm tenant house. Photo: author.

from her again. Don't know where she went to." Stuckey recalled that his father was first a slave of a man who made turpentine, and later was sold to a man who owned a "liberty stable." His name was Stuckey. He said that Stuckey treated his father well, and his father liked and respected him. At the time of emancipation, his father took Stuckey's name, "because he liked him so much," but his two brothers kept their African name, which was "Belin." "So that's why," Stuckey said to the audience, "I carry this old servitude name."[4]

Arthur Raper, whose studies of rural life in the South were instrumental in the formation of the Farm Resettlement Administration, later the Farm Security Administration, seated himself outside the tenant house and showed visitors photographs he had taken of farm tenant houses and families in rural Georgia in the late 1920's and 1930's (figure 116). His portrayals of life in the Deep South helped place the house on exhibit in a broader context. He related these tenant houses to the present by explaining that many of the problems in the cities today resulted from tenant farmers having to leave farms, to become "surplus people."[5]

Among the hundreds of people who attended the sessions were

numerous relatives, neighbors, and friends of the participants. I had sent letters and fliers about the festival to the county school systems in southern Maryland, and notices were included in the paychecks of Charles County teachers. Among the school groups that came on field trips were several classes of the elementary school in Howard County, Maryland, where Octavia (Proctor) Carter was principal. She is the daughter of Octavia Proctor, who lived next door to the tenant house as a child. With the guidance of Mrs. Carter and her mother, the students practiced butter churning and learned about other traditional ways of life, lessons in history that they are not likely to forget, having learned them from their principal in a personal, informal context.

In recent years, the Smithsonian is increasingly inviting persons associated with exhibits to come to its museums to share their recollections with the public at large. In this occasion at the tenant house, for example, people were given rare glimpses behind the curtain of time as participants described their experiences with farming, raising children, doing household chores, going to school, entertaining, making things, and making do. The informants' participation was especially important because historical experiences like theirs are not often written down. If they are, they are rarely available in a popular form to most Americans. In ways such as this, the farm tenant house, as well as other exhibits, can offer a setting for those "experiments in history teaching" that the educator John Dewey called for in historical museums. Evaluating the educational benefits of the oral informants in this session, historian Wilcomb Washburn said that there was "no final measure for their contributions."[6]

But folk festivals end, and meanwhile the way of life of rural black families, like that of other people on the land, is rapidly disappearing. Tenants and farm laborers have had their jobs replaced by machines, and black landowning farmers have rarely been able to accumulate sufficient land and capital to keep abreast of the changes in modern agriculture. As a result, the few black families who still farm for a living in southern Maryland must supplement their incomes by working at other occupations. Not one family located in this survey of over two hundred sites in southern Maryland and Montgomery County depends exclusively on farming for its income.

As the farmlands are abandoned or give way to subdivisions and shopping centers, the historical houses of rural blacks disappear. Examples are numerous, and represent the fate of many farmhouses throughout the South and the nation: the Ross tenant house is gone;

the slave house at River View is collapsing; the Cusic-Medley house, the Harrod house, the Robert Collins house are abandoned, vandalized, falling in; perhaps the home of McKinley Gantt will follow in a few years. All the survivals represent only a few of the total number of houses that once dotted the southern Maryland country-side, numbering many thousands for a black population of more than 50,000 in 1900. The abandonment of these farmhouses is in keeping with the national trend: only 4 percent of our national labor force work on the farm today, compared with 20 percent in 1935 and 90 percent in 1776.[7]

The loss of land in recent years has been especially severe for blacks. Throughout the eleven states of the South (not including Maryland), blacks lost 6,500,000 acres of farmland from 1950 to 1969, a loss of more than 50 percent. In Maryland, the amount of land used for farming by both blacks and whites diminished by 1,954,557 acres between 1920 and 1969. Throughout the state there are scores of once-prosperous rural black communities of landowners that are depopulated today in comparison with the past. Ben's Creek is only one example. This is a study of a vanishing way of life.[8]

What can we do to preserve this vital, imperiled legacy? One approach is to consider the houses, people, and traditions as national cultural resources, and to record them in historical surveys funded by federal, state, local, and private sources. To a large measure, this study is the product of such a survey. There are many more historical black communities in southern Maryland that desperately need attention, yet could not be surveyed within the time and budget allowed to this study. Indeed, many historical communities throughout the South and the nation warrant the recognition and expertise of scholars. Their studies can help validate the significance of these communities to governments and historical preservation organizations and can enable citizens to participate on a more informed basis in the planning and development of their communities. The attention such studies generate can also stimulate economic assistance to help the elderly improve their old houses, and legal advice to help them hold on to their land. Professional scholars, planners, and preservationists can also advise the young who are returning to their home communities, and who wish to learn about their history and to maintain and repair their family homes, the physical symbol of their heritage.

In the more distant future, the written descriptions, photographs, and taped and filmed interviews will constitute a valuable archives of the people's history, like the photographs of the Farm Security Administration and the WPA ex-slave narratives of the 1930's. All of these could help educate future generations about ways of life and material culture that will be radically different from theirs in the twenty-first and twenty-second centuries.

Student projects on preserving the people's history could also be included in the history, English, economics, or social studies curricula of local schools and community colleges. Projects like Foxfire, Inc., in north Georgia have demonstrated the educational benefits of such endeavors. The projects could be connected to community organizations, local or state historical societies, or local commissions for the elderly. The projects could help give students a sense of place and a personal, historical perspective, and in turn help give dignity to the lives of the elderly. Schools, libraries, shopping centers, churches, courthouses, and other community centers could offer places to show traveling exhibits produced by these projects.

During the 1930's, a former slave advised his interviewer, "If you want Negro history, you will have to get [it] from somebody who wore the shoe, and by and by from one to another, you will get a book." This study is a product of such an effort to "get" Negro history. We have learned from those "who wore the shoe" how black families in the past have striven to rise above enslavement and the poverty of the post–Civil-War era by adapting African traditions to New World needs, utilizing the natural resources around them to their own advantage, making their own houses, furnishings, medicines, and clothes, and founding communities. Such life stories as those of Joseph Ross, William Jordan, Albert Gantt, and Cecilia Golder Harrod showed how many freed slaves preserved their identity, continued with traditions of self-sufficiency, and passed on their sense of self and of family pride to their descendants. Even impoverished farm tenants, such as Abraham Medley and his family or the residents of the farm tenant house at the Smithsonian, did not break under the pressure of poverty. Continuing with earlier traditions, they created and sustained a world familiar to them, not alien.[9]

When I first began this work in southern Maryland, I had only heard of one or two extant slave houses in St. Mary's County; the rest was a blank. When I was first told of William Diggs, he was characterized as a "kook"—such was the bias against a person desperately involved in the preservation of his people's history. But without his assistance and that of others, both black and white, these re-creations of the physical world of black people would not have been possible. The historical evidence these people offered and the houses they led me to illustrate the rich potential that awaits further exploration in southern Maryland and throughout the nation. I hope that the reader will join other historians, folklorists, museum professionals, architectural historians, and lay people in reconsidering the black contributions to our built environment and in reevaluating the places, things, and memories that we study for "history." Now is the time.

APPENDIX I
Sites Surveyed in Southern Maryland and Montgomery County, Maryland

The following list identifies the black historical sites that I surveyed in southern Maryland and in Montgomery County, Maryland, upon which this study is based. I located and recorded these sites as part of a Summer Graduate Internship with the Smithsonian Institution in 1974, and with a grant from the Center for the Study of Man, Smithsonian Institution, in 1975, and as a Predoctoral Fellow, Smithsonian Institution, in 1975–76. In 1976–77 I was a Historic Sites Surveyor with the Maryland Commission on Afro-American History and Culture and the Maryland Historical Trust in Annapolis, and surveyed black historical sites in southern Maryland. In 1978–79 I recorded black historical sites in upper western Montgomery County as a Historic Sites Surveyor with Sugarloaf Regional Trails, with support from the Montgomery County Office of Community Development and the Maryland Historical Trust. The Montgomery County Office of Community Development funds are received from HUD block grants, and the Maryland Historical Trust funds from the National Park Service. The architectural descriptions, black-and-white prints, and slides of each site in southern Maryland and Montgomery County are on file at the Maryland Historical Trust and are open to use by the public. They are cataloged by the county, the name of the site, and the inventory number as given in this list. The Montgomery County sites are also on file at the Rockville Public Library, Rockville, Maryland.

Sites Surveyed in Anne Arundel County

1. AA-94a   Grasslands slave house
2. AA-109   Smith house, Pindell farm (overseer or tenant house)
3. AA-141a   Cedar Park slave or tenant house
4. AA-177a   Bunker Hill slave house
5. AA-200a   Indian Range
6. AA-225a   Ivy Neck house (slave, overseer, or tenant house)
7. AA-225b   Ivy Neck house #2 (tenant)
8. AA-230a   Collison Farm slave or tenant house

9. AA-232a   Gresham slave house
10. AA-233a   Ivy Neck, Whall Residence (artisan or slave house)
11. AA-236a   Essex slave house
12. AA-240a   Batchellor's Choice tenant house
13. AA-326a   Whitehall overseer's slave quarters
14. AA-339a   Goshen slave house
15. AA-340   Basil Smith farm, slave house
16. AA-GM-1   Wayson Farm slave houses

Sites Surveyed in Calvert County

17. CLVT-7a   Hawkins tenant house
18. CLVT-61a   Morgan's Fresh slave house or outbuilding
19. CLVT-106   Holt-Whittington house (slave, tenant, or landowner house)
20. CLVT-107   Hopsie Johnson house (slave or tenant and later landowner's house)
21. CLVT-108   Benjamin and Sophie Foote house (slave or tenant and later landowner's house)
22. CLVT-109   Ireland-Mills-Gantt house (landowner)
23. CLVT-110   Gross-Johnson (Albert) house (slave or tenant and later landowner's house)
24. CLVT-111   Alex Rice house (slave or tenant and later landowner's house)
25. CLVT-112   John A. and Thomas Gray house (landowner)
26. CLVT-164   David Gray house (landowner)
27. CLVT-178   Walter A. Curtis house (landowner)
28. CLVT-179   Thomas Foote house (landowner)
29. CLVT-180   John and Mamie Jackson house (landowner)
30. CLVT-181   Locks-Bannister house (landowner)
31. CLVT-182   Parran-Gray house (tenant)
32. CLVT-183   John Rice house and blacksmith forge (landowner)
33. CLVT-184   Thomas Rice house (landowner)
34. CLVT-185   Isaac Saunders house (landowner)
35. CLVT-186   Edward Egans house (landowner)
36. CLVT-187   Harold Parker house (landowner)
37. CLVT-200   George Virgil Gantt house (landowner)

Partial List of Sites at Ben's Creek

38. CLVT-188a   Bourne log house (landowner)
39. CLVT-188b   Brooks log house (landowner)
40. CLVT-188c   Chase-Gross house (landowner)
41. CLVT-188d   Chew-Locks house (landowner)
42. CLVT-188e   James Harrod house (landowner)
43. CLVT-188f   Ethelbert Parker house (site) (landowner)

44. CLVT-188g Sam Parker house (landowner)
45. CLVT-188h James Wilson, Jr., house (landowner)
46. CLVT-188i James Wilson, Sr., house (landowner)

Sites Surveyed in Charles County

47. CH 128   Chicamuxen Negro School
48. CH 151   Westwood Manor tenant house
49. CH 306   Hawkins house (tenant)
50. CH 307   Preston Janifer house (landowner)
51. CH 308   Hart-Diggs house (landowner)
52. CH 309   Jordan Chapel, Alexandria United Methodist Church and
                Cemetery
53. CH 310   Hancock-Ross house (slave or tenant house)
54. CH 311   Sinkfield house (landowner)
55. CH 312   George Barbour house (landowner)
56. CH 313   Eddy Boston house (landowner)
57. CH 314   Bridgett-Thomas house (tenant)
58. CH 315   Butler-Cooke house (landowner or tenant)
59. CH 316   Frances Collins house (school and landowner's house)
60. CH 317   Cooksey Farm tenant house
61. CH 318   Harrison and Janie Dent house (landowner)
62. CH 320   Dyson-Mahoney house (tenant)
63. CH 321   Hill house (landowner)
64. CH 322   Jameson-Tolson house (tenant)
65. CH 323   Annie Johnson house (landowner)
66. CH 325   Nyce Manor tenant house
67. CH 326   Saint Ignatius slave house
68. CH 327   Reginald and Annie Scott house (landowner)
69. CH 328   Luther Stuckey house (landowner)
70. CH 329   Rodella Swann house (landowner)
71. CH 330   Frank and Nannie Thomas house (landowner)
72. CH 360   Crain Farm slave house

Sites Surveyed in Prince George's County

73. PG 62-15   Johnson-Crump house (landowner)
74. PG 62-16   Augustus Ross house (landowner)
75. PG 62-17   Edward Gross house (landowner)
76. PG 73-19   Northampton frame slave quarters (site)
77. PG 73-20   Northampton brick slave quarters (site)
78. PG 74-17   Countee house (landowner)
79. PG 76-15   Henry and William D. Butler house (landowner)

Sites Surveyed in St. Mary's County

80. STMA-1a   Mulberry Fields slave house
81. STMA-1b   Howard Young house (slave or tenant)
82. STMA-3a   Cross Manor slave house (site)
83. STMA-7a   Sotterley slave house
84. STMA-7b   Sotterley slave house and gate house
85. STMA-27a   Rose Croft slave house
86. STMA-33a   Brome Farm slave house
87. STMA-93a   Cremona slave house
88. STMA-98a   St. Cuthbert's Fortune slave house (site)
89. STMA-110a Bushwood Manor slave house
90. STMA-110b Bushwood Manor tenant house
91. STMA-120a River View slave house
92. STMA-125a Blair's Purchase slave house
93. STMA-243   Cusic-Medley house (slave or tenant)
94. STMA-291   John C. Dyson house (landowner)
95. STMA-292   Thomas Ally Hebb house (landowner)
96. STMA-293   Joseph B. Herbert house (landowner)
97. STMA-294   George Taylor house (landowner)
98. STMA-295   James Scriber house (landowner)
99. STMA-303   James G. Curtis house (landowner)
100. STMA-306 Raley outbuilding: kitchen, alleged "slave quarters"
101. STMA-307 Joseph Statesman house (landowner)
102. STMA-308 William B. and Ella Thompson house (landowner)
103. STMA-309 Bowling-Countee tenant house
104. STMA-310 William Marshall house (landowner)
105. STMA-322 Butler-Davis-Gross house (landowner)

Sites Surveyed in Beachville Community

106. STMA-283 Thomas Christopher Butler house (landowner)
107. STMA-284 Samuel Carroll house (landowner)
108. STMA-285 John D. Woodland–Willie Carroll house (landowner)
109. STMA-286 Mortimer Cole house (landowner)
110. STMA-287 Charles Medley house (landowner)
111. STMA-288 John Medley house (landowner)
112. STMA-289 Richard Medley house (landowner)
113. STMA-290 Ignatius Smallwood–Raleigh Wilson house (landowner)

Sites Surveyed in Abell Community

114. STMA-277 Abell Negro School
115. STMA-278 Robert Henry Collins house (landowner)

116. STMA-279 Dickerson-Clark house (landowner)
117. STMA-280 Steven and Lucy Jones house (landowner)
118. STMA-281 Love and Charity Social Club Hall
119. STMA-311 Robert Ed Coles tenant house
120. STMA-312 Beverly Collins house (landowner)
121. STMA-313 Edward Collins house (landowner)
122. STMA-314 John Dickerson Collins house (landowner)
123. STMA-315 Robert Henry Collins (birthplace) log house (site)
124. STMA-316 Taylor Green house (landowner)
125. STMA-317 Hotel
126. STMA-318 Maddox-Lee house (landowner)
127. STMA-319 Milestone School
128. STMA-320 Tommy Thompson–J. B. Clark house (landowner)
129. STMA-321 Branson House

Sites in Montgomery County
Unless indicated otherwise, all houses were landowners' dwellings.

Sites Surveyed in Blocktown

130. M-18-40-1 Daniel Thomas Jackson house
131. M-18-40-2 Gladys (Jackson) and William Luckett house
132. M-18-40-3 Harry Jackson house
133. M-18-40-4 William Jackson house
134. M-18-40-5 Jackson family house

Sites Surveyed in Clarksburg

135. M-13-10-1 Clarksburg Negro School
136. M-13-10-2 William and Laura Davis house
137. M-13-10-3 Foreman Hill house
138. M-13-10-4 Arthur and Ella Mae Gibson house
139. M-13-10-5 Lloyd Gibbs house
140. M-13-10-6 William L. Hackey house
141. M-13-10-7 Hawkins family house
142. M-13-10-8 Jeremiah Lyles house
143. M-13-10-9 Maurice and Sarah Mason house (Payne)
144. M-13-10-10 William and Rachel Mason house (rec. center)
145. M-13-10-11 Moore house (site behind Mason house)
146. M-13-10-12 Pleasant Grove Church
147. M-13-10-13 Clifton Snowden house
148. M-13-10-14 Thomas and Henrietta Snowden house
149. M-13-10-15 John Wesley M.E. Church
150. M-13-10-16 Benjamin Wims house
151. M-13-10-17 John Henry Wims house
152. M-13-10-18 Warner Wims house (Disney)

Sites Surveyed in Hyattstown

153. M-10-58 Montgomery Chapel
154. M-10-70-1 Lyles family house

Sites Surveyed in Jerusalem

155. M-17-51-1 Clarke family house
156. M-17-51-2 David Copeland house
157. M-17-51-3 Frank Dorsey house
158. M-17-51-4 George Dorsey house
159. M-17-51-5 James Dorsey house
160. M-17-51-6 William H. Dorsey house
161. M-17-51-7 Lizzie Grimes house
162. M-17-51-8 John and Mary Hallman house
163. M-17-51-9 Dennis Hamilton house
164. M-17-51-10 Wallace and Horace Hamilton house
165. M-17-51-11 John and Annie Harper house
166. M-17-51-12 Jerusalem Baptist Church and Cemetery
167. M-17-51-13 Jerusalem Church Parsonage
168. M-17-51-14 George and Ora Lyles house
169. M-17-51-15 Ann Maria and William Moore house
170. M-17-51-16 William and Mary Lyles house
171. M-17-51-17 Charles and Josephine McPherson house
172. M-17-51-18 Hartley Moore house
173. M-17-51-19 Poolesville School
174. M-17-51-20 Susie Proctor house
175. M-17-51-21 William and Jenny Robinson house
176. M-17-51-22 Robert Williams house
177. M-17-51-23 Elijah's Rest United Methodist Church
178. M-17-51-24 Wims-Moore house
179. M-17-51-25 Johnson family house

Sites Surveyed in Jonesville

180. M-17-8-1 Basil Bailey house
181. M-17-8-2 Mary Genus Davis house
182. M-17-8-3 Horace Genus house
183. M-18-8-4 Thomas Harper house
184. M-17-8-5 Jones-Hall house
185. M-17-8-6 Dennis and Henry Jones house
186. M-17-8-7 Elmar Jones house
187. M-17-8-8 Frank Jones house
188. M-17-8-9 George M. Martin house
189. M-17-8-10 Noland house
190. M-17-8-11 Solomon Owens house

Sites Surveyed in Martinsburg

191. M-16-12-1 Betters house

192. M-16-12-2   Dorsey-Scott house
193. M-16-12-3   Fairfax house
194. M-16-12-4   Fisher-Diggs house
195. M-16-12-5   Graham house
196. M-16-12-6   Graham house (site)
197. M-16-12-7   Green-Hebron house
198. M-16-12-8   Gilmore Green house
199. M-16-12-9   Hood house
200. M-16-12-10 Jenkins Log house (site)
201. M-16-12-11 Love and Charity Hall
202. M-16-12-12 Martinsburg School
203. M-16-12-14 Oak Hill Post Office–Green house
204. M-16-12-15 Peters log house (site)
205. M-16-12-16 Poole-Peters Blacksmith Shop (site)
206. M-16-12-17 Ridout house
207. M-16-12-18 Thompson house
208. M-16-12-19 Warren M.E. Church Cemetery
209. M-16-12-20 Warren M.E. Church

Sites Surveyed in Sugarland

210. M-27-41-1   John Adams house (site)
211. M-17-41-3   Sam Beander house (site)
212. M-17-41-4   James Beckwith house (site)
213. M-17-41-5   Tilghman Beckwith house (site)
214. M-17-41-6   Isaac Bell log house
215. M-17-41-7   John Branison house (site)
216. M-17-41-8   Raf Branison house (site)
217. M-17-41-9   Coates family house (two sites)
218. M-17-41-10 Joe Curtis log house (site)
219. M-17-41-11 John Henry Diggs house (site)
220. M-17-41-12 Basil Dorsey house (site)
221. M-17-41-13 Garnett family house (site)
222. M-17-41-14 Levi Hall house (site)
223. M-17-41-15 Luke and Vinie Hebron house (site)
224. M-17-41-16 Patrick and Amelia Hebron house (site)
225. M-17-41-17 Robert and Harriet Hebron house (site)
226. M-17-41-18 John Higgins house (site)
227. M-17-41-19 Charles Jackson house (site)
228. M-17-41-20 Horace Jackson house (site)
229. M-17-41-21 Peter Jackson house (site)
230. M-17-41-22 Nathan Johnson house (site) and Sugarland Post Office (site)
231. M-17-41-23 Phillip Johnson house (site)
232. M-17-41-24 Sam Johnson house (site)
233. M-17-41-25 Sam and Martha Lee house (site)
234. M-17-41-26 Tilghman Lee house
235. M-17-41-28 Luke Lynch house (site)

236. M-17-41-29 Tom Nichols house (site)
237. M-17-41-30 St. Paul's Community Church and Cemetery
238. M-17-41-31 Sugarland School
239. M-17-41-32 Sugarland Store
240. M-17-41-33 William Taylor house

Sites Surveyed in Turnertown Community, Boyd's

241. M-18-1 David and Susie Turner house
242. M-18-2 Douglas Turner house
243. M-18-3 Harry Turner house
244. M-18-4 Mallie (Turner) Talley house
245. M-18-5 Richard and Alverta Turner house

Sites Surveyed in White Grounds Community, Boyd's

246. M-18-11-1 St. Marks' Church and Boyd's School
247. M-18-11-2 St. Marks' Parsonage
248. M-18-11-3 Martha Carter house
249. M-18-11-4 Williams-Diggins house
250. M-18-11-5 Addison and Celia Duffin house
251. M-18-11-6 Duffin family house
252. M-18-11-7 Gibbs-Coates house
253. M-18-11-8 George Hawkins house
254. M-18-11-9 Odd Fellows' Lodge
255. M-18-11-10 Joshua Duffin house
256. M-18-11-11 Nathan Duffin house
257. M-18-11-12 Parker family house

Sites Surveyed in the Big Woods Community, Dickerson

258. M-12-42-1 Awkard family cemetery
259. M-12-42-2 Lewis Brown house
260. M-12-42-3 Tom Crumpton house
261. M-12-42-4 Mt. Zion M.E. Church Cemetery
262. M-12-42-5 Dan Diggins house (site)
263. M-12-42-6 Owens-Diggins family property
264. M-12-42-7 Awkard-Diggins property
265. M-12-42-8 Gene Hackett house
266. M-12-42-9 Henry Hackett house (site)
267. M-12-42-10 Fred Hamilton house
268. M-12-42-11 Lawrence Hamilton house
269. M-12-42-12 Adolphus Higgins house (site)

270. M-12-42-13 Louise Hutchinson house (site)
271. M-12-42-14 Robert Vinton Hutchinson house
272. M-12-42-15 Elbert Johnson–Thomas Johnson house (site)
273. M-12-42-16 Richard King house (site)
274. M-12-42-17 Lee-Simms house (site)
275. M-12-42-18 Noah Lee house (site)
276. M-12-42-19 Richard Lee house (site)
277. M-12-42-20 James Lee house (site)
278. M-12-42-21 Richard Mercer house (site)
279. M-12-42-22 Mt. Zion M.E. Church
280. M-12-42-23 Henry T. Onley house (site)
281. M-12-42-24 Henry Thomas Onley, Jr., house
282. M-12-42-25 James Onley house
283. M-12-42-26 John T. Onley house
284. M-12-42-27 Onley-Campbell house
285. M-12-42-28 Ned Onley house (site)
286. M-12-42-29 Owens-Diggins house
287. M-12-42-30 Payne house
288. M-12-42-31 Sellman Lodge
289. M-12-42-32 Sellman School (site)
290. M-12-42-33 Mary Smith house
291. M-12-42-34 Spencer family cemetery
292. M-12-42-35 Mose Tibbs house (site)

Sites Surveyed in Mount Ephraim Community, Comus

293. F-7-1-1   Bell's Chapel and Cemetery
294. F-7-1-2   Comstock School
295. F-7-1-3   Cosgrove-Naylor house
296. F-7-1-4   Bene and Barbara Hallman house (site)
297. F-7-1-5   James and Malinda Hallman house (site)
298. F-7-1-6   Moses Hallman house (site)
299. F-7-1-7   William and Hannah Hallman house (site)
300. F-7-1-8   Frank Nichols house
301. F-7-1-9   Morris and Agnes Proctor house
302. F-7-1-10   Charles and Laura Proctor house
303. F-7-1-11   David and Sally Proctor house (site)
304. F-7-1-12   Frank and Maggie Proctor house
305. F-7-1-13   Linwood Proctor house
306. F-7-1-14   William and Mary Proctor house (site)
307. F-7-1-15   William and Rachel Proctor house
308. F-7-1-16   Wood-Bowie house

APPENDIX II
Oral Informants and Interviews

Anne Arundel County

Bowie, Captain John, interviews by George McDaniel, Grasslands Farm, Annapolis Junction, Maryland, and Bethesda, Maryland, February 1976.

Bridgeman, Eucleth W., interview by George McDaniel, Harwood, Maryland, February 1976.

Lansdale, Colonel John, interview by George McDaniel, Harwood, Maryland, January 1976.

Rich, Edward, interview by George McDaniel, Annapolis, Maryland, January 1976.

Smith, Arthur, and William Smith, interviews by George McDaniel, Pindell, Maryland, January, February, and March 1976.

Smith, Basil, interview by George McDaniel and Mary Warren, Severn, Maryland, March 1977.

Calvert County

Bourne, Edward, interview by George McDaniel and Wayne Nield, Island Creek, Maryland, May 1977.

Gantt, McKinley, interview by George McDaniel and Merry Stimson, Mutual, Maryland, July 1974.

———, interview by George McDaniel and Amy Kotkin, Mutual, Maryland, May 1976.

———, interview by George McDaniel, Mary Sue Nunn, and William Diggs, Mutual, Maryland, February 1978.

———, interview by George McDaniel, Mutual, Maryland, July 1978.

Gross, Viola Foote, interviews by George McDaniel, Lusby, Maryland, November 1976 and July 1978.

Johnson, Albert, interviews by George McDaniel, Mutual, Maryland, December 1976 and February 1977.

Johnson, "Hopsie," interview by George McDaniel, Lusby, Maryland, November 1976.

———, interview by George McDaniel, Mary Sue Nunn, and John Pearce, Lusby, Maryland, March 1977.

Reichart, Jennie Tongue, interviews by George McDaniel, Lusby, Maryland, November 1976 and July 1978.

Wilson, Blanche, interview by George McDaniel, Island Creek, Maryland, March 1977.

————, interviews by George McDaniel and Mary Sue Nunn, Island Creek, Maryland, May 1977 and December 1978.

————, telephone interviews by George McDaniel, October and December 1980 and April 1981.

Charles County

Diggs, Rachel, interviews by George McDaniel, Chicamuxen, Maryland, November 1976, July 1978; National Museum of American History, Smithsonian Institution, Washington, D.C., October 1978.

Diggs, William, interviews by George McDaniel, Indian Head, Maryland, November 1976; National Museum of American History, Smithsonian Institution, Washington, D.C., October 1978.

————, interview by George McDaniel, Mary Sue Nunn, John Pearce, and Alix Sommer, Indian Head, Maryland, February 1978.

————, interview by George McDaniel and Mary Sue Nunn, Sotterley Plantation, Hollywood, Maryland, February 1978.

————, interview by George McDaniel, Mary Sue Nunn, and John Pearce, Eagle Harbor, Maryland, June 1979.

————, telephone interviews by George McDaniel, April 1980 and March 1981.

Ross, Benjamin, and Nellie Ross, interviews by George McDaniel, Riverside, Maryland, February 1977 and June 1978.

Ross, Benjamin, Nellie Ross, and William Diggs, interview by George McDaniel and Mary Sue Nunn, Riverside, Maryland, January 1978.

Ross, John, interview by George McDaniel, Riverside, Maryland, June 1978.

Stuckey, Luther, interviews by George McDaniel, Pisgah, Maryland, April and May 1977, June and August 1978; National Museum of American History, Smithsonian Institution, Washington, D.C., October 1978.

Stuckey, Luther, and Edna Jones, interview by George McDaniel, Carl Scheele, and Richard Ahlborne, National Museum of American History, Washington, D.C., March 1978.

Williams, Preston, interview by George McDaniel, Mary Stokely, and Ellen Hughes, National Museum of American History, Smithsonian Institution, Washington, D.C., March 1978.

Prince George's County

Butler, William, interviews by George McDaniel, Oxon Hill, Maryland, July and November 1976, March 1978.

————, interview by George McDaniel and Louise Hutchinson, Oxon Hill, Maryland, May 1977.

Crump, Oscar, and Sadie Crump, Muirkirk, Maryland, October and November 1976.

Furr, Frank, telephone interview by George McDaniel, February 1978.

Harley, Edward, and Vivian Harley, interview by George McDaniel, National Museum of American History, Smithsonian Institution, Washington, D.C., March and October 1978.

Heidelbach, Mrs. Walter, telephone interview by George McDaniel, October 1980.

Howell, Margaret (Spragins), telephone interviews by George McDaniel, January, February, and October 1978.

James, Bill, and Edith James, interview by George McDaniel, Lanham, Maryland, January 1978.

James, Bill, and Edith James, Richard James, and Helen (Turner) James, interview by George McDaniel and Rodris Roth, National Museum of American History, Smithsonian Institution, Washington, D.C., February 1978.

James, Richard, and Helen (Turner) James, interviews by George McDaniel, Lanham, Maryland, January and June 1978; National Museum of American History, Smithsonian Institution, Washington, D.C., October 1978.

Johnson, Elizabeth ("Mamie"), and George Johnson and family, interviews by George McDaniel, National Museum of American History, Smithsonian Institution, Washington, D.C., March and October 1978.

Parker family: Octavia Parker Proctor, Mary Parker, Elizabeth Parker Merrill, Octavia Proctor Carter, interviews by George McDaniel, Seat Pleasant, Maryland, February 1978; National Museum of American History, Smithsonian Institution, Washington, D.C., March and October 1978.

Savoy, Mary Agnes, interview by George McDaniel, National Museum of American History, Smithsonian Institution, Washington, D.C., March 1978.

Slinguff, Margaret, interview by George McDaniel, Bowie, Maryland, February and March 1978.

Spragins, Samuel, telephone interviews by George McDaniel, February and March 1978, October 1980, and April 1981.

Wood, Eugene, interview by George McDaniel, National Museum of American History, Smithsonian Institution, Washington, D.C., April 1978.

Wood, Joe, interviews by George McDaniel, Mitchellville, Maryland, February and March 1978.

St. Mary's County

Buckler, J. Gwynn, interview by George McDaniel, Mechanicsville, Maryland, September 1978.

Burch, Colonel Colin, interview by George McDaniel, Oakley, Maryland, July 1974.

Carroll, George, interviews by George McDaniel, Beachville, Maryland, November and December 1976.

Curtis, James G., interview by George McDaniel, Mechanicsville, Maryland, July 1974.

Cusic, Elwood, telephone interview by George McDaniel, July 1978.

Cusic, Nora, interview by George McDaniel, Mechanicsville, Maryland, September 1978.

Dickerson, John, interview by George McDaniel, Abell, Maryland, April 1977.

Dyson, Clem, interviews by George McDaniel, Bushwood, Maryland, June 1978; National Museum of American History, Smithsonian Institution, Washington, D.C., October 1978.

Fowler, Zack, interview by George McDaniel, Malcolm Watkins, and Nancy Groce, National Museum of American History, Smithsonian Institution, Washington, D.C., March 1978.

Jansson family, interviews by George McDaniel, Beauvue, Maryland, July 1974 and March 1976.

Johnson, Joseph Julius, interviews by George McDaniel, Bushwood, Maryland, March 1976 and June 1978.

Knott, Charles, and James Knott, interview by George McDaniel, Hollywood, Maryland, June 1978.

Knott, Edward, interviews by George McDaniel, Hollywood, Maryland, February 1977 and June 1978.

Medley, Abraham, interview by George McDaniel and Cary Carson, Mechanicsville, Maryland, July 1974.

———, interviews by George McDaniel, Mechanicsville, Maryland, January and March 1976 and April 1977.

Medley, Abraham, and Charles Medley, interview by George McDaniel and Mary Sue Nunn, Mechanicsville, Maryland, September 1978.

Milford, Alex, interview by George McDaniel, Beachville, Maryland, November 1976.

Nelson, Amanda, interview by George McDaniel, Malcolm Watkins, and Nancy Groce, National Museum of American History, Smithsonian Institution, Washington, D.C., March 1978.

———, interview by George McDaniel, National Museum of American History, Smithsonian Institution, Washington, D.C., October 1978.

———, telephone interview by George McDaniel, March 1980.

Scriber, James, interview by George McDaniel and Bill Bishop, Hollywood, Maryland, February 1977.

———, interviews by George McDaniel, Hollywood, Maryland, July 1974, March and November 1976, June 1977, June 1978, and June 1980.

Young, Howard, and family, interview by George McDaniel, Beauvue, Maryland, July 1974.

Montgomery County

Foreman, Ethel, interview by George McDaniel, Clarksburg, Maryland, January 1979.

Graham, Lemuel, interview by George McDaniel, Martinsburg, Maryland, May 1978.

Hallman, Florence, interviews by George McDaniel and Ida Hallman, Big Woods Community, Dickerson, Maryland, July, August, and September 1978 and July 1979.

Hawkins, Arnold, and Joe Hawkins, interview by George McDaniel, Purdum, Maryland, January 1979.

Herbert, Evelyn, interviews by George McDaniel, Martinsburg, Maryland, May and June 1978.

Lee, Tilghman, and Bessie Lee, Sugarland, Maryland, July, August, and November 1978.

————, telephone interview by George McDaniel, July 1979.

Lyles, Howard, interview by George McDaniel, Martinsburg, Maryland, January 1979.

Miscellaneous

Bachand, Ronald, telephone interview by George McDaniel, March 1980.

Cameron, Moselle, and Janie Cameron Riley, interview by George McDaniel, Durham, North Carolina, July 1975.

Dyson, William, interview by George McDaniel, Washington, D.C., June 1976.

Harris, Julia, interview by George McDaniel, Durham, North Carolina, November 1974.

Kinard, Jesse Beulah, telephone interviews by George McDaniel, January 1978 and March 1980.

McDaniel, James G., telephone interviews, March and September 1978.

Pearce, John, interviews by George McDaniel, Washington, D.C., May 1977, July and December 1978, and March 1979.

Raper, Arthur, interviews by George McDaniel, Oakton, Virginia, March and October 1978.

NOTES

Preface

1. William Shakespeare, *Henry IV*, Part II, quoted in Thomas Schlereth, "The History behind, within, and outside the History Museum," a paper presented in the George Washington Guest Lecture Series in Museum Education, George Washington University, Washington, D.C., March 27, 1980.
2. Peter H. Wood, "Whetting, Setting, and Laying Timbers: Black Builders in the Early South," *Southern Exposure* 8, no. 1 (spring 1980): 3–8.
3. Woodward quoted in Eugene Genovese, *Roll, Jordan, Roll: The World the Slaves Made* (New York: Vintage, 1976), p. xv.
4. By material culture, I mean the traditional definition, "the objects that man has learned to make," particularly the houses, furnishings, and other related artifacts. For further explanation of material culture, see Henry Glassie, *Pattern in Material Folk Culture in the Eastern United States* (Philadelphia: University of Pennsylvania Press, 1968), p. 2.
5. Letitia Woods Brown, *Free Negroes in the District of Columbia, 1790–1846* (New York: Oxford University Press, 1972), pp. 17, 21. In the nineteenth century, the slave population leveled off and the number of free blacks increased. After the general emancipation, many blacks remained in southern Maryland, continuing their agricultural way of life as farm tenants or fledgling landowners, and a black majority persisted in much of the region until the late 1800's. See James M. Wright, *The Free Negro in Maryland, 1634–1860* (New York: Columbia University Press, 1921), p. 86; Margaret Law Callcott, *The Negro in Maryland Politics: 1870–1912* (Baltimore: Johns Hopkins University Press, 1969); U.S., Bureau of the Census, *Negro Population in the United States, 1790–1915* (New York: Arno Press, 1968), p. 783; Benjamin Quarles, "Introduction," *Maryland Historical Magazine* 56, no. 1 (spring 1971): ix.
6. For information on this house of ante-bellum free blacks, and for copies of family photographs, see my descriptions and photographs of the Henry and William D. Butler House (PG 76-15), on file at the Maryland Historical Trust, Annapolis, Maryland.
7. For a more detailed architectural history of black sites in southern Maryland, see George W. McDaniel, "Preserving the People's History: Traditional Black Material Culture in Nineteenth- and Twentieth-Century Southern Maryland" (Ph.D. diss., Duke University, 1979). The descriptions and photographs of the

sites in this survey are on file at the Maryland Historical Trust, Annapolis, Maryland, referred to hereafter as the Southern Maryland Afro-American Survey.
8. Bayly Ellen Marks, "Economics and Society in a Staple Plantation System: St. Mary's County, Maryland, 1790–1840" (Ph.D. diss., University of Maryland, 1979), pp. 153, 218, 258, 396.
9. James Scriber interview, June 1978.

Introduction

1. For a more complete description of the tenant house, see George W. McDaniel, "Preserving the People's History: Traditional Black Material Culture in Nineteenth- and Twentieth-Century Southern Maryland" (Ph.D. diss., Duke University, 1979), pp. 413–513, and McDaniel, "The Sharecropper's House in the Hall of Everyday Life in the Museum of History and Technology," a report on file with the Division of Domestic Life, Department of Cultural History, National Museum of American History, Smithsonian Institution, Washington, D.C., April 17, 1978.
2. Conversations with members of the Smithsonian staff, such as Silvio Bedini, former deputy director, National Museum of American History, currently special assistant-keeper of rare books; Malcolm Watkins, senior curator, Department of Cultural History; Richard Ahlborn, chairman, Division of Community Life; Carl Scheele, curator, Division of Community Life; Anne Golovin, associate curator, Division of Domestic Life.
3. Ellis Yochelson telephone interview, December 1977; Bill and Edith James interview, January 1978; Richard and Helen James interviews, January, February, and June 1978. All interviews taped from January to April 1978 for the Smithsonian project are on deposit at the Division of Domestic Life, National Museum of American History. Those taped in October are on file at the Office of the Folklife Program, Smithsonian Institution, Washington, D.C.
4. Will of Beale D. Mulliken, 1904, Registry of Wills, Prince George's County Courthouse, Upper Marlboro, Maryland; Deed of John C. Jones to Samuel H. Spragins, 1909, Registry of Deeds, Prince George's County Courthouse; Deed of Mattie Spragins to Henry H. Canton, 1959, Registry of Deeds, Prince George's County Courthouse; George M. Hopkins, *Prince George's County Atlas of 1878* (Upper Marlboro, Maryland: Prince George's County Historical Society, 1976).
5. Parker family interviews, March and October 1978.
6. Edward and Vivian Harley interviews, March and October 1978.
7. Elizabeth "Mamie" Butler Johnson and George Johnson interviews, March and October 1978.
8. Joe Wood interview, March 1978; Eugene Wood interview, April 1978.
9. Samuel H. Spragins interviews, March 1978 and October 1980.
10. Margaret Slingluff interview, March 1978; Zack Fowler interview, March 1978; Preston Williams interview, March 1978.

158–59; Alex W. Bealer and John O. Ellis, *The Log Cabin: Homes of the* ~~rth~~ *American Wilderness* (Barre, Massachusetts: Barre Publishing, 1978), pp. ~~8~~; Henry Glassie, "The Types of the Southern Mountain Cabin," ~~an~~ Harold Brunvard, ed., *The Study of American Folklore: An Introduction* ~~w~~ York: Norton, 1978), pp. 345–59; Fred Kniffen and Henry Glassie, "Build-~~in~~ Wood in the Eastern United States: A Time-Place Perspective," *Geo-~~hical~~ Review* 56 (January 1966): 58–65.

Chapter II

~~iam~~ Diggs interview, February 1978.

~~hern~~ Maryland Afro-American Survey. See also George W. Rawick, *The American Slave: A Composite Autobiography*, vol. 16, *Maryland Narratives* ~~st~~port, Connecticut: Greenwood, 1972), pp. 44, 49, 51; Mr. and Mrs. ~~er~~ Jansson and family interviews, July 1974 and March 1976.

~~les~~ Ball, *Fifty Years in Chains, or, The Life of an American Slave* ~~mi~~, Florida: Mnemosyne, 1969); Rawick, *Maryland Narratives*, pp. 66, 24; ~~Ellen~~ Marks, "Economics and Society in a Staple Plantation System: St. ~~s~~ County, Maryland, 1790–1840" (Ph.D. diss., University of Maryland, ~~pp.~~ 560–62.

~~s,~~ "Economics and Society," p. 562.

~~k,~~ *Maryland Narratives*, p. 20; Letitia Brown and Elsie Lewis, *Washington* ~~Banneker~~ *to Douglass, 1791–1870* (Washington, D.C.: Education De-~~ent~~, National Portrait Gallery, 1971), p. 6; James Wright, *The Free Negro* ~~yland~~, *1634–1860* (New York: Columbia University Press, 1921), ~~4–55~~; Marks, "Economics and Society," p. 562.

~~k,~~ *Maryland Narratives*, p. 26; Southern Maryland Afro-American Survey; W. McDaniel, *Black Historical Resources in Upper Western Montgomery* ~~,~~ *Maryland* (Rockville, Maryland: Montgomery County Govern-~~nd~~ Sugarloaf Regional Trails, 1979).

~~M.~~ Brodie, *Thomas Jefferson: An Intimate Biography* (New York: Norton, ~~p.~~ 87; farm journal of William Anderson, 1853–75, manuscript ~~ession~~ of Captain John Bowie, Bethesda, Maryland.

~~lach~~, *The Afro-American Tradition in Decorative Arts* (Cleveland: ~~nd~~ Museum of Art, 1978), pp. 42, 108–38 *passim*; Peter H. Wood, ~~ng~~, Setting, and Laying Timbers: Black Builders in the Early South," *Exposure* 8, no. 1 (spring 1980): 3–8.

Maryland Narratives, p. 6.

49, 51, 44; George W. Rawick, ed., *The American Slave: A* ~~te~~ *Autobiography*, vol. 16, *Virginia Narratives* (Westport, ~~icut~~: Greenwood, 1972), p. 26; Ronald Killian and Charles ~~eds.~~, *Slavery Time When I Was Chillun Down on Marster's Plantation* ~~h~~, Georgia: Beehive Press, 1973), pp. 35–36.

~~.~~ Washington, *Up from Slavery* (New York: Avon, 1965); Frederick ~~My~~ *Bondage and My Freedom* (New York: Arno Press, 1969), p. 37;

11. Southern Maryland Afro-American Survey; Lee H. Nelson, "Nail Chronology as an Aid to Dating Old Buildings and Paint Color Research and Restoration," *History News* 19, no. 2 (December 1963): 1–3.

12. Richard and Helen James interviews; Parker family interviews; Arthur Raper, *Preface to Peasantry* (New York: Atheneum, 1974), p. 61; Sam Spragins interview, October 1980; Mrs. Walter Heidelbach interview, October 1980.

13. Parker family interviews; "Mamie" Johnson and George Johnson interviews; Edward and Vivian Harley interviews; Richard and Helen James interviews; Samuel Spragins interviews.

14. Parker family interviews; Deed of Samuel Spragins to Lewis Parker, 1920, Registry of Deeds, Prince George's County Courthouse, Upper Marlboro, Maryland.

15. Richard and Helen James interviews; "Mamie" Johnson and George Johnson interviews; Edward and Vivian Harley interviews.

16. Edward and Vivian Harley interviews; "Mamie" Johnson and George Johnson interviews; Parker family interviews.

17. Richard and Helen James interviews; "Mamie" Johnson and George Johnson interviews; Edward and Vivian Harley interviews; Parker family interviews.

18. Frank Furr interview, February 1978; Parker family interviews; "Mamie" Johnson and George Johnson interviews; Richard and Helen James interviews; Edward and Vivian Harley interviews.

19. Edward and Vivian Harley interviews.

20. Claire C. Cooper, *Easter Hill Village: Some Social Implications of Design* (New York: Free Press, 1975).

21. "Mamie" Johnson and George Johnson interviews; Parker family interviews; Richard and Helen James interviews; Samuel Spragins interviews.

22. Richard and Helen James interviews; Parker family interviews; Edward and Vivian Harley interviews. My thanks to Rodris Roth, curator of the Division of Domestic Life, who alertly picked up on Mrs. James's comments on the correct historical uses of these rooms during our interview.

23. Henry Glassie, "The Types of the Southern Mountain Cabin," in Jan Harold Brunvard, ed., *The Study of American Folklore: An Introduction* (New York: Norton, 1978), pp. 402–11; Cooper, *Easter Hill Village*.

Chapter I

1. Charles Ball, *Fifty Years in Chains, or, The Life of an American Slave* (Miami, Florida: Mnemosyne, 1969), p. 15; see John Michael Vlach, *The Afro-American Tradition in Decorative Arts* (Cleveland: Cleveland Museum of Art, 1978), for a fine study of African elements in Afro-American material culture; also Robert Farris Thompson, "African Influence on the Art of the United States," in Armstead L. Robinson, Craig C. Foster, and Donald H. Ogilvie, eds., *Black Studies in the University: A Symposium* (New Haven: Yale University Press, 1969), pp. 128–77; Thomas Jefferson quoted in Vlach, *Afro-American Tradition*, p. 25; Peter H. Wood, *Black Majority:*

Negroes in Colonial South Carolina from 1670 through the Stono Rebellion (New York: Norton, 1974), pp. 35–62, 95–131 *passim.*

2. Susan Denyer, *African Traditional Architecture* (New York: Africana, 1978), pp. 55, 80, 82, 175; see also René Gardi, *Indigenous African Architecture* (New York: Van Nostrand Reinhold, 1973); Paul Oliver, *Shelter in Africa* (New York: Barrie and Jenkins, 1978); Bernard Rudofsky, *Architecture without Architects* (Garden City, New York: Doubleday, 1964).

3. Denyer, *African Traditional Architecture*, pp. 2, 56–57, 79; Richard Hull, *African Cities and Towns before the European Conquest* (New York: Norton, 1976), p. 105; Labelle Prussin, *Architecture in Northern Ghana: A Study of Forms and Functions* (Berkeley: University of California Press, 1969), p. 10.

4. See Gardi, *Indigenous African Architecture*, and Labelle Prussin's review of Gardi, *Indigenous African Architecture*, in *African Arts* 9, no. 1 (1975): 83; Oliver, *Shelter in Africa*; Rudofsky, *Architecture without Architects*; G. J. Afolabi, "Traditional Yoruba Architecture," *African Arts* 1, no. 3 (1967): 14–17, 70–72; J. S. Mbiti, *African Religions and Philosophy*, quoted in Denyer, *African Traditional Architecture*, p. 4; Julius F. P. S. Gluck, "African Architecture," in Douglas Fraser, ed., *The Many Faces of Primitive Art: A Critical Anthology* (Englewood Cliffs, New Jersey: Prentice-Hall, 1966), pp. 224–43; Vlach, *Afro-American Tradition*, pp. 124–25; Denyer, *African Traditional Architecture*, pp. 2–4, 133–42, 159; Prussin, *Architecture in Northern Ghana*, e.g., pp. 21–37.

5. Ira Berlin, "Time, Space, and the Evolution of Afro-American Society in British Mainland North America," *The American Historical Review* 85, no. 1 (February 1980): 58–67; Wood, *Black Majority*, especially chs. 5 and 6.

6. Vlach, *Afro-American Tradition*, p. 136; Ronald Bachand interview, March 1980. Bachand, who is chief of operations, African region, U.S. Peace Corps, lived in Zaire for several years and speaks Kikongo, the language of the Kongo people. See Denyer, *African Traditional Architecture*, pp. 42–43, for photographs of Kongo houses and granaries.

7. Georgia Writers' Project, *Drums and Shadows: Survival Studies among Georgia Coastal Negroes* (Athens: University of Georgia Press, 1940), pp. 179–81; Suzanne S. McFarlane, "The Ethnoarchaeology of a Slave Community: The Couper Plantation Site" (M.A. thesis, University of Florida, 1975), pp. 60–73.

8. Russell Menard, "The Maryland Slave Population, 1658 to 1730: A Demographic Profile of Blacks in Four Counties," *The William and Mary Quarterly* 32, no. 1 (January 1975): 37.

9. John M. Vlach, "Shotgun Houses," *Natural History* 86, no. 2 (February 1977): 50–57.

10. Ira Berlin, "Time, Space, and the Evolution," pp. 67–77; William A. Diggs, "Black History: Here at the Beginning," in Jack D. Brown et al., eds., *Charles County, Maryland: A History* (South Hackensack, New Jersey: Custombook, 1976), p. 225; Russell R. Menard, "Maryland Slave Population," pp. 29–54.

11. Menard, "Maryland Slave Population," pp. 29–54.

12. *Ibid.*

13. Denyer, *African Traditional Architecture*, p. 4; Pruss[...] *Ghana*, p. 57.

14. Denyer, *African Traditional Architecture*, pp. 92–9[...] *Indigenous African Architecture*, pp. 53–61, 159, 1[...]

15. Gardi, *Indigenous African Architecture*, pp. 35–43; [...] *Northern Ghana*, pp. 42–44; Henry Chandler For[...] *Furniture in Tidewater Maryland* (Cambridge, Ma[...] 6; Alec Clifton-Taylor, *The Pattern of English Bu[...] Faber, 1972), pp. 288, 298, 304, 353; C. F. Inn[...] *English Building Construction* (Devon, England: [...] 1971), pp. 125–34; Denyer, *African Traditional* [...]

16. Forman, *Old Buildings and Gardens*, p. 6.

17. Denyer, *African Traditional Architecture*, p. 93; [...] *Building*, pp. 289–93. A rammed-earth house w[...] Prince George's County (Forman, *Old Building*[...] eighteenth-century example stood at 1300 Rh[...] ton, D.C., built when the area was still part [...] (*Washington Star*, April 20, 1947). John W. C[...] *can Farmer* 3, no. 20 (August 10, 1821): 151 [...] p. 135.

18. Denyer, *African Traditional Architecture*, pp. [...]

19. *Ibid.*, pp. 40–51, 87–89, 97; Hull, *African C*[...] 106; Gardi, *Indigenous African Architecture*, [...]

20. Innocent, *English Building Construction*, pp. [...] *English Building*, pp. 336–48; Denyer, *African* [...] Forman, *Old Buildings and Gardens*, p. 5; W[...]

21. Denyer, *African Traditional Architecture*, pp. [...]

22. Menard, "Maryland Slave Population," pp. [...]

23. Cheryl Hayes, "Cultural Space and Family [...] tecture, Queen Anne's County, Maryland, [...] Georgetown University, 1974); Eugene Ge[...] *the Slaves Made* (New York: Vintage, 1976[...] *Farmhouses and Cottages* (London: Routled[...] For a discussion of colonial housing of ter[...] Carson, "English Vernacular Architecture [...] the Society of Architectural Historians, [...] His more thorough study of impermanent [...] Virginia will appear in *Winterthur Portfol*[...]

24. Allan Kulikoff, "The Beginnings of the A[...] Aubrey C. Land, Lois Green Carr, and [...] *Society, and Politics in Early Maryland* (B[...] Press, 1974), pp. 171–96; Russell Mena[...] pp. 49–53.

25. Arnold R. Shurtleff, *The Log Cabin M*[...] *English Colonists in North America* (Glo[...]

pp[...]
No[...]
9–[...]
in [...]
(N[...]
ing[...]
gra[...]

1. Wil[...]
2. Sou[...]
   ed.,[...]
   (We[...]
   Holg[...]
3. Cha[...]
   (Mia[...]
   Bayl[...]
   Mary[...]
   1979[...]
4. Mark[...]
5. Rawi[...]
   from[...]
   partm[...]
   in Ma[...]
   pp. 15[...]
6. Rawi[...]
   Georg[...]
   Count[...]
   ment [...]
7. Fawn [...]
   1974),[...]
   in poss[...]
8. John V[...]
   Clevela[...]
   "Whet[...]
   Souther[...]
9. Rawick[...]
10. *Ibid.*, [...]
    Compos[...]
    Connec[...]
    Waller,[...]
    (Savann[...]
11. Booker [...]
    Douglass[...]

Josiah Henson, *Father Henson's Story of His Own Life* (Northbrook, Illinois: Metro, 1972), p. 18.

12. Benjamin and Nellie Ross and William Diggs interview, January 1978; James Scriber interview, November 1976.

13. Marks, "Economics and Society," pp. 46–67; Gregory A. Stiverson, "Landless Husbandmen: Proprietary Tenants in Maryland in the Late Colonial Period," in Aubrey C. Land, Lois Green Carr, and Edward C. Papenfuse, eds., *Law, Society, and Politics in Early Maryland* (Baltimore: Johns Hopkins University Press, 1974), pp. 202–5; Southern Maryland Afro-American Survey.

14. Fred Kniffen, "Folk Housing: Key to Diffusion," *Annals of the Association of American Geographers* 4, no. 4 (December 1965): 549–77; Fred Kniffen and Henry Glassie, "Building in Wood in the Eastern United States: A Time-Place Perspective," *Geographical Review* 56 (January 1966): 40–66; Henry Glassie, "The Types of the Southern Mountain Cabin," in Jan Harold Brunvard, ed., *The Study of American Folklore: An Introduction* (New York: Norton, 1978), pp. 338–69; Alex W. Bealer and John D. Ellis, *The Log Cabin: Homes of the North American Wilderness* (Barre, Massachusetts: Barre Publishing, 1978), pp. 9–28; Charles van Ravenswaay, *The Arts and Architecture of German Settlements in Missouri: A Survey of a Vanishing Culture* (Columbia: University of Missouri Press, 1977), pp. 111–43.

15. Vlach, *Afro-American Tradition*, pp. 122–31; James Deetz, *In Small Things Forgotten: The Archaeology of Early American Life* (Garden City, New York: Anchor, 1977), pp. 138–55; Susan Denyer, *African Traditional Architecture* (New York: Africana, 1978), pp. 55, 80, 82, 133–42, 159.

16. James Scriber interview, November 1976; Ross/Diggs interview, January 1978; "Hopsie" Johnson interview, March 1977; Blanche Wilson interview, December 1978.

17. Marks, "Economics and Society," p. 121; Ross/Diggs interview, January 1978.

18. Ross/Diggs interview, January 1978.

19. *Ibid.*

20. "Hopsie" Johnson interview, March 1977; William Diggs interview, February 1978.

21. Southern Maryland Afro-American Survey; Kniffen and Glassie, "Building in Wood," pp. 53–65.

22. Southern Maryland Afro-American Survey; James Scriber interview, June 1978; William Diggs interview, February 1978; Clem Dyson interview, June 1978; Cary Carson, conversation with John Pearce, St. Mary's City, Maryland.

23. Southern Maryland Afro-American Survey.

24. *Ibid.*

25. *Ibid.*; Rawick, *Maryland Narratives*, p. 6; James Scriber interview, February 1977; Bealer and Ellis, *The Log Cabin*, p. 10; Glassie, "Types," p. 404.

26. Ross/Diggs interview, January 1978; Rawick, *Maryland Narratives*, p. 51; Henson, *Father Henson's Story*, p. 18. An example of a plank floor added over the original dirt floor is in the slave house at Brome Farm, St. Mary's City, Maryland, which was included in the Southern Maryland Afro-American Survey.

27. McKinley Gantt interview, February 1978; Ross/Diggs interview; James Scriber interview, June 1978; William Diggs interview, February 1978; Edward Knott interview, June 1978.

28. Scriber interview, June 1978.

29. William Diggs, presentation to a class in the Graduate Program of Historical Preservation, George Washington University, Washington, D.C., June 1979.

30. W. C. Handy, *Father of the Blues: An Autobiography* (New York: Collier, 1941), pp. 1–2.

31. James Scriber interview, February 1977.

32. Unidentified National Park Service guide, interview by George McDaniel, February 1980, Old Stone House, Georgetown, D.C.

33. M. W. Barley, *The English Farmhouses and Cottages* (London: Routledge and Kegan Paul, 1961), p. 8; C. F. Innocent, *The Development of English Building Construction* (Devon, England: David and Charles Reprints, 1971), pp. 157–61, 143–44.

34. Labelle Prussin, *Architecture in Northern Ghana: A Study of Forms and Functions* (Berkeley: University of California Press, 1969), pp. 57–58; Denyer, *African Traditional Architecture*, p. 94; Werner E. Knuffel, *The Construction of the Bantu Grass Hut* (Graz, Austria: Akademische-Druck-U. Verlagsantstalt, 1973), pp. 45–46; Vlach, *Afro-American Tradition*, p. 135.

35. Southern Maryland Afro-American Survey; William Diggs interview, June 1979.

36. McKinley Gantt interview, February 1978; "Hopsie" Johnson interview, March 1977; Albert Johnson interview, February 1977; Benjamin and Nellie Ross interview; Douglass, *My Bondage*, p. 37; Rawick, *Maryland Narratives*, p. 51; Genovese, *Roll, Jordon, Roll*, p. 525; Ross/Diggs interview.

37. Southern Maryland Afro-American Survey; Diggs interview, February 1978; Vlach, *Afro-American Tradition*, p. 135; "Hopsie" Johnson interview, March 1977.

38. William Diggs interview, June 1979; Genovese, *Roll, Jordon, Roll*, p. 525; James Scriber interview, June 1978.

39. Rawick, *Maryland Narratives*, p. 6; Douglass, *My Bondage*, p. 37.

40. Ross/Diggs interview.

41. Benjamin and Nellie Ross interview; Ross/Diggs interview.

42. James Scriber interview, February 1977.

43. William Diggs interview, June 1980; Luther Stuckey interview, June 1978.

44. William Diggs interview, February 1978.

45. William Diggs interview, June 1979; Genovese, *Roll, Jordon, Roll*, p. 525.

46. William Diggs interview, June 1979.

47. Southern Maryland Afro-American Survey; Genovese, *Roll, Jordon, Roll*, p. 527; James Scriber interview, June 1978; Clem Dyson interview.

48. William Diggs interview, February 1978; William Dyson interview, June 1976.

49. Southern Maryland Afro-American Survey; Douglass, *My Bondage*; James Scriber interview, February 1977; Genovese, *Roll, Jordon, Roll*, p. 529; Clinton A. Weslager, *The Log Cabin in America* (New Brunswick: Rutgers University Press, 1969), p. 67.

50. Southern Maryland Afro-American Survey; John Demos, *A Little Common-*

wealth: Family Life in Plymouth Colony (New York: Oxford University Press, 1970); Glassie, "Types," p. 396; René Gardi, *Indigenous African Architecture* (New York: Van Nostrand Reinhold, 1973), p. 107.

51. James Scriber interview, June 1977.
52. William Diggs interview.
53. Southern Maryland Afro-American Survey.
54. James Scriber interview, February 1977.
55. William Diggs interview, June 1979; Clem Dyson interview; Marks, "Economics and Society," p. 59.
56. William Diggs interview, June 1979.
57. *Ibid.*
58. This description is based on William Diggs's demonstration to John Pearce, Mary Sue Nunn, and George McDaniel, Eagle Harbor, Maryland, June 1979.
59. *Ibid.*
60. Vlach, *Afro-American Tradition*, p. 136; see painting of Mulberry Plantation by Thomas Coram, Gibbs Street Gallery, Charleston, S.C.; Diana S. Waite, "Roofing for Early America," in Charles E. Peterson, ed., *Building Early America: Contributions toward the History of a Great Industry* (Radnor, Pennsylvania: Chilton, 1976), pp. 135–36.
61. Denyer, *African Traditional Architecture*, p. 163.
62. William Diggs interview, June 1979.
63. Southern Maryland Afro-American Survey; Rawick, *Maryland Narratives*, p. 71; Marks, "Economics and Society," pp. 53–58.
64. "Hopsie" Johnson interview, March 1977; Albert Johnson interview, December 1976; McKinley Gantt interview, February 1978; Southern Maryland Afro-American Survey.
65. Southern Maryland Afro-American Survey; Basil Smith interview, March 1977.
66. Rawick, *Maryland Narratives*, p. 24; Henry C. Forman, *Tidewater Maryland Architecture* (New York: Bonanza, 1956), pp. 127–29; Jansson family interview, March 1976.
67. Southern Maryland Afro-American Survey; Marks, "Economics and Society," p. 56.
68. Marks, "Economics and Society," p. 161; Rawick, *Maryland Narratives*, p. 19, and *Virginia Narratives*, p. 38; Julia Harris interview, November 1974; Southern Maryland Afro-American Survey.
69. William Diggs interview, June 1979; James Scriber interview, June 1978; Southern Maryland Afro-American Survey; Frederick Law Olmsted, *A Journey in the Seaboard Slave States with Remarks on Their Economy* (New York: Dix and Edwards, 1960), p. 159.
70. James Scriber interview, June 1980; Clem Dyson interview, June 1978; Alex Milford interview, November 1976; Southern Maryland Afro-American Survey.
71. August Meier and Elliott Rudwick, *From Plantation to Ghetto* (New York: Hill and Wang, 1976), p. 67; John W. Blassingame, *The Slave Community: Plantation Life in the Antebellum South* (New York: Oxford University Press, 1972), p. 159; Lerone Bennett, Jr., *Before the Mayflower: A History of the Negro in America, 1619–1964* (New York: Penguin, 1978), p. 75.

Chapter III

1. James Scriber interview, February 1977; Amanda Nelson interview, March 1978.

2. Josiah Henson, *Father Henson's Story of His Own Life* (Northbrook, Illinois: Metro, 1972), p. 18.

3. Charles L. Perdue, Jr., Thomas E. Borden, and Robert K. Philips, *Weevils in the Wheat: Interviews with Ex-Slaves* (Charlottesville: University of Virginia Press, 1976), p. 149; Benjamin and Nellie Ross interview, February 1977; James Scriber interview, February 1977.

4. Eugene Genovese, *Roll, Jordon, Roll: The World the Slaves Made* (New York: Vintage, 1976), p. 528.

5. McKinley Gantt interview, May 1976; James Scriber interview, June 1978; Howard Lyles interview, January 1979; Blanche Wilson interview, December 1978.

6. George W. Rawick, ed., *The American Slave: A Composite Autobiography*, vol. 16, *Virginia Narratives* (Westport, Connecticut: Greenwood, 1972), p. 37; Jansson family interview, March 1976.

7. George W. Rawick, ed., *The American Slave: A Composite Autobiography*, vol. 16, *Maryland Narratives* (Westport, Connecticut: Greenwood, 1972), pp. 52, 6, and *Virginia Narratives*, p. 37; William Diggs interview, June 1979.

8. Ronald Killion and Charles Waller, eds., *Slavery Time When I Was Chillun Down on Marster's Plantation* (Savannah, Georgia: Beehive Press, 1973).

9. William Diggs interview, March 1981. For a study of quilting, see Gladys Marie Frye, "Harriet Powers: Portrait of a Black Quilter," in Georgia Council for the Arts, *Missing Pieces: Georgia Folk Art, 1770–1976* (Athens, Georgia: Whittet and Shepperson, 1976). Professor Frye is now conducting a study of slave-made quilts in Maryland and throughout the nation. See also Maude Southwell Wahlman, "The Art of Afro-American Quiltmaking: Origins, Development, and Significance" (Ph.D. diss., Yale University, 1980).

10. James Scriber interview, February 1977.

11. William Green, *Narrative of Events in the Life of William Green (Formerly a Slave)* (Springfield, Mass.: L. M. Guernsey, 1853), pp. 8–9.

12. Austin Steward, *Twenty-Two Years a Slave, and Forty Years a Freeman* (New York: Negro Universities Press, n.d.), p. 13.

13. Blanche Wilson interview, March 1977; William Diggs interview, February 1978; Henry Glassie, *Pattern in the Material Folk Culture of the Eastern United States* (Philadelphia: University of Pennsylvania Press, 1968), p. 116.

14. William Diggs interview, February 1978.

15. William Diggs interview, June 1979.

16. William Diggs interview, February 1978.

17. Rawick, *Maryland Narratives*, pp. 7, 54; Rawick, *Virginia Narratives*, p. 38; William Diggs interview, February 1978.

18. Henson, *Father Henson's Story*, p. 17.

19. Rawick, *Maryland Narratives*, p. 76; James Scriber interview, February 1977.

20. Rawick, *Maryland Narratives*, pp. 76, 54.

21. Charles Ball, *Fifty Years in Chains, or, The Life of an American Slave* (Miami, Florida: Mnemosyne, 1968), p. 17.
22. Rawick, *Virginia Narratives*, p. 38.
23. Ball, *Fifty Years in Chains*, pp. 10, 16; Rawick, *Maryland Narratives*, p. 19.
24. Rawick, *Maryland Narratives*, pp. 4, 8, 49, 56, 67; William Diggs interview, October 1978.
25. Rawick, *Maryland Narratives*, pp. 8, 56.
26. *Ibid.*, pp. 62, 6–7; Bayly Ellen Marks, "Economics and Society in a Staple Plantation System: St. Mary's County, Maryland, 1790–1840" (Ph.D. diss., University of Maryland, 1979), pp. 114–21.
27. William Diggs interview, June 1979.
28. James Scriber interview, February 1977.
29. *Ibid.*; William Diggs interview, February 1978; U.S., Department of Agriculture, Office of Experiment Stations, *Dietary Studies with Reference to the Food of the Negro in Alabama in 1895 and 1896*, by W. O. Atwater and Charles D. Woods (Washington, D.C.: G.P.O., 1897), pp. 12–15.
30. Jessie Beulah Kinard interviews, January 1978 and March 1980; Mr. and Mrs. Howard Young interview, July 1974.
31. Rawick, *Maryland Narratives*, pp. 26, 75, 62; Simon J. Martenet, *Map of Maryland* (Baltimore: Simon J. Martenet, 1866).
32. Amanda Nelson interview, March 1980; Howard Lyles interview, January 1979; Florence Hallman interview, July 1979.
33. Rawick, *Maryland Narratives*, p. 7; McKinley Gantt interview, July 1978; Blanche Wilson interview, December 1978; George Butler interview, November 1976; James Scriber interview, February 1977.
34. Rawick, *Maryland Narratives*, pp. 6, 75, 53; William Diggs interview, February 1978.
35. Rawick, *Maryland Narratives*, pp. 53, 7; Rawick, *Virginia Narratives*, p. 38.
36. U.S., Department of Agriculture, *Nutritive Value of Foods*, Home and Garden Bulletin No. 72 (1977), pp. 9–29 *passim*. For further discussion of the importance of slaves' efforts to provide for themselves, see John Blassingame, *The Slave Community: Plantation Life in the Antebellum South* (New York: Oxford University Press, 1972), e.g., pp. 92–93, 206–7.
37. Marks, "Economics and Society," pp. 550–51; Rawick, *Maryland Narratives*, pp. 17, 9, 76, 49; Moselle Cameron and Janie Cameron Riley interview, July 1975.
38. Lewis Thomas, *The Medusa and the Snail: More Notes of a Biology Watcher* (New York: Viking, 1979), pp. 102–5. For a more complete discussion of endorphins, see the transcript of "Nova No. 610, 'Keys to Paradise,'" produced by WGBH Educational Foundation, Boston, Massachusetts.
39. W. C. Handy, *Father of the Blues: An Autobiography* (New York: Collier, 1941), p. 6.
40. Rawick, *Maryland Narratives*, p. 56; Marks, "Economics and Society," pp. 550–51.
41. Rawick, *Maryland Narratives*, pp. 14–15.
42. William Diggs interview, January 1978.

43. "World Psychosis," *Science 80*, 1, no. 6 (September/October 1980): 7.

44. Rawick, *Maryland Narratives*, pp. 9, 60.

45. William A. Diggs, "Black History: Here at the Beginning," in Jack D. Brown et al., eds., *Charles County, Maryland: A History* (South Hackensack, New Jersey: Custombook, 1976), pp. 228–31; Rawick, *Maryland Narratives*, p. 71; Albert J. Raboteau, *Slave Religion: The "Invisible Institution" in the Antebellum South* (New York: Oxford University Press, 1978), p. 239.

46. Raboteau, *Slave Religion*, pp. 216–17; George W. Rawick, ed., *The American Slave: A Composite Autobiography*, vol. 1, *From Sundown to Sunup: The Making of the Black Community* (Westport, Connecticut: Greenwood, 1972), pp. 39–45; John Szwed cited in Genovese, *Roll, Jordon, Roll*, p. 237.

47. Raboteau, *Slave Religion*, pp. 250–66.

48. *Ibid.*

49. Rawick, *Maryland Narratives*, pp. 61–62.

50. William Diggs interview, November 1976. Among the manuscripts in Diggs's private possession is the list of slaves to be emancipated on the plantation where William Tubman lived. Tubman's name is included.

51. Diggs, "Black History," pp. 230–31; William Diggs interview, November 1976.

52. John Vlach, *The Afro-American Tradition in Decorative Arts* (Cleveland: Cleveland Museum of Art, 1978), p. 150; John M. Vlach, "Phillip Simmons: Afro-American Blacksmith," in Linn Shapiro, ed., *Black People and Their Culture: Selected Writings from the African Diaspora* (Washington, D.C.: Smithsonian Institution, 1976), p. 50.

Chapter IV

1. Leon F. Litwack, *Been in the Storm So Long: The Aftermath of Slavery* (New York: Alfred A. Knopf, 1979), p. xiii.

2. McKinley Gantt interview, July 1974; Albert J. Raboteau, *Slave Religion: The "Invisible Institution" in the Antebellum South* (New York: Oxford University Press, 1978), p. 251.

3. Jeffrey R. Brackett, *Notes on the Progress of the Colored People of Maryland since the War* (Baltimore: Johns Hopkins University Press, 1890), pp. 15–32, 72–77; Pete Castello et al., "Government: We the People," in Jack D. Brown et al., eds., *Charles County, Maryland: A History* (South Hackensack, New Jersey: Custombook, 1976), p. 207.

4. Brackett, *Progress of the Colored People*, pp. 29–35; Clayton Colman Hall, *Baltimore: Its History and Its People* (New York: Lewis Historical Publishing Co., 1912); pp. 235–36.

5. Labor Contracts, Freedmen's Bureau Collection, Record Group 105, National Archives, Washington, D.C.

6. Labor Contracts.

7. Labor Contracts; Nina Clarke and Lillian Brown, *History of Black Public Schools in Montgomery County, 1872–1961* (New York: Vantage, 1976); Brackett, *Progress of the Colored People*, p. 55.

8. Southern Maryland Afro-American Survey; W. E. B. Du Bois, "The Problem of Housing the Negro: The Home of the Country Freedman," *Southern Workman* 30, no. 3 (September 1901): 535–38; W. D. Weatherford, *Negro Life in the South: Present Conditions and Needs* (New York: Association Press, 1915), pp. 63–65; U.S., Department of Agriculture, Office of Experiment Stations, *Dietary Studies with Reference to the Food of the Negro in Alabama in 1895 and 1896,* by W. O. Atwater and Charles D. Woods (Washington, D.C.: G.P.O., 1897), p. 16; Luther Stuckey interview, March 1978.

9. Southern Maryland Afro-American Survey; Du Bois, "Home of the Country Freedman," p. 537.

10. Southern Maryland Afro-American Survey; Donald McDauley, "The Urban Impact on Agriculture in Prince George's County, 1850–1880," in Aubrey C. Land, Lois Green Carr, and Edward C. Papenfuse, eds., *Law, Society, and Politics in Early Maryland* (Baltimore: Johns Hopkins University Press, 1974); Clem Dyson interview, June 1978.

11. Clem Dyson interview, June 1978.

12. Benjamin and Nellie Ross and William Diggs interview, January 1978.

13. Benjamin and Nellie Ross interview, February 1977.

14. Ross/Diggs interview, January 1978; Benjamin and Nellie Ross interviews, September and July 1978.

15. Ross/Diggs interview, January 1978.

16. *Ibid.*; James Scriber interview, February 1977; McKinley Gantt interview, February 1978.

17. Ross/Diggs interview, January 1978; James Scriber interview, February 1977; McKinley Gantt interview, February 1978.

18. Ross/Diggs interview, January 1978.

19. *Ibid.*

20. *Ibid.*

21. Preston Williams interview, March 1978; Ross/Diggs interview, January 1978.

22. Ross/Diggs interview, January 1978.

23. *Ibid.*

24. *Ibid.*

25. *Ibid.*

26. Benjamin and Nellie Ross interview, February 1977.

27. *Ibid.*

28. *Ibid.*

29. *Ibid.*

30. Wilcomb E. Washburn and Frederick Gutheim, *The Federal City: Plans and Realities* (Washington, D.C.: Smithsonian Press, 1976), pp. 22–31; John Ross interview, June 1978; Benjamin and Nellie Ross interview, February 1977.

31. Benjamin and Nellie Ross interview, February 1977.

32. *Ibid.*

33. Southern Maryland Afro-American Survey.

34. Abraham Medley interview, July 1974; Nora Cusic interview, September 1978; J. Gwynn Buckler interview, September 1978.

35. Southern Maryland Afro-American Survey.

36. *Ibid.*

37. J. Gwynn Buckler interview; Abraham Medley and Charles Medley interview, September 1978.

38. Nora Cusic interview, September 1978.

39. *Ibid.*

40. *Ibid.*

41. *Ibid.*

42. Abraham Medley/Charles Medley interview, September 1978. When I first located and investigated this house, I did not know of Medley's son, Charles, or of the Cusics. It was only in 1978, during one of a half-dozen return visits, that I located and interviewed them.

43. Abraham Medley/Charles Medley interview, September 1978.

44. Arthur Raper, *Preface to Peasantry* (New York: Atheneum, 1974), p. 397.

45. William P. Hedgepeth, *The Hog Book* (New York: Doubleday, 1978); Abraham Medley/Charles Medley interview, September 1978; Tilghman Lee interview, July 1979.

46. Abraham Medley/Charles Medley interview, September 1978.

47. *Ibid.*

48. Dr. James G. McDaniel interview, September 1978. Dr. McDaniel, a native of rural Georgia, was a practicing physician in Georgia for over forty years.

49. Raper, *Preface to Peasantry,* pp. 67–68; Abraham Medley/Charles Medley interview, September 1978.

50. Nora Cusic interview, September 1978; Abraham Medley/Charles Medley interview, September 1978; Wayne Nield interview, March 1981.

51. Abraham Medley/Charles Medley interview, September 1978; Edward and Vivian Harley interview, March and October 1978.

52. Abraham Medley/Charles Medley interview, September 1978; Amanda Nelson interview, March and October 1978.

53. Abraham Medley/Charles Medley interview, September 1978.

54. *Ibid.*

55. *Ibid.*

56. *Ibid.*

57. Abraham Medley interviews, January and March 1976.

58. *Ibid.*

59. Abraham Medley/Charles Medley interview, September 1978.

60. Abraham Medley interviews, January and March 1976 and April 1977.

61. Abraham Medley/Charles Medley interview, September 1978.

62. McKinley Gantt interview, July 1974; Benjamin and Nellie Ross interview, February 1977.

Chapter V

1. Roger L. Ransom and Richard Sutch, *One Kind of Freedom: The Economic Consequences of Emancipation* (New York: Cambridge University Press, 1977), p. 82.

2. Arthur Raper, *Preface to Peasantry* (New York: Atheneum, 1974), pp. 138–41, 139. See George W. McDaniel, *Black Historical Resources in Upper Western Montgomery County, Maryland* (Rockville, Maryland: Montgomery County Government and Sugarloaf Regional Trails, 1979), for further descriptions and photographs of black community institutions, such as schools and lodges, founded by freed men and women.

3. W. E. B. Du Bois, *Black Reconstruction in America, 1860–1880* (New York: Atheneum, 1973), p. 603; Raper, *Preface to Peasantry*, p. 118; U.S., Bureau of the Census, *Negro Population in the United States, 1790–1915* (New York: Arno Press, 1968), p. 486.

4. Two pioneering studies of black towns are Norman L. Crockett, *The Black Towns* (Lawrence, Kansas: Regents Press of Kansas, 1979), and Nell Irvin Painter, *Exodusters: Black Migration to Kansas after Reconstruction* (New York: Alfred A. Knopf, 1977).

5. Southern Maryland Afro-American Survey; Sugarloaf Regional Trails Survey. My *Black Historical Resources* is a study in words and photographs of thirteen historical black landowning communities in Montgomery County, Maryland, founded after emancipation.

6. Du Bois, *Black Reconstruction*, p. 601; August Meier and Elliot Rudwick, *From Plantation to Ghetto* (New York: Hill and Wang, 1976), p. 166; A. R. Lightfoot quoted in Ransom and Sutch, *One Kind of Freedom*, p. 81.

7. Paul Bohannan and Philip Curtin, *Africa and Africans* (Garden City, New York: Natural History Press, 1971), pp. 119–28.

8. Jeffrey R. Brackett, *Notes on the Progress of the Colored People of Maryland since the War* (Baltimore: Johns Hopkins University Press, 1890), pp. 81–93; Sugarloaf Regional Trails Survey; Montgomery County Courthouse, Registry of Deeds, Deed R/217, Rockville, Maryland; Southern Maryland Afro-American Survey; John N. Pearce interview, March 1979.

9. Ransom and Sutch, *One Kind of Freedom*, pp. 86–87.

10. Raper, *Preface to Peasantry*, pp. 121–25; Blanche Wilson interviews, March and May 1977; George Carroll interview, December 1976.

11. Jennie Tongue Reichart interview, July 1978.

12. M. Johnson and J. Karpaik, "Agriculture: Still a Tobacco Economy," in Jack Brown et al., eds., *Charles County, Maryland: A History* (South Hackensack, New Jersey: Custombook, 1976), p. 8; U.S., Bureau of the Census, *Negro Population*, pp. 486, 514.

13. Southern Maryland Afro-American Survey; Sadie Crump interview, October 1976; George Carroll interview, December 1976; Tilghman Lee interview, November 1978.

14. Edwin W. Beitzell, *Life on the Potomac River* (Abell, Maryland: E. W. Beitzell,

1973), pp. 77, 67; William Diggs interview, January 1978. For descriptions of houses of black watermen, see my survey of Abell, Maryland, on file at the Maryland Historical Trust, Annapolis, Maryland.

15. W. E. B. Du Bois, "The Problem of Housing the Negro: The Home of the Country Freedman," *Southern Workman* 30, no. 3 (September 1901): 536; Bernard L. Fontana, "The Tale of a Nail: On the Ethnological Interpretation of Historic Artifacts," *The Florida Anthropologist* 18, no. 3: 85–89.

16. For informative examples of builders' and design manuals popular in the last half of the nineteenth century, see A. J. Downing, *The Architecture of Country Houses, Including Designs for Cottages and Farm-Houses and Villas* (D. Appleton, 1850; reprint ed., New York: Dover Publications, 1969); George E. Woodward, *Woodward's Country Homes: A New, Practical, and Original Work on Rural Architecture* (New York: George E. Woodward, 1865; reprint ed., Watkins Glen, New York: American Life Foundation, n.d.); and George E. Woodward, *Woodward's Victorian Architecture and Rural Art: A Facsimile of Volume One (1867) and Volume Two (1868)* (Watkins Glen, New York: American Life Foundation, 1978).

17. Southern Maryland Afro-American Survey.

18. *Ibid.*

19. *Ibid.*; Sugarloaf Regional Trails Survey.

20. *Ibid.*

21. Herbert Gutman, *The Black Family in Slavery and Freedom, 1750–1925* (New York: Pantheon, 1976), pp. 89–90.

22. Blanche Wilson interviews, March and May 1977. My thanks to Wayne Nield, former historical sites surveyor for the Maryland Historical Trust, who led me to Ben's Creek, introduced me to Blanche Wilson, and assisted in the study of this community.

23. Blanche Wilson interviews, March and May 1977; Calvert County Courthouse, Registry of Deeds, Deed A.A.H. 10/201, Prince Frederick, Maryland.

24. *Ibid.*; Blanche Wilson interviews, March and May 1977; National Archives, R.G. 29, U.S. 1880 Census, Maryland, Calvert County, First Election District, p. 24.

25. Calvert County Courthouse, Deeds J.L.B. 43/461, J.S. 3/466, A.A.H. 10/201, S.S. 6/322; Blanche Wilson interview, December 1978.

26. Blanche Wilson interview, March 1977; Jennie Tongue Reichart interview, November 1976; Raper, *Preface to Peasantry*, pp. 122–25; Ransom and Sutch, *One Kind of Freedom*, pp. 86–87.

27. Blanche Wilson interview, March 1977.

28. Blanche Wilson interview, December 1978.

29. *Ibid.*; Southern Maryland Afro-American Survey; Fred Kniffen and Henry Glassie, "Building in Wood in the Eastern United States: A Time-Place Perspective," *Geographical Review* 56 (January 1966): 54–55.

30. Southern Maryland Afro-American Survey; Sugarloaf Regional Trails Survey; William Diggs interview, February 1978.

31. Southern Maryland Afro-American Survey; Sugarloaf Regional Trails Survey.

32. Southern Maryland Afro-American Survey; Blanche Wilson interview, December 1978; Sugarloaf Regional Trails Survey.
33. Southern Maryland Afro-American Survey; Sugarloaf Regional Trails Survey; Du Bois, "Home of the Country Freedman," pp. 537–38.
34. Blanche Wilson interviews, March and May 1977, December 1978.
35. *Ibid.*
36. *Ibid.*
37. *Ibid.*
38. *Ibid.*
39. *Ibid.*
40. Blanche Wilson interview, March 1977; Edward and Vivian Harley interviews, March 1977 and October 1978; Luther Stuckey interview, March 1978; Richard and Helen Turner James interview, February 1978; James Scriber interview, June 1978.
41. Blanche Wilson interview, December 1978.
42. National Archives, R.G. 29, U.S. 1870 Census, Maryland, Calvert County, First Election District, pp. 29–30; National Archives, R.G. 29, U.S. 1880 Census, Maryland, Calvert County, First Election District, p. 24.
43. Henry Glassie, *Folk Housing in Middle Virginia: A Structural Analysis of Historic Artifacts* (Knoxville: University of Tennessee Press, 1976).
44. Maryland Afro-American Survey; Blanche Wilson interview, May 1977.
45. Blanche Wilson interviews, May 1977 and December 1978.
46. *Ibid.*
47. *Ibid.*
48. *Ibid.*
49. *Ibid.*; William Seale, *The Tasteful Interlude: American Interiors through the Camera's Eye, 1860–1917* (New York: Praeger, 1975), p. 32.
50. Blanche Wilson interviews, May 1977 and December 1978.
51. *Ibid.*
52. *Ibid.*
53. *Ibid.*
54. McKinley Gantt interview, July 1978.
55. *Ibid.*
56. *Ibid.*
57. *Ibid.*; John Vlach, *The Afro-American Tradition in the Decorative Arts* (Cleveland: Cleveland Museum of Art, 1978), pp. 97–107.
58. McKinley Gantt interview, July 1978.
59. *Ibid.* Two fires in 1883 destroyed the Calvert County Courthouse and its records, including the original deeds to the Gantt property. A few deeds in the possession of owners survived and were reregistered. Among these were the deeds to the Harrod, Wilson, and other properties in Ben's Creek.
60. McKinley Gantt interview, July 1978.
61. *Ibid.*
62. *Ibid.*
63. *Ibid.*; U.S., Bureau of the Census, *Negro Population*, p. 727.

64. *The 1902 Edition of the Sears, Roebuck Catalogue* (New York: Bounty, 1969), pp. 781, 181, 752; Fred L. Israel, ed., *1897 Sears, Roebuck Catalogue* (New York: Chelsea, 1968), 643.
65. Israel, *1897 Sears, Roebuck Catalogue*, p. 653.
66. *The 1902 Edition of the Sears, Roebuck Catalogue*, pp. 117, 802; Israel, *1897 Sears, Roebuck Catalogue*, p. 300.
67. *The 1902 Edition of the Sears, Roebuck Catalogue*, p. 827.
68. Arthur Smith interview, February 1976.
69. McKinley Gantt interview, July 1978.
70. Blanche Wilson interview, March 1981.
71. Vlach, *Afro-American Tradition*, pp. 122–23. For further discussion of these ideas, see Edward T. Hall, *Silent Language* (Garden City, New York: Doubleday, 1959), and Glassie, *Folk Housing*.

Epilogue

1. Vivian Harley, panel discussion at the Festival of American Folklife, National Museum of American History, Smithsonian Institution, Washington, D.C., October 4–9, 1978. The tapes of these panels are on file with the Office of the Folklife Program, Smithsonian Institution, Washington, D.C.
2. Amanda Nelson, panel discussion at the Festival of American Folklife.
3. William Diggs, panel discussion at the Festival of American Folklife. His stories with the puppets were not given as part of the panel and may not have been taped.
4. Luther Stuckey, panel discussion at the Festival of American Folklife.
5. Arthur Raper, panel discussion at the Festival of American Folklife.
6. John Dewey quoted in Thomas J. Schlereth, "The History behind, within, and outside the History Museum," a paper presented in the George Washington Guest Lecture Series in Museum Education, George Washington University, Washington, D.C., March 1980; Wilcomb Washburn, conversation with the author, Festival of American Folklife.
7. U.S., Bureau of the Census, *Negro Population in the United States, 1790–1915* (New York: Arno Press, 1968), p. 783; John Rupnow and Carol Ward Knox, *The Growing of America: 200 Years of U.S. Agriculture* (Fort Atkinson, Wisconsin: Johnson Hill Press, 1975), p. 130.
8. Black Economic Research Center, *Only Six Million Acres: The Decline of Black-Owned Land in the Rural South* (New York: Black Economic Research Center, 1973), p. 3; Harold E. Vokes and Jonathan Edwards, Jr., *Geography and Geology of Maryland* (Baltimore: Geological Survey, 1974), p. 151.
9. Lawrence W. Levine, *Black Culture and Black Consciousness: Afro-American Folk Thought from Slavery to Freedom* (New York: Oxford University Press, 1977), p. 443.

BIBLIOGRAPHY

Afolabi, G. J. "Traditional Yoruba Architecture." *African Arts* 1, no. 3 (1967).

Agee, James, and Walker Evans. *Let Us Now Praise Famous Men.* New York: Ballantine, 1973.

Atkinson, Frank. "Yorkshire Miners' Cottages." *Folk Life Journal of the Society for Folk Life Studies* 3 (1965).

Baker, Ray Stannard. *Following the Color Line.* New York: Harper and Row, 1964.

Ball, Charles. *Fifty Years in Chains, or, The Life of an American Slave.* Miami, Florida: Mnemosyne, 1968.

Barley, M. W. *The English Farmhouses and Cottages.* London: Routledge and Kegan Paul, 1961.

Bealer, Alex W. *Old Ways of Working Wood.* Barre, Massachusetts: Barre Publishers, 1972.

Bealer, Alex W., and John O. Ellis. *The Log Cabin: Homes of the North American Wilderness.* Barre, Massachusetts: Barre Publishers, 1978.

Beitzell, Edwin. *Life on the Potomac River.* Abell, Maryland: E. W. Beitzell, 1973.

Berlin, Ira. "Time, Space, and the Evolution of Afro-American Society in British Mainland North America." *American Historical Review* 85, no. 1 (February 1980).

Black Economic Research Center. *Only Six Million Acres: The Decline of Black-Owned Land in the Rural South.* New York: Black Economic Research Center, 1973.

Blassingame, John W. *The Slave Community: Plantation Life in the Antebellum South.* New York: Oxford University Press, 1972.

Blumenson, John J. G. *Identifying American Architecture.* Nashville, Tennessee: American Association for State and Local History, 1977.

Bohannan, Paul, and Philip Curtin. *Africa and Africans.* Garden City, New York: Natural History Press, 1971.

Boles, Nancy G. "Notes on Maryland Historical Society Manuscript Collections." *Maryland Historical Magazine*, spring 1971.

Bowie, Captain John. Private manuscript collection. Bethesda, Maryland.

Brackett, Jeffrey R. *Notes on the Progress of the Colored People of Maryland since the War.* Rpt. ed., Freeport, New York: Books for Libraries Press, 1971.

Brodie, Fawn M. *Thomas Jefferson: An Intimate Biography.* New York: Norton, 1974.

Brown, Jack D., et al., eds. *Charles County, Maryland: A History.* South Hackensack, New Jersey: Custombook, 1976.

Brown, Letitia Woods. *Free Negroes in the District of Columbia.* New York: Oxford University Press, 1972.

Brown, Letitia Woods, and Elsie Lewis. *Washington from Banneker to Douglass, 1791–*

1870. Washington, D.C.: Education Department, National Portrait Gallery, 1971.

Brown, Lillian, and Nina Clarke. *History of Black Public Schools in Montgomery County, 1872–1961.* New York: Vantage, 1976.

Brunskill, Ronald W. *Vernacular Architecture.* London: Faber and Faber, 1971.

Brunvard, Jan Harold. *The Study of American Folklore: An Introduction.* New York: Norton, 1978.

Callcott, Margaret Law. *The Negro in Maryland Politics, 1870–1912.* Baltimore: Johns Hopkins University Press, 1969.

Calvert County Courthouse, Prince Frederick, Maryland. Registry of Deeds. Deeds A.A.H. 10/201; J.L.B. 43/461; J.S. 3/466; S.S. 6/322.

Charles County Courthouse, La Plata, Maryland. Registry of Deeds. Deeds JST 1/572; JST 1/573.

Clark, Thomas D. *The Southern Country Store.* Norman, Oklahoma: Oklahoma Press, 1974.

Clifton-Taylor, Alec. *The Pattern of English Building.* London: Faber and Faber, 1972.

Conrat, Maisie, and Richard Conrat. *The American Farm.* San Francisco: California Historical Society, 1977.

Cooke, Alistair. *America.* New York: Knopf, 1973.

Cooper, Claire C. *Easter Hill Village: Some Social Implications of Design.* New York: Free Press, 1975.

Cothran, Kay C. "Pines and Pineywoods Life in South Georgia." *Proceedings of the Pioneer American Society* 2 (1979).

Crockett, Norman L. *The Black Towns.* Lawrence, Kansas: Regents Press of Kansas, 1979.

Curtis, John O. "The Introduction of the Circular Saw in the Early 19th Century." *Bulletin of the Association for Preservation Technology* 5, no. 2 (1973).

Dabbs, Edith M. *Face of an Island.* Columbia, South Carolina: B. L. Bryan, 1970.

Deetz, James. *In Small Things Forgotten: The Archeology of Early American Life.* Garden City, New York: Anchor, 1977.

Demos, John. *A Little Commonwealth: Family Life in Plymouth Colony.* New York: Oxford University Press, 1970.

Denyer, Susan. *African Traditional Architecture.* New York: Africana, 1978.

Douglass, Frederick. *My Bondage and My Freedom.* New York: Dover, 1969.

Downing, A. J. *The Architecture of Country Houses, Including Designs for Cottages and Farm-houses and Villas.* D. Appleton, 1850. Rpt. ed., New York: Dover, 1969.

Dozier, Richard. "The Black Architectural Experience in America." *AIA Journal,* July 1976.

Du Bois, W. E. B. "The Problem of Housing the Negro: The Home of the Country Freedman." *Southern Workman* 30, no. 3 (September 1901): 535–42.

———. *Black Reconstruction in America, 1860–1880.* New York: Atheneum, 1973.

Edwards, Jonathan, Jr. *Geography and Geology of Maryland.* Baltimore: Geological Survey, 1974.

Fitch, James Marston. *American Building: The Historical Forces That Shaped It.* New York: Schocken, 1973.

Fogel, Robert W., and Stanley L. Engerman. *Time on the Cross: The Economics of American Negro Slavery.* Boston: Little, Brown, 1974.

Fontana, Bernard L. "The Tale of a Nail: On the Ethnological Interpretation of Historic Artifacts." *The Florida Anthropologist* 18, no. 3, part 2.

Forman, Henry Chandlee. *Tidewater Maryland Architecture and Gardens.* New York: Bonanza, 1956.

———. *Old Buildings, Gardens, and Furniture in Tidewater Maryland.* Cambridge, Maryland: Tidewater, 1967.

Foster, Craig C., Donald H. Ogilvie, and Armstead L. Robinson, eds. *Black Studies in the University: A Symposium.* New Haven: Yale University Press, 1969.

Fraser, Douglas, ed. *The Many Faces of Primitive Art: A Critical Anthology.* Englewood Cliffs, New Jersey: Prentice-Hall, 1966.

Frye, Gladys Marie. "Harriet Powers: Portrait of a Black Quilter." In Georgia Council for the Arts, *Missing Pieces: Georgia Folk Art, 1770–1976.* Athens, Georgia: Whittet and Shepperson, 1976.

Gardi, René. *Indigenous African Architecture.* New York: Van Nostrand Reinhold, 1973.

Genovese, Eugene. *Roll, Jordan, Roll: The World the Slaves Made.* New York: Vintage, 1976.

Georgia Writers' Project. *Drums and Shadows: Survival Studies among Georgia Coastal Negroes.* Athens: University of Georgia Press, 1940.

Glassie, Henry. *Pattern in the Material Folk Culture of the Eastern United States.* Philadelphia: University of Pennsylvania Press, 1968.

———. *Folk Housing in Middle Virginia: A Structural Analysis of Historic Artifacts.* Knoxville: University of Tennessee Press, 1975.

Glassie, Henry, and Fred Kniffen. "Building in Wood in the Eastern United States: A Time-Place Perspective." *Geographical Review* 56 (January 1966).

Goodwyn, Lawrence. *Democratic Promise: The Populist Moment in America.* New York: Oxford University Press, 1976.

Green, William. *Narrative of Events in the Life of William Green (Formerly a Slave).* Springfield, Massachusetts: L. M. Guernsey, 1853.

Gutheim, Frederick, and Wilcomb E. Washburn. *The Federal City: Plans and Realities, the History.* Washington, D.C.: Smithsonian Press, 1976.

Gutman, Herbert. *The Black Family in Slavery and Freedom, 1750–1925.* New York: Pantheon, 1976.

Hall, Clayton Colman. *Baltimore: Its History and Its People.* New York: Lewis Historical Publishing Co., 1912.

Hall, Edward T. *Silent Language.* Garden City, New York: Doubleday, 1959.

Handy, W. C. *Father of the Blues: An Autobiography.* New York: Collier, 1941.

Harris, Cyril M. *Dictionary of Architecture and Construction.* New York: McGraw-Hill, 1975.

Hayes, Cheryl. "Cultural Space and Family Living Patterns in Domestic Architecture, Queen Anne's County, Maryland, 1750–1776." M.A. thesis, Georgetown University, 1974.

Hedgepeth, William B. *The Hog Book.* New York: Doubleday, 1978.

Henson, Josiah. *Father Henson's Story of His Own Life.* Northbrook, Illinois: Metro Books, 1972.

Hopkins, George M. *Prince George's County Atlas of 1878.* Upper Marlboro, Maryland: Prince George's County Historical Society, 1976.

Hull, Richard. *African Cities and Towns before the European Conquest.* New York: Norton, 1976.

Hutslar, Donald A. "Log Cabin Reconstruction: Guidelines for the Historical Society." Technical Leaflet 74. *History News* 29, no. 5 (May 1974).

Innocent, C. F. *The Development of English Building Construction.* Rpt. ed., Devon, England: David and Charles Publishers, 1971.

Killion, Ronald, and Charles Waller, eds. *Slavery Time When I Was Chillun Down on Marster's Plantation.* Savannah, Georgia: Beehive Press, 1973.

Kniffen, Fred. "Folk Housing: Key to Diffusion." *Annals of the Association of American Geographers* 55, no. 4 (December 1965).

Knox, Carol Ward, and John Rupnow. *The Growing of America: 200 Years of U.S. Agriculture.* Fort Atkinson, Wisconsin: Johnson Hill Press, 1975.

Knuffel, Werner E. *The Construction of the Bantu Grass Hut.* Graz, Austria: Akademische-Druck-U. Verlagsantstalt, 1973.

Land, Aubrey C., Lois Green Carr, and Edward C. Papenfuse, eds. *Law, Society, and Politics in Early Maryland.* Baltimore: Johns Hopkins University Press, 1974.

Levine, Lawrence W. *Black Culture and Black Consciousness: Afro-American Folk Thought from Slavery to Freedom.* New York: Oxford University Press, 1977.

Library of Congress, Washington, D.C. Historic American Buildings Survey.

Litwack, Leon F. *Been in the Storm So Long: The Aftermath of Slavery.* New York: Knopf, 1979.

Marks, Bayly Ellen. "Economics and Society in a Staple Plantation System: St. Mary's County, Maryland, 1790–1840." Ph.D. diss., University of Maryland, 1979.

Maryland Historical Society, Baltimore, Maryland. Benjamin Latrobe Collection.

Maryland Historical Trust. *Historical Sites Inventory,* vol. I, *Lower Southern Maryland.* Annapolis, Maryland: Department of Economic and Community Development, 1974.

McDaniel, George W. *Black Historical Resources in Upper Western Montgomery County, Maryland.* Rockville, Maryland: Montgomery County Government and Sugarloaf Regional Trails, 1979.

———. "The Sharecropper's House in the Hall of Everyday Life in the Museum of History and Technology." Report on file with the Division of Cultural History, National Museum of American History, Smithsonian Institution, Washington, D.C.

———. "Preserving the People's History: Traditional Black Material Culture in Nineteenth- and Twentieth-Century Southern Maryland." Ph.D. diss., Duke University, 1979.

McFarlane, Suzanne S. "The Ethnoarchaeology of a Slave Community: The Couper Plantation Site." M.A. thesis, University of Florida, 1975.

Meier, August, and Elliott Rudwick. *From Plantation to Ghetto.* New York: Hill and Wang, 1976.

Menard, Russell. "The Maryland Slave Population, 1658 to 1730: A Demographic
    Profile of Blacks in Four Counties." *William and Mary Quarterly* 32, no. 1
    (January 1975).
Montgomery, Charles T. "Survivors from the Cargo of the Slave Yacht *Wanderer.*"
    American Anthropologist 10 (1908).
Montgomery County Courthouse, Rockville, Maryland. Registry of Deeds.
    Deed R/217.
National Archives, Washington, D.C. Record Group 105, Labor Contracts, Freed-
    men's Bureau.
———. Record Group 29, U.S. 1870 and 1880 Census, Calvert County, Maryland.
Nelson, Lee H. "Nail Chronology as an Aid to Dating Old Buildings and Paint
    Color Research and Restoration." *History News* 19, no. 2 (December 1963).
Nova. "Keys to Paradise." Boston, Massachusetts: WGBH Educational Founda-
    tion.
Oliver, Paul. *Shelter in Africa.* New York: Barrie and Jenkins, 1978.
Olmsted, Frederick Law. *A Journey in the Seaboard Slave States, with Remarks on
    Their Economy.* New York: Dix and Edwards, 1960.
Painter, Nell. *Exodusters: Black Migration to Kansas after Reconstruction.* New York:
    Knopf, 1977.
Perdue, Charles L. "Slave Life Styles in Early Virginia." *Proceedings of the Pioneer
    America Society* 2 (1973).
Perdue, Charles L., Thomas E. Borden, and Robert K. Philips. *Weevils in the Wheat:
    Interviews with Ex-Slaves.* Charlottesville: University of Virginia Press, 1976.
Peterson, Charles E., ed. *Building Early America: Contributions toward the History
    of a Great Industry.* Radnor, Pennsylvania: Chilton, 1976.
Prince George's County Courthouse, Upper Marlboro, Maryland. Registry of Deeds.
    Deed J.W.B. 10/133; Deed of Mattie Spragins to Henry H. Canton, 1959;
    Deed of John C. Jones to Samuel Spragins, 1909; and Deed of Samuel Spragins
    to Lewis Parker, 1920.
———. Registry of Wills. Will of Beale D. Mulliken, 1904.
———. Probate Records Office. Inventory of Beale D. Mulliken, 1904.
Prussin, Labelle. *Architecture in Northern Ghana: A Study of Forms and Functions.*
    Berkeley: University of California Press, 1969.
Quarles, Benjamin. "Introduction." *Maryland Historical Magazine* 56, no. 1 (spring
    1971).
Raboteau, Albert J. *Slave Religion: The "Invisible Institution" in the Antebellum South.*
    New York: Oxford University Press, 1978.
Ransom, Roger L., and Richard Sutch. *One Kind of Freedom: The Economic
    Consequences of Emancipation.* New York: Cambridge University Press, 1977.
Raper, Arthur. *Preface to Peasantry: A Tale of Two Black Belt Counties.* New York:
    Atheneum, 1974.
Ravenswaay, Charles van. *The Arts and Architecture of German Settlements in
    Missouri: A Survey of a Vanishing Culture.* Columbia: University of Missouri
    Press, 1977.
Rawick, George W. *The American Slave: A Composite Autobiography,* vol. 16,
    Maryland Interviews. Westport, Connecticut: Greenwood, 1972.

Rosengarten, Theodore. *All God's Dangers: The Life of Nate Shaw*. New York: Avon, 1974.

Rowe, W. John. "Old-World Legacies in America." *Folk Life Journal of the Society for Folk Life Studies* 6 (1968).

Rudofsky, Bernard. *Architecture without Architects*. Garden City, New York: Doubleday, 1964.

Schlereth, Thomas J. "Historic Houses as Learning Laboratories: Seven Teaching Strategies." American Association for State and Local History Technical Leaflet 105. *History News* 33, no. 4 (April 1978).

———. "Collecting Ideas and Artifacts: Common Problems of History Museums and History Texts." *Roundtable Reports*, summer/fall 1978.

———. "The History behind, within, and outside the History Museum." Paper presented in the George Washington Guest Lecture Series on Museum Education, George Washington University, Washington, D.C., March 1980.

Sears, Roebuck. *1897 Sears, Roebuck Catalogue*, ed. Fred L. Israel. New York: Chelsea, 1968.

———. *The 1902 Edition of the Sears, Roebuck Catalogue*. New York: Bounty, 1969.

Shapiro, Linn, ed. *Black People and Their Culture: Selected Writings from the African Diaspora*. Washington, D.C.: Smithsonian Institution, 1976.

Shurtleff, Arnold R. *The Log Cabin Myth: A Study of the Early Dwellings of the English Colonists in North America*. Gloucester, Massachusetts: Peter Smith, 1967.

Sloane, Eric. *A Museum of Early American Tools*. New York: Ballantine, 1973.

———. *A Reverence for Wood*. New York: Ballantine, 1973.

Sotterley Plantation Guide. Privately published; no author, publisher, or date.

Southern Maryland Afro-American Survey. On file at the Maryland Historical Trust, Annapolis, Maryland. See Appendix I.

Steward, Austin. *Twenty-Two Years a Slave, and Forty Years a Freeman*. Rpt. ed., New York: Negro Universities Press, n.d.

Sugarloaf Regional Trails Survey. On file at the Maryland Historical Trust, Annapolis, Maryland, and at the Rockville Public Library, Rockville, Maryland. See Appendix I.

Thomas, Lewis. *The Medusa and the Snail: More Notes of a Biology Watcher*. New York: Viking, 1979.

U.S., Bureau of the Census. *Negro Population in the United States, 1790–1915*. New York: Arno Press, 1968.

U.S., Department of Agriculture. *Nutritive Value of Foods*. Home and Garden Bulletin No. 72, 1977.

U.S., Department of Agriculture, Office of Experiment Stations. *Dietary Studies with Reference to the Food of the Negro in Alabama in 1895 and 1896*, by W. O. Atwater and Charles D. Woods. Washington, D.C.: G.P.O., 1897.

Vaux, Calvert. *Architecture and Decorative Art*, vol. 12, *Villas and Cottages*. New York: Da Capo Press, 1968.

Vlach, John M. "Shotgun Houses." *Natural History* 86, no. 2 (February 1977).

———. *The Afro-American Tradition in Decorative Arts*. Cleveland: Cleveland Museum of Art, 1978.

Wahlman, Maude Southwell. "The Art of Afro-American Quiltmaking: Origins, Development, and Significance." Ph.D. diss., Yale University, 1980.

Walsh, Richard, and William Lloyd Fox, eds. *Maryland: A History, 1632–1974.* Baltimore: Maryland Historical Society, 1974.

Washington, Booker T. *Up from Slavery.* New York: Avon, 1965.

Weatherford, W. D. *Negro Life in the South: Present Conditons and Needs.* New York: Association Press, 1915.

Weslager, Clinton A. *The Log Cabin in America.* New Brunswick, New Jersey: Rutgers University Press, 1969.

Whiffen, Marcus. *American Architecture since 1780: A Guide to Styles.* Cambridge, Massachusetts: MIT Press, 1976.

Wigginton, Eliot, ed. *The Foxfire Book.* Vols. 1, 2, 3, and 4. Garden City, New Jersey: Doubleday, 1972, 1973, 1975, 1977.

Williams, Henry Lionel, and Ottalie K. Williams. *A Guide to Old American Houses, 1700–1900.* South Brunswick, New York: A. S. Barnes, 1962.

Wood, Peter. *Black Majority: Negroes in Colonial South Carolina from 1670 through the Stono Rebellion.* New York: Norton, 1974.

Wood, Peter H. "Whetting, Setting, and Laying Timbers: Black Builders in the Early South." *Southern Exposure* 8, no. 1 (spring 1980).

Woodward, C. Vann. *Origins of the New South, 1877–1913.* Baton Rouge: Louisiana State University Press, 1971.

Woodward, George E. *Woodward's Country Homes: A New, Practical, and Original Work on Rural Architecture.* New York: George E. Woodward, 1865. Rpt. ed., Watkins Glen, New York: American Life Foundation, n.d.

———. *Woodward's Victorian Architecture and Rural Art: A Facsimile of Volume One (1867) and Volume Two (1868).* Watkins Glen, New York: American Life Foundation, 1978.

"World Psychosis." *Science 80* 1, no. 6 (September/October 1980).

Wright, James Martin. *The Free Negro in Maryland, 1634–1860.* New York: Columbia University Press, 1921.

INDEX

Numerals in italics indicate illustrations.